NATURE-MAN-SPIRIT COMPLEX IN TRIBAL INDIA

RANCHI ANTHROPOLOGY SERIES—3

Ranchi Anthropology Series

No. 1 Process, Performance and Pilgrimage : A Study in Comparative Symbology—**Victor Turner,** Rs. 50

No. 2 Development of Researches in Anthropology in India : Bihar : A Case Study—**L.P. Vidyarthi** and **V.S. Upadhyay,** Rs. 65

No. 3 Nature-Man-Spirit Complex in Tribal India—**R.S. Mann,** Rs. 70

RANCHI ANTHROPOLOGY SERIES—3

Gen. Editor : L.P. VIDYARTHI

NATURE-MAN-SPIRIT COMPLEX IN TRIBAL INDIA

Edited by
R.S. MANN

Assisted by
VIJOY S. SAHAY

CONCEPT PUBLISHING COMPANY, NEW DELHI

First Published 1981

Published and Printed by
Ashok Kumar Mittal
Concept Publishing Company
A/15-16, Commercial Block, Mohan Garden,
NEWDELHI-110059 (India)

Phones: 25351460, 25351794
Fax: 091-11-25357103
***E-mail:* publishing@conceptpub.com**

FOREWORD

THE Department of Anthropology of Ranchi University has celebrated its Silver Jubilee in 1978. Again, it has received the récognition of being the only U.G.C. Centre of Special Assistance in Anthropology in the country almost in the same year. During the tenure of my Presidentship of the International Union of Anthropological and Ethnological Sciences (1973-78) as well as of the Xth ICAES (1978), the Department was also called upon to perform several academic and professional roles involving it at the international level.

With this background, with the financial assistance of the University Grants Commission, we ventured to launch a new series of publications entitled "Ranchi Anthropology Series" in the year 1980. This series is designed to provide short but scholarly treatments of key problem-areas in anthropology. Under this series, in addition to learned lectures delivered at Ranchi by scholars of national and international repute, we publish the theoretically-oriented research work of local scholars as well as proceedings of the national and international level seminars and symposia organised by us.

This series was initiated with the publication of one of our internationally distinguished anthropologists, Professor Victor Turner. Author of several books on symbol, myth and ritual, Professor Turner in this series of lectures delivered at the Department of Special Assistance in Anthropology in Ranchi University, summarises the results of his research in the field of "Comparative Symbology". Published under the title *Process, Performance and Pilgrimage* the book became popular among the scholars of the world within a short span of time.

The second volume is of selected papers presented at a National Symposium on the *Development and Trends in Anthropology in India*, with special reference to Bihar. Edited by me and my collaborator, Dr. V.S. Upadhyay, this volume provides a case study of the development of anthropology in one of the States of India. It is hoped that such exercises will be repeated in other States as well.

The *Nature-Man-Spirit Complex in Tribal India* forms the third volume in this series. The areas of tribal concentration in India are, perhaps, the last bastions of an idyllic existence in tune with Nature. Arising out of Man's close interaction with and dependence on Nature is his belief in the supernatural and the spirit world. The three are thus intertwined inextricably, at times merging into each other. This concept which was first enunciated and described in my study of the Maler was also found useful by other anthropologists in analysing the life styles of simpler communities. The present volume consists of eleven essays bringing out the aspect of this interdependence among several tribes who are relatively outside the pale of modern civilization. Perhaps this will not be for long since "civilization" is creeping imperceptibly into these regions and the tranquil existence of these simple folk in the hills and forests and far-flung isles will change considerably under the impact of modernisation. Man's awe of nature and the elements might well vanish into time altogether, though certain aspects of the complex will continue and find readjustments with changes in them.

I take this opportunity to thank the contributors to this volume who have attempted to test this concept, in cross-cultural and cross-regional situations. In particular I thank Dr. R.S. Mann who kindly agreed to edit the volume and write its introduction in such a short time. I would also like to acknowledge the assistance provided by Dr. Vijoy S. Sahay in preparing the volume.

My grateful thanks are also due to the publishers for their interest in bringing out the book speedily and with care.

L.P. VIDYARTHI

CONTENTS

LIST OF CONTRIBUTORS

Ramesh Chandra
Anthropologist, Anthropological Survey of India, Mysore

Amitava Das Gupta
Head of the Department of Anthropology, G.C. College, Silchar-4, Assam, and U.G.C. Teacher Fellow, Ranchi University, Ranchi

R.S. Mann
Deputy Director, Anthropological Survey of India, Western Regional Office, 1, Old Fathepura, Udaipur, Rajasthan

S.G. Morab
Anthropologist, Anthropological Survey of India, Mysore

Vijoy S. Sahay
Research Associate, Department of Anthropology, Ranchi University, Ranchi

Pradip Singh
U.G.C. Research Fellow, Department of Anthropology, Ranchi University, Ranchi

R.K. Sinha
Associate with the Anthropological Survey of India, Central Region, Nagpur, Maharashtra

Julian Steward
Department of Anthropology, University of Illinois

R.K. Prasad
Head, Department of Anthropology, K.B. College, Bermo, University of Ranchi, Ranchi

INTRODUCTION

TO EXPLORE man, his society and culture, anthropologists have suggested a variety of approaches as part of their research methodology. Among the more important of these, in the twentieth century, can be included 'pure functionalism' (Bronislaw; Malinowski), 'structure functionalism' (Radcliffe-Brown), 'structuralism' (Claude Lévi-Strauss), 'ethnolinguistics' (F.C. Wallace; Strutevant), 'neo-evolutionism' (Leslie White) and' 'cultural ecology' (Julian Steward). The anthropological ideas grew more forcefully in the second and third quarters of the present century. Some of these suggested for mere revival, with minor additions here and there, of what had already been said. Others, however, professed to be new. In most of the cases the idea has not been to altogether discard or delete a specific theoretical front, but to suggest for betterment in terms of richness of data and its deep insight and interpretation. The strength of various approaches has been proved in different social situations, though areas of objection are also met with. But then the attitude should not be to quarrel about the superiority or inferiority of an approach or idea, or method, but to make use of it to the full extent along with its effectivity. And this might provide impetus to the overall growth of an academic discipline.

'Cultural ecology', in association with 'spirits' forms the soul of this book. The academic infrastructure, raised in all the eleven chapters of the book, certifies an important place for the cultural ecological approach in attempting a more exhaustive ethnography. Looking to the Indian tribal situation, the world of spirits is also found to have a very close interaction with man, his social structure, and the natural environments. L. P. Vidyarthi's concept of 'nature-man-spirit complex', thus, provides a sharp tool in understanding and describing the cultural matrix of Indian tribes. The usefulness of the tool has been supported by the empirical studies made use of in this volume.

Cultural ecology, one of the important current theoretical strategies, subscribes to the view point that an intimate relationship exists between a culture and its surrounding environments. For Marshall Sahlins (1969) cultures are human adaptations. In most of its areas, latent as well as manifest, a culture assigns relevance to typical external conditions. And the arrangement helps survive the members of the group in terms of its practical requirements, and polity ideology. Human beings have sufficient capacity to adapt with the ecology for the sake of their existence. The cultural ecologists search for adaptation of societies to specific environments. It is done on the plea (Honigmann 1976) that natural features, whether cognitively or through physical means, lead to changes in cultural milieu, and this necessitates a new kind of adaptation. Julian Steward (1969) feels that cultural ecological adaptations are responsible for distinctive cultural traditions. Even the functioning of a culture is considered by the local environmental conditions. Julian H. Steward, as the first exponent of cultural ecology, eliminates biological ecology from its orbit, though Andrew Vayda, Roy Rappaport, Robin-Fox (1970) spoke for an important place for biological ecology in the study of cultural ecology.

Some studies, at practical level, have supported man-nature interaction. The study of Evans-Pritchard on Nuers is an excellent example where his reasoning is strictly ecological. But the idea of natural interaction between culture and environment is comparatively of late origin; Redfield (1955), Vidyarthi (1963), Laura Thompson (1961). In addition to Julian H. Steward the method of cultural ecology also influenced Sidney Mintz (1956), Eric Wolf (1957) and Morton Fried (1952). Some of their works prove that cultural ecology links emic phenomena with the etic conditions of nature. The group structure and ideology are responsive to material conditions provided by ecology. Rather, there is a causal connection between culture and environment. The cultural determinism of Marvin Harris (1968) also involves technology, economy and natural environment.

Since the 1930s Julian Steward stressed that the element of adaptation formed the central concept in ecological studies. Such an adaptation is dynamic because the organism and environment do not remain constant. And it is through adaptation that culture change is reflected. For Steward (1955), the study of cultural ecology should take note of interrelationship between behaviour pattern and productive technology. And a very closely related aspect of it is to see how behaviour patterns affect other sectors of culture. Hence, there is dialectic interplay between culture and environment. And to understand the same, the native view of environment, that is, how people construe it, would be more useful. A still broader purview of cultural ecology could be provided by Anderson (1973). He thinks cultural change as part of adaptation. The origin of particular cultural features/structures could also be known by analysing socio-cultural environmental adaptations. Culture and environment could also be divided into relevant and irrelevant parts. And it is the functional relationship of relevant environmental factors that cause organisational relationships. Anderson even went to the extent of saying that 'creative cultural core-environmental nexus' is little affected by historical factors and inter-societal relationships. The equilibrium of socio-cultural-environmental systems is long lasting. The hypcthesis of adaptation of man to environmental conditions through socio-cultural institutions and behaviour has been widely employed, (e.g. Cohen 1968; Fortier 1957; Frake, 1956; Gerlick, 1965; M. Harris, 1966; R. Harris, 1962; Howard 1966; Sahlins, 1962, 1964; Steward, 1965; Strehlow, 1965 and Tindale,1959), with interesting interpretations. And this has happened in spite of certain limitations of the method.

Within the broader purview of cultural ecology, as enunciated in the above paragraphs in terms of its attributes of interrelatedness, adaptation and interaction between socio-cultural phenomena and environment, the present exercise on "Nature-Man-Spirit Complex in Tribal India" has been made. However, an added dimension of this work is the analysis of spirits and other religious attributes, in their relationship to man and his culture on the one hand and nature on the other. As products of man, numerous elements, events, rituals, institutions and practices of culture have been explored in terms of their relationship and interaction with nature and spirits. Whether the ingredients of the latter determine the former, or it is an equation of more adaptations is also made clear in the context of nine tribes whose account forms the explanations in this book. One gathers an impression, through certain presentations included herewith, that ecology has a lot of say even in the religious complex, as also vice versa. Since the religious format can broadly be taken as part of culture, it may not be out of place to say that this work presents an exhaustive account of socio-cultural-environmental phenomena in the case of Indian tribes. Where ecological variation, as broad as sea, forest, hills, plains, high altitudes etc. mark the Indian tribal scene, with deep rooted religious organization, the method of "cultural ecology" is of quite a significance in exploring the tribal cultural nexus.

In chapter one, "The Maler: A Study in Nature-Man-Spirit Complex of a Hill Tribe in Bihar", Julian Steward presents his observations on L.P. Vidyarthi's book *The Maler: A Study in Nature-Man-Spirit Complex*. Social structure elements like family, lineage and village community, the variety of supernatural attributes and the basic drives and anxieties, including those connected with survival of a people, are analysed in interrelatedness and interdependence. Adaptation of social arrangement for survival is, as part of the cultural ecology, well explained. Steward argues that the study makes it obvious that the little traditions perpetuate in spite of certain links with the larger society. Such a persistence is attributed to the ecological conditions and religion.

"Nature-Man-Spirit Complex of a Hill Tribe: A Restudy" forms the second chapter wherein Pradip Singh analyses the social organisation of the Maler in the context of ecology and religious structure with special reference to changing situations. He restudied the same Maler villages after a period of over two decades, which L. P. Vidyarthi did in the fifties. Highlighting "determinism" and "possibilism" phenomena of ecology, he boils down to a mutual interaction purview of cultural ecology. Under the latter, Singh observes that certain elements of culture have been susceptible to change; the reasons being Hinduisation, Christianization, industrialization, welfare agencies, political parties etc. Now a little indifferent attitude to slash and burn cultivation has developed among the Maler. Hunting is on the decline. Likewise, some religious performances and worship are done more as a tradition and less as devotion, though pig and fowl sacrifice is still made. There is a growing favourable attitude to paddy cultivation, formal education and medical care. The Maler are now comparatively more conscious of these provisions. This is reflected through the formation of the Parahaiya Uthan Samiti. To some extent the traditional Panchayats (councils) have been influenced by the formal and legal system of social control. But these new trends, in general, have to assume a viable practical shape. These are, so far, reported in case of scanty population, and that too with very little force. The major areas of Maler life and culture have continued to be intact because the ecology and supernatural world continue largely to remain the same. Nature and spirit still determine the Maler life.

In an other paper, Singh works out a mathematical abstraction of the concept and goes to establish that inspite of changes, the nature-man-spirit complex remains constant.

Das Gupta, in chapter three "A Study in Nature-Man-Spirit Complex", has again concentrated on the study of interaction of man with spirit and nature with reference to the Ho tribe of Kolhan. Like in chapter two, Das Gupta has also divided his presentation in three distinct sections, that is, nature, man and spirit. In the first part is expressed the ecological basis of culture. Man to man interaction is searched in the second part covering family, clan, village community and tribe. The influence of the supernatural world on Ho life is exhibited in part three. This is attempted in the background of sacred geography, sacred specialists and sacred performances.

Ecology has limited Ho rice cultivation to three types of agricultural plots. The Ho system of therapeutics and pharmacopia depends on the forest. Rituals, festivals and even love making are adjusted with the cycle of nature. The village community seeks protection from spirits, against epidemics, drought, crop-failure etc. The tribe collectively maintains social discipline for fear of annoyance of spirits. The totemic base of Ho clans is again sought in religion. Both nature and spirit interact while contracting a marriage. The prescribed code of conduct is adhered to for fear of the Creator, village god and ancestral spirits. Construction of a hut is related to both ecology as well as the supernatural dimensions. The belief system and philosophy of life are governed by the spirits. Village rituals are held only with the invoking of spirits. The latter are believed to cause rain, control epidemics and look after livestock and human life.

R.K. Prasad, in chapter four "The Parahaiyas : A Study in Nature-Man-Spirit Complex" outlines three different ecological settings (hill, valley and plain) which determine Parahaiyas economic activities, social organisation and their relationship with the world of spirits. His paper is based on his Ph.D. dissertation. The gathering economy of the Parahaiyas is forest-based, and is the chief means of subsistence for hill and forest dwellers. Economic earnings and expenditure also vary as per the environmental categorisation. A very interesting feature of Parahaiya social organisation is that it is territory based. This holds true for all the three sections of Parahaiyas, that is, plain, hill and forest. The dimensions of social groupings go as per the territorially defined limits. The village community, descent groups like family and lineage (Parahaiyas have no clans) have a defined leadership pattern which is not uniform among the three settlement categories. This part of the social ecology is typical of each. The nature of interaction with caste groups is again determined by the nature of settlement, plain, valley and hill. More exposed to the caste society are the plain and valley people than those living in the hills. Accordingly goes the pattern of social stratification, intra-tribe, tribe versus caste and tribe versus tribe situation. The process of Hinduisation is more prominent among the plain dwellers than others. Ancestral spirits of the three categories of Parahaiyas also differ. The deities of three groups forbid them to inter-marry with one another. In major elements of the Parahaiya life style, environmental variations have quite a deep say.

In chapter five "A Note on the Nature-Man-Spirit Complex of a Tribe (Pando)" R.K. Sinha has adopted the approach of studying the complex of nature, man and spirit on the lines similar to the one adopted by L.P. Vidyarthi in the case of the Maler. Interactions and interconnections between nature, man and spirit have thus been explored. Sinha also makes use of K.N. Sahay's model of interpreting change in the three cornered complex, in the light of forces of change around. The Pando are living in Surguja district of Madhya Pradesh. Their economy of food-gathering, hunting and basket-making is dependent on the forest around. Some families change their village very often because of the gathering economy. As made clear in his explanations, Pando life and culture have developed and flourished in the lap of nature. A Pando retaliates if he/she is asked to leave the forest because it is the latter which provides him food material, drinks, oils, medicine, shelter and raw material for basketry. Formation of hunting groups is again related to the forest. Some fibrous material, obtained from the trees, is used to ward off evil spirits, and as an antidote to snake bite. A variety of material equipment, including nets, traps etc. are obtained from the forest. Though the Pando maintain social solidarity, they are ranked into higher and lower social groups. Ranking or inequality is also explained in the context of other ethnic groups, both tribes and castes of the region. Some clan names are associated with hills and territories. Clan and family deities provide happiness and prosperity to the family. The head of a family worships them on festivals and other occasions. There is a religious centre for the village community too and the same ensures safety to community interests. The supernatural world of the Pando provides for the observance of superstitions during pregnancy. Benevolent spirits are approached for safe delivery. The supernatural elements, specially spirits, influence other areas of Pando life and culture. Misfortunes, ailments, accidents, disease, death, abortion, failure of crops, scarcity of forest produce etc., are attributed to spirits. Details of gods, goddesses, deities, rituals, worship, spirits, festivals etc., have been given in terms of their implications in practical life, social and economic. since the Pando have not remained immune to the forces of change, the old complex of the nature-man-spirit has inducted shake of various forms and magnitude. The same has been highlighted towards the close of the chapter. Forest laws, contact with caste, cultivation of land, protective legislations, Panchayati Raj etc. have had their own place. However, the major ingredients of the complex have not weakened considerably.

"Cultural Ecological Approach to the Study of the Bhil" forms the sixth chapter wherein R.S. Mann starts with the search of the theoretical frontiers of society, culture and ecological inter-relatedness and adjustment in tribal India. The social and cultural life has a strong bearing on the external ecology. As a specific case Mann explores the cultural milieu of the Bhil of South Rajasthan in terms of its association to the environmental conditions. This relates to the areas of dispersed village settlement, Pal organisation, separation of son from father immediately after his marriage, uni-clan hamlets, clan names, social divisions of Palia and Kalia Bhils and certain aspects of marriage. The Bhil gods, goddesses, spirits, ghosts etc., marking their supernatural world, have close relationship with physical environments, especially the hills, forest, water source and agriculture fields.

Reciprocity and cooperation as part of economic relations in agriculture and irrigation are ecology based. Otherwise, where ecological condition is not pressing, individualism marks Bhil society. However, interaction of culture and ecology has been influenced through acculturation. But the relationship is reframed rather than being broken. However, like the Maler and Pando tribes the traditional persistence of the culture-ecology relationship is still leading over change. And man-to-man interaction, in many instances, continues to be intervened by environmental conditions. And, therefore, the knowledge of environmental features is helpful in describing certain elements of the cultural matrix. Even to explain changes in the socio-economic framework, ecological shake, if any, might prove of relevance. Thus, cultural ecological approach further adds to the deeper exploration of the cultural nexus, and is a welcome addition to the other existing approaches.

In chapter seven "The Soliga : A Study in Ecology, Society and Religion of a Hill Tribe in South India", S.G. Morab has examined L.P. Vidyarthi's concept of nature-man-spirit complex in Soliga tribe of Biligiri Ramgana Hills, Mysore District, Karnataka. This paper is an outcome of his Ph.D. thesis. The stress of the paper is on the analysis of ecological system, social system, religious aspects and economic organisation. Soliga are explained to have complete harmony with their physical environment. They depend on shifting cultivation and collection of forest produce. The forest provides them food, drink, shelter, fuel and raw material of various other kinds used in Soliga technology. Socialization of Soliga children depends on forest ecology. Division of labour in family and Swidden cultivation have an intimate relationship with ecology. Formation of 'local community' is ecology-based. Some Soliga rituals are connected to their movements in the forest, and to the selection of settlement sites. Various operations of shifting cultivation are taken care of by the priest through worship. Sacredness of Swidden fields is maintained. Deities are propitiated prior to honey collection. Agriculture yield depends on the blessings of gods and spirits. Part of good yield is first offered to the deity. Birth and death are attributed as the creations of God. In general, the rites of passage are related to nature, man and supernaturals. As a matter of fact the world of spirits prevails in selecting a new patch for shifting cultivation, in setting up a hut, in life-cycle ceremonies and in the tribal council. In many instances the abode of spirits is the forest, and they cause harm to human beings. The beliefs and practices regarding the supernatural world express the devotion and anxiety of the people at the socio-cultural interaction level too.

"Animism, Economy, Ecology and Change among Negrito Hunters and Gatherers" forms the eighth chapter. R.S. Mann, the author of this chapter, has explained the intimate relationship and interaction between ecology, religion, social life and economy of the Onge tribe of Little Andaman island. The tassel, worn by an Onge woman, is an outcome of forest product. With this tassel are connected certain rituals and superstitions. The clay obtained for painting the body is again an ecological product. In addition to other functions (like mourning, decoration, display of affection for the husband) of clay painting, it also protects the Onge from ticks and mosquitoes which are in abundance in the island climate. The clay, while being put on the body, is mixed with turtle fat obtained from the sea. In addition to ochre, clay, turtle fat, ficus bark is also used to get rid of certain diseases. Pulmonary and skin diseases are attributed to excessive rains, forest and sea conditions. Certain birds are recognised as totems and, thus, their killing and eating are taboo. Clan-like groupings among the Onge are based on totemic objects. Accepting a new-born as a member of the Onge tribe is done through a ritual involving passing fish, obtained from sea or creek, from father to Kuvera (religious person) and back to father.

The spirits, malevolent and benevolent, recognised by the Onge have a bearing on the surrounding ecology. Tomonje spirit survives on pork obtained from wild boar. Likewise, Gay Boratekada spirit is believed to reside in the interior of the forest, and survives on crocodile flesh. Any sudden death in the forest is attributed to this spirit. The abode of Tejawala Lange spirit is the sky. A woman conceives only when blessed by Tejawala Lange. Hunting, gathering and fishing form the chief economy of the Onge. With this is connected their nomadism. Division of Onge into bands, and their mobility are governed by the weather conditions to which the Onge have adapted. Turtle hunting and creek hunting are also adjusted as per weather conditions. Spirits are appeased for the safe return of hunters. A large influx of non-Onge immigrants to Little Andaman has reacted adversely to Onge forest ecology and their economy. Some impact of new inductees, and their activities, has also been left on Onge band organisation and on some of their psychological attitudes. The groups and their respective territorial sanctity have also been affected. Now, in the social organisation of the Onge, one finds instances of adaptation and interaction with ecological conditions, as also with the changes that have taken place thereof. Within the framework of the prevalent ecology, nomadic living and gathering economy, the domestication of plants and animals is not being taken up by the Onge. But a form of indirect trading has been initiated.

In chapter nine "The Nicobarese: A Study in Nature-Man-Spirit Complex", V.S. Sahay explains the complex of nature, man and spirit as prevalent among the Nicobarese of Nicobar Islands. To start with, he introduces the inhabited settlement of the Nicobar group of islands, and the background of their contact with the outsiders. Like others in this book the focus of Sahay remains on horticulture (Nicobarese grow coconut, arecanut and some fruits and vegetables), forest and sea ecology vis-a-vis their interaction and relationship with social organisation and religion. The hut is constructed near the garden which a Nicobarese raises. Spirits are believed to reside in forests. When someone dies of falling from a tree, they observe taboo and do not visit the forest for three days. Sacrifices are offered to appease the garden and forest spirits. Forest is the source of livelihood and provides material for making canoe, mat, basket, hut etc. Herbs of medicinal value are also obtained from the forest. Installation of Takoya, after the death of a person, in the coconut garden marks certain rituals to appease the spirits. A coconut occupies an important place in rituals connected with birth, death, decision-making, marriage, canoe race, witchcraft etc. The witch doctor suggests the place for raising a coconut garden. He is again consulted at various other stages where he performs rituals. Because of excessive rainfall, and hence the dampness of the ground, the Nicobarese erect huts on raised platforms. House construction is marked by the propitiation of spirits; the same holds true for pot-making, canal-making, as also for their safety. Earthen pots, made by Chowrians, are sacred, and so are the canoes. From the sea are obtained fish, octopus, turtle, crocodiles etc. As protection against sea devastation, the spirits are worshipped. The day and time of each sea expedition are fixed by the witch doctor. The canoe-race of the Nicobarese has a socio-religious segnificance. The size of family depends upon the availability of food on the island. Life-cycle rituals, ecology and spirits interact. Benevolent spirits cause conception. The umbilical cord is cut with a sharp bamboo stick. Many religious rituals are associated with adolescent stage. Pre and extra-marital sex relations are attributed to forest ecology. Patrilocal or matrilocal residence is determined by the economic resource. Funeral procession is led by a witch doctor. Purificatory rites connected to the life-cycle are also observed. A large number of Nicobarese ceremonies and festivals are organised to scare away the spirits. Malevolent and benevolent spirits are the cause of various fortunes and misfortunes. Cliffs are said to be the abode of spirits and devils. Offerings, in addition to pig and fowl sacrifice, are made of garden products like coconut, yam, banana, pandanus etc,

"Ecology and Religion of the Kinner : Mountain Dwellers of North-Western Himalayas" forms the tenth chapter. In this chapter Ramesh Chandra initiates with the argument that culture has a great bearing on ecology, specially through adaptation. He picks up religion as major ingredient of culture, and argues that "Religion, both as a dogma and as a way of life helps maintaining a well adjusted plane with the ecology ; thus satisfying people to fulfil their requirements—in terms of

(1) deriving remedial treatment to their problems, and (2) achieving psychological satisfaction. This thesis of Chandra has been tested among the Kinner (who include Kanet, Badhi, Lohar, Koli and Nagaloo), a polyandrous community of North-Western Himalayas. In three distinct divisions of his paper, Chandra starts with the ecological context, goes on to the description of people, and finally lands into religious attributes vis-a-vis their reciprocity to ecological setting. Harder ecological conditions contribute to strong religious faith. Temples are built of locally available material provided by the ecology—it differs in the higher and lower altitudes of Kinnaur. The two elevations are even otherwise marked by Buddhism and Hinduism. Sacrifice of goat to the deity is interpreted in terms of ecological environment. Ecological hazards pose for Kimshoo worship. Shirgal deity presides over domestication of sheep and goat. Likewise, Bansheer deity protects the forest. Concepts of purity and pollution, and the pattern of worship have strong interaction with ecological setting. Reciprocity between religion and ecology is also observed in life-cycle ceremonies.

The above explanations make it obvious that in tribal India there is an intimate relationship and interaction between social organisation/social system on the one hand, and religious complex and ecological conditions on the other. In certain instances it appears that the nature and spirits condition some of the social ways and practices; while in others it sounds as a case of adjustment for a smooth living. At times the relationship appears unavoidable; its avoidance would cause hardship to the people. But at other places the shift in some of the life-styles has been reported leading thereby to the easing of severity traditionally defined in nature, man, spirit complex. The changes, mainly because of the alien influence, are of minor form. In major areas of socio-cultural life of all the eight tribes (Maler, Parahaiya, Pando, Bhil, Soliga, Nicobarese, Kinner, Onge and Ho) studied there is a strong network of linkages between social structure, elements, and those provided by religious attributes and environmental conditions. The restudy of Maler has well certified this explanation.

The tribes, covered for the purpose of this study, are of wide variance. They include hunters and collectors, shifting cultivators and settled agriculturists. Except in the case of the Onge and Nicobarese, where sea ecology is an added dimension, the rest hold similarity in the sense that forests reflect on the life and culture of the tribes. That the forests house some of the spirits is almost uniformly true. Other than the supernaturals the dominance of sacred specialists is also reported. However, some of the details of sacred performances do differ. And these have accordingly designed the belief system of the tribals.

Another important element could be reported from tribes where some kind of ecological change, at times imbalance, has taken place. This specially applies to the Onge and certain sections of the Bhil and Soliga. People are in the stage of making readjustment as regards some of their ways of life. This holds true for religious life too. But in terms of their attitude, the tribals still express their preference for 'traditional' rather than 'transitional' where adjustment, many a time, is becoming difficult. This has specially been reflected in the case of Parahaiya. Many of them are in close physical proximity to the Santhal, but prefer, and continue to subscribe to the old complex of nature-man-spirit.

Both economic necessity and socio-psychological protection have directed man to keep the closest possible liaison with the forces of nature, environmental and supernatural. For the above considerations, man is submissive to, and is sometimes dominated by the apparent as well as non-apparent forces of the natural and supernatural worlds. Among the tribes studied, no alternatives seem to have been provided, or exist to these two requirements of the tribals. And if some viable substitutes are provided, people's old links with their centuries old beliefs will take time to assume any new form. And there, too, the triangular links, that is, between nature, man and spirit, might assume new forms, correspondingly reformulating the concerned socio-economic and cultural network.

The study of tribes, as widely scattered as from Chhota Nagpur/Santhal Pargaṇa, to Kinnaur of Himachal Pradesh to South-West Rajasthan, to Karnataka, to Andaman and Nicobar, within the perspective of nature-man-spirit complex does certify that one can certainly have deeper insights in tribal life and culture with the help of cultural ecological methodology. The latter provides a broad based frame to further enrich a social analyst's capacity for analysis and interpretation of socio-cultural phenomena. In the baggage of social anthropological methodology, the cultural ecological approach is quite a rewarding experience in researching man, his society and culture.

R.S. MANN

ONE

Julian Steward

THE MALER
A Study in Nature-Man-Spirit Complex of a Hill Tribe in Bihar*

PROFESSOR Vidyarthi presents a vivid, penetrating and sympathetic analysis of the Maler, a primitive hill tribe of India. The Maler, or Paharia, constitute an enclave within the great civilization of India and are even linked tenuously with the larger society in several ways, but they fail to share the basic institutions of that society. The "little tradition" of the Maler, to use Redfield's terms, does not reflect the "great tradition" of India. It has no castes, occupational specialists, urban concentrations, or states. Its supernaturalism has been influenced little if at all by Buddhism, Islam, or Christianity. Particulars show considerable borrowing from their neighbours on the plains, the Santhal, but much less from Hinduism.

Like several other hill peoples of India, the Maler live in an infertile and rather inaccessible habitat which has insulated them from fundamental impacts of the larger society. Moreover, their local traditions, which are very old ones, are unable to assimilate alien patterns. They represent social and spiritual adjustments to omnipresent threats of starvation, sickness and death. The Maler's anxieties are deep, constant and rarely below the surface of consciousness.

Despite the extreme difficulties of field work, Professor Vidyarthi and his students from Bihar University (now Ranchi University) made extended visits to the Maler over the course of several years. They were able to win the confidence of the

*This article appeared as the Foreword to L. P. Vidyarthi's *The Maler: A Study in Nature-Man-Spirit Complex*, 1963, Bookland Ltd., Calcutta.

people, analyze their economic, social and religious life and record other special kinds of data. This volume is a basic ethnographic monograph, which covers virtually all aspects of culture, but the emphasis is upon the subsistence activities, social arrangements, and supernaturalism involved in the struggle to survive. Professor Vidyarthi has wisely relegated other materials to a series of appendices.

The central theme is that the Maler are motivated by two basic drives, hunger for food and need for sex, which the Maler also conceive as a hunger. The unrelenting anxieties that surround subsistence, health and sex are expressed in a religious system, which includes a considerable complex of supernatural beings, religious personnel, and ceremonialism. Professor Vidyarthi's analysis makes the religious complex extremely interesting, not because its ingredients are unique, but by demonstrating how the Maler have related the beliefs and practices functionally to the needs and fears of the people and to different levels within the social structure : the individual, the family, the lineage, the village, and the region. Professor Vidyarthi shows how the structuring of society within each of these levels in turn represents organisations of the people for the purposes of subsistence, sexual satisfaction, procreation, socialization of children, and patterns of interaction and co-operation appropriate to these goals. An important orienting concept is that of cultural ecology, or the adaptation of social arrangements to the requirements of surviving in this harsh environment by means of a certain technological inventory.

The relationships of the family, lineage and community to one another and to productive processes are especially provocative in view of their significance for comparative studies. Despite a fairly rich inventory of crops, including maize and rice, domesticated animals, including cattle, goats, hogs and chickens, and forest products, the rocky, hilly and forested lands make subsistence very precarious. Slash-and-burn cultivation requires a new clearing each year, for land is usually cultivated a second time only after the lapse of at least five years. Frequently, the crop is partly or entirely lost owing to wild animals, insects, and other adversities.

Social structure consists of interpersonal arrangements adapted to the exploitation of resources, satisfaction of sex, child rearing, and manipulation of supernatural beings. The basis of society is the nuclear family, which, in six villages averages only 3.8 persons. The family, which is sometimes polygynous occupies its own hut, own forest lands for slash-and-burn farming, and is the ultimate unit of consumption. But the isolated family is unable to cope with many crucial tasks. In clearing and preparing the forests for planting, in constructing houses, and in other chores, it needs assistance. The first call for co-operative help is always to other members of the patrilineage.

Professor Vidyarthi's detailed analysis of the Maler lineage raises some interesting questions. The lineage is reckoned through only 3 generations, and it consists of an average of 4 nuclear families. Each family has an average of 3.8 persons—a total of 15.2 lineage. Marriage is forbidden within 3 generations of each line of descent. The Maler have a term to distinguish the lineage from other social units, but it seems structurally to be little more than an extended family which is patrilineal in inheritance of farm lands. These lineages are very small as compared with lineage segments or primary lineages elsewhere. They are minimal in size, perhaps subminimal. Families average only 1.8 children, and the population of Professor Vidyarthi's principal village has shrunk to one quarter of its size of 50 years ago. The patrilineal hunting bands among the Australians, Bushmen, Fuegians, and others consist of lineages of forty or more persons. Some of the single-house lineages of the Northwest Amazon are still larger. Lineages in Africa and Asia discussed by Leach, Bohannan, Forts, Evans Pritchard and others are so large as to have segmented into many primary corporate units.

A population which barely perpetuates its numbers must average two offspring per family who in turn produce two offspring and so on. If relationship is traced through the male line for only three generations, the minimum cannot be less than three families—grandfather, father and son with additional kin and children of the son. The total lineage membership might range between 10 and 20 persons. A large lineage means either that the population is expanding or that descent is reckoned beyond three generations.

In the light of Professor Vidyarthi's data, two ways of enlarging the sphere of co-operation of the lineage or extended family suggest themselves. First, the family or minimal lineage may be enlarged by reckoning relationship back to five or six generations. Thus, four generations would double the average of 15 persons of the three generations lineage to 30 persons. Five generations would make it 60 persons, and so on. Knowledge of ancestry to five or six generations among a people without a sense of history or genealogy would be lost only if there were taboos which erased knowledge of deceased ancestors. Extension of lineage beyond five or six generations ordinarily occurs only where there is a fairly sophisticated society, large population, and sense—or myth—of genealogy. Second, instead of lineage expansion, other lineages within the same community may participate in co-operative enterprises. The Maler village consists of three to seven lineages, which are related through inter-marriage and co-operate in many village-level functions. Without detailed cross-cultural comparisons, one cannot be sure in any instance whether co-operation within an enlarged lineage of 4 to 6 generations or between smaller lineages within the village is a function of the nature of land use, residence patterns, and other factors. It seems clear that patrilineal hunting bands reckon relationship within five or six generations because lineage land tenure and co-operative hunting within territories of optimum size would be badly disjoined if lineages were to split after three generations. Maler land tenure is on a family basis, and there appears to be no reason why regulation of sex ceremonialism and other activities within the village cannot be carried on by inter-lineage co-operation.

Among other provocative features of Professor Vidyarthi's monograph is the relationship of various types of social interaction, especially of co-operation, to levels and territories of integration. The village achieves cohesion through marriages between its lineages, through common shrines, ceremonies and sacrifices, through an hereditary priest (*majhiye*) who is also secular leader, through a youth dormitory, and through association of village members in daily activities which creates bonds that cross out kinship ties.

The nuclear family, extended family or lineage and village are the basic, and probably the oldest, patterns. Social interaction fades beyond the village, but it is not absent. Members of a Maler village may inter-marry, offer co-operative assistance, attend ceremonies and visit weekly markets at other Maler villages. The Maler area or region of social interaction includes about 80 villages within a radius of 8 to 10 miles. That of the lowland Santhal includes 500 villages within a 40 mile radius. "The Maler have a regional headman, Sardar, whose office dates from pre-British times, but whose duties are ill-defined. Today, he collects taxes and maintains law and order. Interaction with the lowland peoples, especially the Santhal, is largely economic. The Maler sell local forest products, borrow money, and sometimes hire labour. Borrowing of money and hiring labour, however, seem to be functions of a marginal, transitional situation. Plough cultivation with its greater cash requirements is moving up from the lowland but it has not penetrated the culture of the true hill Maler. These inter-regional cash transactions have introduced money to the Maler to the extent that fines for breaches of taboos or customary behaviour are paid in rupees, but this has not affected the older subsistence patterns nor the structure and functions of the family, lineage and community.

Professor Vidyarthi has also related the beliefs and practices concerning the supernatural very clearly to the basic drives and anxieties of the people and to the levels of socio-cultural integration and co-operation. The religious complex is surprisingly rich for so simple a society, owing partly to fairly extensive borrowing from the lowland Santhal and slightly to infiltration of Hindu ingredients. There are nature spirits, both beneficient and evil, and deceased ancestors which need to be placated. There are innumerable fetishes, household and village shrines, and sacred places. Religious personnel includes shamans, curers, oracles, ceremonial leaders, and witches, sacrifices, offerings, magic, and counter-magic are all prominent.

Among malicious forces, there is witchcraft, in which everyone believes but to which no one admits. The Maler, like so many societies that consist of tight in-groups which suppress hostilities, ascribe many misfortunes to the malevolence of some neighbour. But there are also many evil nature spirits, which may cause abortions, sickness, death, starvation and other calamities. These must be avoided, propitiated, and guarded against.

The more benign spirits are called upon to prevent sickness and other misfortunes and to further food production, but ceremonial lapses and violations of taboos may turn them against the people. The religious functionaries include shamans and curers who deal with individual troubles and illness, the family heads who conduct household rites, and oracles and ceremonial leaders who operate on behalf of the village.

It is apparently a function of the extremely small size of the primary lineage and of the fairly tightly integrated village that while the lineage operates ceremonially mainly in life cycle functions, the village as a whole carries out the principal ceremonials. The village and the nuclear family, however, are usually counterparts of the same religious activities, which relate principally to the two basic "hungers", food and sex. That is, village ceremonies are accompanied by household rites.

The principal annual village ceremony follows the harvest. It includes offerings to the spirits for the harvest (but smaller offerings if the harvest is not good—a kind of chastisement of the spirits), feasting and merry-making and sexual licence. Since blood sacrifice is efficacious in proportion to the size of the animal, buffalos, which can be purchased only through contributions from the whole community are sacrificed at the major ceremonies. The sex play at the harvest ceremony relates to the marriage system and to the nature of controls of pre- and extra-marital sexual relations. The sexual hunger of unmarried Maler youths leads to many affairs, but, since these are prohibited, they are carried out clandestinely in the forests. Affairs between youths or between married persons are matters of village concern. One who denies them is put under oath and subjected to the ordeal of licking salt or a hot axe head. While maintenance of pre-marital chastity or marital faithfulness is not usually treated so rigorously in primitive societies, the Maler regard these as offences against the village as well as the family or lineage. The sexual licence permitted at the annual harvest festival is essentially an occasion of the selection of marriage partners, and it therefore has village approval. Thus, oaths, ordeals and ceremonies serve to enforce customary law in the absence of formal law and law enforcement agencies.

In these vital areas of Maler life it appears that the lineage is frequently bypassed. The nuclear family operates in some measure as the basic productive, consumption, sexual, and ceremonial unit. The several other families within the lineage, or extended family, co-operate in production and some ceremonialism. But, because the lineage is small and the multilineage village has deep interest in such matters as maintenance of the family against promiscuity, insurance of subsistence productivity, protection against disease, disaster, predatory animals and other threats of concern to all village members, the multilineage village, instead of an expanded lineage of five or six generations has become the integrated unit that deals with the problems arising from the hungers for food and sex and with the ever-present threats to existence.

Professor Vidyarthi's generous request that I write this Foreword has led me to speculate about a number of interesting matters. A monograph less rich in a sense of problem and less incisive in relevant detail would not stimulate such thought. The highest compliment I can pay Professor Vidyarthi is that his analysis is so provocative even though its substantive reporting is not vitiated by excessive theorizing or imposition of preconceived notions upon the data.

TWO

Pradip Singh

NATURE-MAN-SPIRIT COMPLEX OF A HILL TRIBE
A Restudy

I

IT has long been established that ecology plays a vital role in conditioning the culture of a given area, and that the geographical situation of a locale goes a long way in shaping the needs, customs, behaviour and thoughts of the people. The interaction between man and nature is a two-way process. Both affect and alter each other, the degree of impact depending upon the technological advancement of the people concerned. The greater the technological achievement of the people, the lesser the impact of nature, and vice-versa.

So, in different ecological settings, different types of cultures developed and flourished, each with its own distinct economy, social organization, material artifacts, religious beliefs, ethos and world-view. An anthropologist has to take into account every factor which affects man's life and culture, so it was but natural that he be interested in the study of ecology. Considerable emphasis has been given on this aspect by a host of anthropológists, who view it in two ways—determinism and possibilism. The former view is that nature determines the culture while the latter view is that it only conditions or limits the culture. Nobody however denies that it has a great impact on life and culture.

Anthropologists of all hues and complexions, right from Ratzel through Graebena, Wissler, Kroeber, Redfield, Steward and Vidyarthi have emphasized this point, and all are influenced by the same view-point : Nature-Man. It is now realised that the true relationship between man and his environment is that of mutual interaction, which has led to a sub-discipline of cultural ecology.

Both Wissler (1917) and Kroeber (1939) have explained the relationship between man and his ecology in terms of culture area and human and environmental traits. Steward (1955) proposed three fundamental procedures of cultural ecology : (1) The relation between environment and exploitative or productive technology; (2) the behaviour patterns involved in the exploitation of a particular area by means of a particular technology; (3) the extent to which the behaviour patterns entailed in exploiting the environment affect other aspects of culture. Steward used these procedures to examine the cultures of the hunting stage to modern civilization. Redfield (1955) reviews the studies to bring out the ecological basis of culture and comes up with the view that "both man and nature are the twin-agents of the perennial revolution that shapes and reshapes the face of the earth". On the same topic an international symposium was organized by the Wenner Gren Foundation (1956) also.

Researches on these lines in the Indian context were unknown until the publication of Vidyarthi's paper (1958) and his book (1963). This was a pioneering work and a landmark on cultural ecological researches in India. In his paper "Cultural Types in Tribal Bihar" (1958), Vidyarthi described the cultural types and levels of socio-cultural integration of the tribal societies on the basis of their ecological settings and resultant economy. He made out four cultural types :

(a) Hunters and gatherers
(b) Shifting cultivators
(c) Settled agriculturists
(d) Simple artisans

But the most monumental piece of work in this direction was his book, *The Maler: A Study in Nature-Man-Spirit Complex* (1963), in which he describes the culture of a hill tribe—the Maler—in terms of Nature-Man-Spirit Complex, where the three ingredients of the complex are interdependent and mutually complementary. This was a useful theoretical and methodological model, which was later on used successfully to study different tribes in different natural environments. The studies of Korwa (Sandhwar, A. N., 1978), Parhaiya (Prasad, R. K., 1978), Pando (Sinha, R. K., 1977), Nicobarese (Sahay, V. S., 1979) and Soliga (Morab, S. G., 1980), clearly establish that this concept of Nature-Man-Spirit Complex is an important and useful tool in studying not only the pre-literate, but also the peasant and modern societies.

II

Vidyarthi's study of the Maler signalled an interesting departure from the established tradition of writing a monograph. His approach of Nature-Man-Spirit Complex arose from the practical exigency of arranging the data in a meaningful way—to depict the 'soul' instead of just the 'bones' of Maler culture. This added a new dimension to the cultural ecological studies.

While analysing his data, he discovered a close inter-relationship between Nature, Man and Spirit and their mutual interactions. He believed that theoretical and methodological interests were as important as the ethnographic one, and in order to combine all these in a conceptual manner, he came up with this concept.

The book was divided into three parts with the headings Nature, Man and Spirit respectively, which were further sub-divided into eight chapters. In the first part, he demonstrates the ecological basis of Maler Culture, showing the importance of hills and forests as well as the typical Swidden cultivation (Khallu) around which the entire Maler life revolved. In the second part, dealing with Man, he examines the network of relationships in all its aspects, including the structure and organization of the family, different social institutions and the life cycle of a typical Maler. In the third part, on Spirit, he describes the religious beliefs in supernatural beings, sacred centres, sacred performances and sacred specialists.

He discovered that every moment of the Maler life was profoundly influenced by nature on the one hand and spirit on the other. These two ingredients of the complex play a paramount role in the life cycle of the Maler people. The existence of one simply cannot be thought of in the absence of another.

Laying stress on ecology, Vidyarthi asserts that Maler

culture originated, developed and flourished in the lap of nature. The Maler are surrounded by forests, and a comprehensive understanding of this culture, he points out, can be had mainly by examining it in the context of its forests. In addition to providing land for slash-and-burn (or Swidden) cultivation—a main source of Maler economy—the forests provide them with food, drink, shelter, medicine, raw materials for cottage industries, love-nests and graveyards.

An average Maler is motivated by two basic drives—hunger for food and sex. The interpersonal relations have been arranged in adaptation to that exploitation of resources, satisfaction of sex, child rearing. etc. They do not have a clan system and kinship is reckoned through lineage up to three generations.

The ceaseless anxieties for survival are expressed in a religious system which includes a considerable complex of supernatural beings, religious personnel and ceremonialism, and which have been functionally related to the needs and fears of the people. Every moment of the Maler life is woven with some spirit or other—both malevolent and benevolent—which are to be placated in a precise way for a happy and prosperous life.

Vidyarthi's book brought into light an isolated and obscure tribe living in "extreme primitiveness". More than two decades have passed since his study. Modern democratic institutions and social reforms as well as new leadership patterns are creating an atmosphere in which even the most conservative and rigid systems become susceptible to change. The relative impact of the traditional and modern processes of change (Hinduisation, Christianization, Industrialization and welfare agencies including political parties, etc.) is to be examined to know the changes—their level and direction—that are going on unnoticed behind the curtain of isolation.

It was felt that in the light of these processes of change the concept of Nature-Man-Spirit Complex needs to be re-examined. And what better unit than the Maler tribe itself where it all began! My paper aims essentially at this. The ethnographic data used in this paper have been collected from the same villages which were studied by Vidyarthi earlier.

III

The latest census data on the tribe level are not available, but the figures of the Welfare Department (Paharia Welfare) indicate that the population of the Maler (the Sanvaria Paharia) is on the decline.

NATURE

The Forest Economy

The economy of the Maler still pivots around the forest. It provides them with roots, fruits, liquor, fuel-wood, logs, cotton and *kher* which they either consume or sell in the market. The forest is so much embedded in their life pattern that they simply cannot think of parting with it.

The main fruits which the forest yields are mango, mahua, bair, bel, sharifa, palm and papita. The first two are sold as cash crop. In fact, mango provides them with a sort of seed money for the coming *khallu* cultivation, since every family earns on an average about Rs. 200 during summer in addition to providing food in this lean season.

Semul trees, which yield cotton are another cash-earning source. Most of the families have about 4 or 5 semul trees, which are also sold at an average of Rs. 300 per year.

Bamboo is another valuable forest product, though very few families own bamboo-groves. An average bamboo is sold for Rs. 6. A family which has bamboo-groves is considered rich since it can raise money any time by selling bamboo. Shyam Malto, son of Guia Sardar of village Bendori who spent a record Rs. 2,000 during his marriage, managed it by selling his bamboo alone.

The forest also provides kendu leaves, but these are not sold by the villagers. They are used to prepare their indigenous *biris* (chutti) for smoking.

Among the roots, nape, kendu, cholango, pangdo, pusre, dumberi and tiso are important and are found in abundance. Most of these are available in June-July, when people devote their time in *Khallu*. According to them, a man can live on these roots alone during these months.

But the most important item that forests provide in abundance is fire wood. Every member of the family, male or female, adult or child, cuts and collects fuel wood in the jungle and brings it home and leaves it to dry. On market day one or two members of each family go to the market and sell their wood. During summer each man earns about Rs. 2.50 and during winter these yield as much as Rs. 5. This money is very useful in buying mustard oil and kerosene, spices, vegetables and sometimes rice, too. Actually, the expenses on oil and spices are met by selling fuel wood alone.

From October to March, wooden logs are also in demand. Contractors buy these from villagers and export them to markets in Bengal and to the southern parts of Santhal Parganas. A log of about 6′×5″×4″ fetches Rs. 6. So, during winter, the male can be seen roaming in the jungles to select suitable pieces of such wood, while the female collects fuel wood.

Forests also provide many types of raw materials for building houses, many indigenous medicines, herbs and so on.

Kurwa or Khallu

The main agricultural activity of the Maler centres around Khallu. This is a sort of slash-and-burn cultivation.

Formerly, the Maler loved this method of cultivation but now they do it only because there is no alternative. Every person complains about the huge amount of capital and the hard labour that Kurwa requires, while the yield is comparatively low. There is a marked shift in their attitude about Kurwa, which they wish to give up for its obsolescence. Moreover, they say that Kurwa is very life-consuming. That is, an average Paharia dies early only because he has to go through so much rigours in his life. The example of the neighbouring plain-dweller Santhals who work only once and eat the whole year round is too alluring and enticing for them. Every Maler wants to cultivate paddy lands. In Benderi, one family has about 200 bighas of paddy lands, about 35 bighas on hill-tops. It concentrates on paddy cultivation and ignores Kurwa. Those who have such lands down in the plains give them to Santhals on *bataai* (50 per cent share), because the amount of land they own is not enough to support them for the whole year, and so they cannot make it a full-time operation themselves.

And Kurwa is expensive indeed. A Kurwa plot of about 3 acres needs at least Rs. 1,000 in cash and intensive labour 4 times during the entire operation, excluding harvesting. They sow maize, millet, arhar, sutri and barbatli, all in the same plot.

Khallu is an eight-stage operation. The first stage is the selection of the site. This is done usually a year in advance, sometimes two or three years earlier. The plot is selected on the basis of vegetation which must be dense. A plot which is being cultivated for the first time yields more than the one where it is repeated. In maize specially the produce is much lower in the latter type of plots.

So, a plot is left for 5 to 8 years for the vegetation to grow again. By sheer necessity, even a person who has a great amount of land may have to borrow Kurwa fields from others. Leno Pradhan, the Manjhiya of the village Benderi who has about 1,500 bighas of Kurwa and bari lands, had to take on lease the Kurwa plot in 1979, and has given to six persons in 1980.

The charges for the lease are nominal. A plot of two acres is charged Rs. 6 and that of about 4 acres, Rs. 10 or Rs. 12. The lessee is expected to offer liquor while asking for the lease, and again to give the products as gifts to the land owner.

From March or April, the site selected for Kurwa begins to witness activity. The trees and shrubs are cut. The Maler have begun to earn from this also. Fuel wood is in great demand among Santhals, who have to buy it from the Maler.

It is usual to actually give the land on lease a year earlier than the one agreed upon to the Santhal so that the earth can be prepared for cultivation. The Santhals cut the wood themselves or employ Maler labourers (another source of income). The wood thus chopped is left to dry up and is brought down to Santhal villages just before the rainy season. In return, the Maler get two to three maunds of paddy, depending upon the area and denseness of the vegetation. Mahua, semul, mango and such other trees are spared.

Whatever is left by Santhals, is collected by the Maler, either for their own consumption, or, if suitable, for sale. The shrubs are ignored.

Before the monsoon breaks out, these shrubs are lit. The fire burns every bit of left out wood and shrubs, thus clearing the plot. The monsoon showers wash up the ashes. Sometimes, even lighting the fire is done by Santhals, who do so when they go out in group hunting, but they do not give the share to Maler, even if they kill the game on the hills.

In late June, when it has rained for at least three or four days continuously, sowing operation begins. Wooden sticks, suitably tapered and pointed at one end are used for this purpose.

Arhar is sown first, because it can grow even after a little rain. With the arhar, sutri (a type of pulse) is also mixed and sown. A few days later, when rains become regular, maize and barbatti (beans) are sown. Either three seeds of maize or two seeds of maize plus one seed of barbatti are sown in the holes, dug by pointed wooden sticks.

Just before sowing, the Manjhiya Than (Singpate-Nadu) is worshipped on village level, the worship (*puja*) is called *kudchake*. A pig is sacrificed by the Manjhiya, which is shared by all the villagers. The Manjhiya utters, amme oaee jati...... which means, "Let the crop be good. Please don't let any body cut his hands or feet by sickles and kulhari. Don't let the snake and scorpion come out while we work. Don't let pests and animals destroy the crop or we shall die."

After this worship, every villager is free to sow the seeds in the respective Kurwa fields.

An average plot of three acres requires seed in the following quantities:

Name	*Quantity* (Kgs)	*Seed price* (Rs per Kg)	*Yield price* (Rs)
Maize	15	2.50	2
Millet	8	2.00	1
Arhar	3	3.00	2
Barbatti	5	5.00	4
Sutri	10	1.50	1

About 15 days after sowing, the first weeding begins. By this time the maize plants are about a foot in height. The fields are weeded and bajra-seeds are sown. The weeded grass is used to cover the bajra (millet) seeds. If the sutri, sown earlier, has not grown, it shall also be sown again.

The sowing operation requires labour also. Usually 40 to 50, sometimes even 80 persons are required to work for two to four days to finish the task. They are paid both in cash and kind since the barter system also operates here. If a man has enough millet, he pays by it, which amounts to 3 pai (measures) + 1 handful. If the labourers are to be paid in cash, they get Rs. 4 only. The labourers are both Maler of the same village or Santhals of neighbouring villages.

After this, the Maler get a respite for about twenty days. This period is used to construct high *machans* in the Kurwa field. Here a male member of the family stays at night to protect the crops from wild animals. This is called *mache*.

The second round of weeding begins after about one month of the first one. The grasses are cut and left there to wither. The amount of labour and wages are the same as for the first.

After this, protection of the crop is their main problem and pastime. A Maler lives in the Kurwa field day and night, because as soon as the ears of corn appear, jackals, wild dogs, sometime even bears begin their visits to the Kurwa field. Pests are another threat to the crops.

In late October or early November, the corn ripens. But it is harvested only after a black fowl is sacrificed in the Kurwa field in the name of Yam Gossaiyan. One ear of corn is also offered. This worship is done on the family level.

Then the maize is harvested. The straw is left in the field. By late November, barbatti, sutri and arhar are also collected. This harvesting is done by the family members themselves. The male members now devote their time to building a hut in the Kurwa field itself, called *kalkuria*. The former *mache* served until then. The new hut is made large enough to accommodate the whole family. Until then, the cooking is done in the village itself. After the construction of the kalkuria, the entire family moves to this hut with its belongings. If the family is a large one and there is an adult son, he stays back in the village.

The millet ripens in January. Its harvesting is a little delicate because the ears get heavy with grains and can fall on the field. Usually labourers are employed for cutting and winnowing right in the kalkuria, and each gets 4 seers of millet or paddy plus lunch as wages.

Before harvesting the maize, the Yam Gossaiyan is worshipped again. This time a pair of pigeons, betel leaves, nuts, sweets and vermilion are offered.

The whole family then comes back to the village with the grain. The house is cleaned and the Attu (the hearth) Gossaiyan is worshipped by offering a red fowl.

Now is the time to pay back the loan with interest, which they got from the Mahajan in Borio Bazar. All this is done by the end of January after which people make merry and look forward to their main festival Bandana, held in late February.

In addition to Kurwa on the hill slopes, the plain Bari lands on hill tops are also cultivated. The Bari witnesses activities twice annually. Two crops are grown here (a) Bhadai and (b) Aghani.

In bhadai, maize and barbatti are grown. These are harvested in July. Then mustard and kurthi are sown, to be harvested in December. For bhadai crop, Chal Gossaiyan is worshipped by each family sacrificing fowl.

Rice is the staple food of the Maler. Grains (jagu) of maize, millet and paddy are relished in that order. Rice is accompanied by pulse and barbatti and sutri, or, very rarely, vegetables too. Bread is not eaten very much.

The Maler say that though paddy rice is the best in taste, it is worst as food because, one becomes hungry again in three hours, while maize rice keeps the belly full for a whole day.

The people eat only twice a day—once in the morning at about 10 A.M. and then just at nightfall, about 6.30 P.M. If they can get roots and fruits in the jungle, they do eat them, otherwise they eat nothing else. Their water intake is also remarkably low. A man can work in the field for five or six hours continuously without taking even a drop of water.

The Maler drink too, both male and female. But they are not alcoholic like many other tribes. They brew millet and maize beer, but not that of mahua. The latter is brewed exclusively by Santhals from whom the Maler buy at Rs. 4 a bottle.

Maize and millet are brewed only during Bandana. During this festival even a child drinks to his heart's content. For the rest of the year, the Maler drink only on *haat* days, once or twice a week. The women and children drink on festive occasions like marriages only, simply because they cannot afford to drink otherwise.

In taste, they prefer ethyl spirits sold in government approved shops. But one such bottle costs Rs. 5.60, while mahua can be had at only Rs. 4. So, they usually drink the latter.

Liquor is important in entertaining guests too. Whenever a relative arrives, he has invariably to be offered drink, even if it entails taking a loan. A man who can offer his guest enough wine and meat to make him pass out, is considered a good relative and is held in high esteem. If a man does not or cannot offer drink, he is looked down upon, and his villlage is not visited, nor is he invited to other villages.

The Maler are fond of meat but they cannot afford to eat it very often. Pork is preferred to mutton and every family tries to keep a few pigs, which can be sold at time of need. Fowls are also husbanded, but the eggs are not eaten. These are left for hatching. Sometimes chicken is also eaten if a guest arrives. Usually, these are kept for worshipping. Usually a family has to sacrifice five to six fowls a year excluding the deaths, which require two.

Some families have cows too, but they are not milked to make the calves strong.

An average Maler is not dressed as lavishly as a Santhal. Rather, his dress is only the minimum necessary.

The man wears a dhoti wrapped around his waist when he goes to market or to visit his relatives. In addition he wears underwear and a shirt.

Women wear two piece dresses. The upper piece is called jangha. This is a rectangular piece of cloth. Two ends of the cloth are tied around the neck and the rest is used to cover the breasts. The lower piece is called a lungi. The lower portion of jangha is tucked into the lungi. This leaves the entire back and half of the leg exposed.

A girl begins to wear the jangha when she attains puberty. Till then a girl usually wears children's dresses. In fact, the jangha is the symbol of physical maturity.

The women now prefer saris too. They wear saris on festive occasions. Terelyne saris are very much in demand, which are also worn in the fashion of the lungi.

Women are fond of ornaments too. Usually these are made of ordinary metal. Some families do have silver ornaments.

The most common ornament is the ring, worn on the nose, the ear and the fingers. One of the peculiarities of Maler ornaments are their ear-rings. Usually 9 to 12 rings are worn on each ear.

Glass bangles and necklaces are also in vogue. Some women use face powder also during Bandana, marriage-ceremonies and while being photographed. Whenever I wanted to take a photo, every person begged for a few minutes to wash his or her face, put on their Sunday best and hold an article like an umbrella or torch in their hands. They have become very much appearance-conscious.

Tattooing is totally absent.

A Maler hut is one-roomed. They live, eat, sleep and cook food in the same room.

The hut is made of wood, bamboo and *kher*. Every adult Maler is proficient in constructing huts. All the raw materials are available in the forests—even ropes. A man can build a hut by himself in about a week and needs help only in placing the central beam and roof. This help is extended by other villagers readily.

Every hut has at least two doors. The doors are very small, about 4′×3′, and without stooping even a short man cannot enter the hut. The second door is at the back which is used when a man does not want to meet any person—usually money-lenders—who come to his hut.

The household articles are few. Every hut contains at least one cot, a few pitchers, a hearth in a corner, winnowing fans, two or three wooden seats (kando), sickles and kulhari, cooking utensils, bow and arrow and, in some huts, drums also. Corn can be seen hanging from the roof as also hangers for pitchers, and other pots.

Many families have a mortar and pestle (*okhri* and *musal*) also. Three families have got the Janta grinding gadget also.

The cooking utensils of the Maler are bought from the *haat* (market) and are made of aluminium. These are the *degchi* (pan), *karahi* (wok), *kalchul* (ladle) etc. Some have iron buckets too.

Almost every Maler is in debt. He is always short of cash and needs it at the time of the Bandana festival, during marriages and also at Kurwa. The loan in cash and kind, is readily supplied by the *mahajans* (money-lenders) in Borio and other places, at an interest of 50 per cent. If a Maler takes a loan in kind for seeds, the interest rate is 100 per cent.

In the village under study, every person was in debt, ranging from Rs. 50 to Rs. 400. In most cases, the purpose was Kurwa cultivation, while some had taken loans to buy new clothes for Bandana festival and marriage. The proposed way of return is by selling the agricultural produce from Kurwa. Usually, bajra (millet) and barbatti (beans) are used to repay the loan.

Usually, a Maler is unable to return the whole amount in one year. The balance is carried over to next year, and after two or three years, the accumulated amount is so great that he can never repay it. When such a situation arrives, the Mahajans take some land away. Now, the debtor works in his own field as a labourer and gives half the produce to the Mahajans. In Bendri, five persons had to part from their lands, all of them bari lands, ranging from 5 to 16 bighas in area.

Debt Redemption Act was enforced in Bihar in 1976, but no positive step was taken by the authorities. The Mahajans, too, mislead the Maler, and Santhals also, that if they take loan from the Banks, and fail to repay their houses and every thing else will be forfeited. Moreover, the Mahajans lend money at any time on demand, a facility which banks can never give. This is also one of the major causes of the stronghold the Mahajans have over the people.

In Bendri, 36 out of 42 families have taken agricultural (taccavi) loans from Borio circle office, the amounts varying from Rs. 30 to Rs.100. This money is given on an interest of 12.5 per cent with a clause that the interest will not exceed the principal. No Maler has ever paid the money back in

Bendri, or for that matter, any other village in Borio circle. The Government usually exempts them from paying the interest, and sometimes writes off the loans altogether.

The bi-weekly market sits every Tuesday and Saturday at Borio Bazar. The Saturday-market is bigger than that on Tuesday.

The people within a radius of ten miles attend this market. On Saturday at least 8-10 thousand Maler, Santhals and non-tribals come here. The vendors from as far as Sahibganj, Tinpahar, Godda and Dumka, set up their shops in addition to hundreds of local businessmen.

Market-day is a day to be looked forward to. The Maler bring fuel wood and other seasonal commodities like mango, mahua, semul, millet, barbatti and mustard for sale.

A bundle of fuel wood fetches about Rs. 2.50 in summer and Rs. 4.50 to Rs. 5 in winter. They buy spices, salt, mustard oil and kerosene and rice, clothes, torches and umbrellas, etc.

In addition to the economic function, the market has social and political functions as well. It helps in meeting relatives and friends in other villages. Marriages are also arranged in the market.

Many types of news are also available in the market—political and otherwise. They come to hear of elections and about political parties. They see non-tribals and learn about their food habits, dress patterns, etc. This also goes a long way in moulding their attitudes and behaviour. In short, the market serves to bring them closer to the outside world and bring them into the stream of national life, albeit slowly.

The division of labour in a Maler family is based on age and sex. The males usually do the hard work, viz. cutting of heavy logs, the Kurwa cultivation, etc., while women do the household chores, viz. fetching water from the spring, cooking, collecting firewood, roots and fruits, rearing children etc. But there is no work which only a man or a woman does. Women also help in every work of men in Kurwa operation, while the man is equally proficient in household work. In fact, there is no specialization of labour among them.

A woman cuts wood in the forest, acts as a labourer, goes to the haat with a bundle of firewood on her head, sells and purchases in the market. A man cooks food quite as deliciously as the woman, washes the utensils and rears the child.

The age factor is also important in the division of labour. A child is not required to do heavy work. A boy and a girl, as soon as they attain the age of five or six, begin to help their parents. The boy grazes the cattle, collects roots and fruits, takes the cooked food to his father out in the Kurwa fields etc. A girl helps her mother by fetching water, collecting firewood for their own consumption, and plays with younger brothers and sisters. Sometimes a girl also goes out for grazing the cattle. Even among younger ones, there is no hard and fast division of labour based on sex.

The Maler men and women, as a rule, do not work as labourers outside their village. They may readily do the work for other Maler or for Santhal if the work, however hard, is to be done within their village boundary. This includes the work required in the various stages of Kurwa operation and carrying the wood from one place to another (for Santhals). The wages vary from Rs. 2 (for half day) to Rs. 4 (for full day) in cash to five seers of paddy plus lunch (for full day) in kind.

The system of co-operative labour in mutual reciprocity is on the decline. One has to pay for every service one gets.

THE MAN

The Social System

The family is the minimum social unit among the Maler and is composed of husband, wife and their unmarried children. As soon as the son marries, he sets up a separate household in the village.

The average size of the family in village Bendri comes to 4.4. The family is essentially nuclear and is the centre of economic, social and religious activities.

The family is patrilineal and patri-local. They do not have a clan system, and kinship is reckoned through lineage, both in father's and mother's line. But since their memory is short they usually remember only up to three generations. Marriage is prohibited among lineage members, but in fourth generation, they all get mixed up, and marriages may, and often does, take place.

The husband is the master of the family and has a final say in everything. Though wives are virtually equal in economic affairs, in the family her position is low.

Usually, the husband-wife relationship is cordial and intimate. They act as equals in all aspects of life. They help and co-operate in each other's activities. The woman is as proficient in Kurwa operation, as the man is in looking after and rearing the child. In fact, at times of necessity, the husband does all the household chores normally assigned to the wife.

The relationship gets sour only when the wife becomes lax in her duties, or develops extra-marital relationship with others —a phenomenon not uncommon among Maler. In such cases, divorce is the only way out. A compromise is neither desired nor tried.

Parent-child relationship is also very cordial and informal. Usually, it is the duty of the wife to look after the children, but the husband is not indifferent either.

The control over children is not very strict. They are loved and treated with affection, and, usually, left to their own devices. If the child goes astray or does not obey his or her parents, the maximum punishment is a severe scolding. Beating of children is rare.

The children, in turn, also respect their parents.

As soon as the child attains the age of about ten, he is treated more as a friend than as a son. He may drink or smoke with his parents. His wishes are usually fulfilled and his advice considered on important family affairs.

Unlike many other tribal and non-tribal societies, the Maler do not treat sons and daughters differently. They do not attach any more importance to the birth of a son than that of a daughter. Both are equally important in all social matters. Even economically, both are equal, because if the son helps in agricultural activities, the daughter helps in domestic work, in addition to fetching a bride-price.

The relationship among siblings is also informal. In childhood, the siblings of both sexes mix and play together. When they grow up their relationship usually becomes that of avoidance. But the mutual love and affection does not cease. They do care for each other for the whole of their lives. In fact, in advanced ages, the sibling relationship is closer than the parent-child relationship.

The Maler do not have a social stratification either vertical or horizontal. All are socially and ritually of the same status.

The interpersonal relationship within the village is usually formal. Though living side by side, they do not take interest in each other's affairs and remain centred around their own family. But it is not to be construed that they are totally individualistic. They do help each other when such help is specifically sought, but this is not extended voluntarily. If a family has nothing to eat and has to remain hungry, he shall normally not disclose it to the villagers in general. If and when help is sought, it is only from near relatives. Even if others come to know of it, they will not go and help.

The Maler do not have a system of greeting. When they meet each other, even if it is after a long time, they do not greet each other in contrast to the neighbouring tribes, the Santhals, who have a very elaborate system of greeting.

Nor do they have any term for offering thanks. The children too are not supposed to address in respectful terms, because there are no such terms. But they do have a word for blessing the younger, called *ujje pachku* (May you live long).

Now some persons are learning to wish and greet. They see such things at the *haat* (market) and among the Santhal. Whenever they meet any non-tribal, he will be greeted with a *pranaam*, or a Santhal will be greeted in his own way.

The Maler's relationship with non-tribals is that of indifference and with Santhal of both co-operation and conflict.

A Diku is a man to be feared and avoided because he usually brings trouble. The forest and other block officials as well as the Mahajans are non-tribals, and represent the authority which collects rent. It is their inherent belief that a Diku will not hesitate to kill a Maler if he gets a chance. For this reason, they will never enter the house of a Diku. Even if he or she has sold a bundle of firewood and asked to put it in the courtyard, he shall not enter the house and put the bundle in front of it. Whenever a Diku walks with the Maler, the latter will always step back and let the former go ahead. Though they fear them, the Maler will not admit it in so many words.

Their relations with the Santhal is a bit different. They live side by side and have economic, if not social, contacts. The Maler of Bendri have close economic relationship with the Santhal of the neighbouring villages—Pathar-ghatta, Goranda and Simaria. The Santhal of these villages buy firewood from the Maler, work in the latter's paddy fields down on the plains, sell them Mahua liquor, serve as labourers in the Kurwa fields, etc. One Santhal of Simaria has even done Kurwa on the hills this year.

Some Maler develop close relationships with the Santhal and visit each other in times of sorrow and happiness.

Despite this apparent co-operation, there are moments of suspicion and hatred too. The Maler have had many quarrels and conflicts with the Santhal in the past, and the memory haunts them even now. A few years ago, there arose a tense situation, when Santhals said that they would take wood and other forest products by force and kill any Maler if he should oppose it. There was great fear and apprehension among the Maler, because they are, by nature, meek and cowardly and cannot resist or fight. Somehow, the situation was controlled by the Block Officials and the Police. There is an underlying feeling that Santhals want to kill every Maler and capture the hills.

The Manjhiya of Bendri told of an incident that happened at his father-in-law's village, Chapri, a few miles south of Bendri in July, 1980. It so happened that a Santhal married woman eloped with her lover when she had gone to collect firewood in the jungle. It was thought that the Maler of Chapri had caught her alone, raped and killed her. The entire Santhal village attacked Chapri and set the huts on fire, looting all the belongings of the Maler. The latter did not even put up a semblance of a fight and fled away to the forest. A few old people were also killed.

This was a deadly news to other Maler of the area, who feared that the Santhal would kill every Maler. The situation, however, was controlled by the police and the incident was not repeated at any other place.

(Later inquiries revealed that the attack was politically motivated and organized by a local Jharkhand leader who wanted to teach the Paharias a lesson for not voting for their party. Though, the allegation has not been officially proved.)

Such incidents which flare up every now and then hamper the relationship between the two tribes, which is never harmonious and cordial.

Marriage among the Maler takes place as soon as the boy reaches the age of about sixteen and the girl attains puberty. If the marriage is deferred at this period it is only due to economic consideration on the boy's part.

A boy selects the girl of his own choice. He may choose any girl, within or without the village, with the exception of those with whom he is related on both father's and mother's lineage. There are many ways by which he comes to know about a girl outside the village—from relatives in different villages, visits to *haats* and fairs, at the annual festival of Bandana, etc.

The first point he considers in selecting his spouse is whether she is hardy. Her beauty comes later. She must be diligent and healthy enough to do all the household chores plus the collection of firewood, selling it in market and helping him in agricultural activities. Such a girl deserves a higher *paun* (bride-price). But a boy does not ignore her appearance altogether. There is a girl in Bendri (25 yrs) who has never been proposed to because the lower portion of her face is wrinkled like an old woman—otherwise she has everything a boy can desire. Apparently she will be married to a widower or divorce of an advanced age.

In the selection of a wife, a boy may or may not ask the opinion of his parents—it is not really necessary, because they usually do not object. Nor does a boy normally discuss his choice with his parents. His wishes are conveyed by his friends.

The bride-price to be paid varies with each individual girl depending on her age, diligence and chastity. Virginity of a girl is not strictly demanded, nor expected. Nowadays the paun varies from Rs. 50 to 150 in cash plus one pig and clothes for the girl in the first marriage. The paun is less in the second or third marriages.

The pig is necessary and has almost ritual significance. The pig is killed by the uncle and maternal uncle of the girl and its meat is distributed among the relatives. This distribution is precise and interesting.

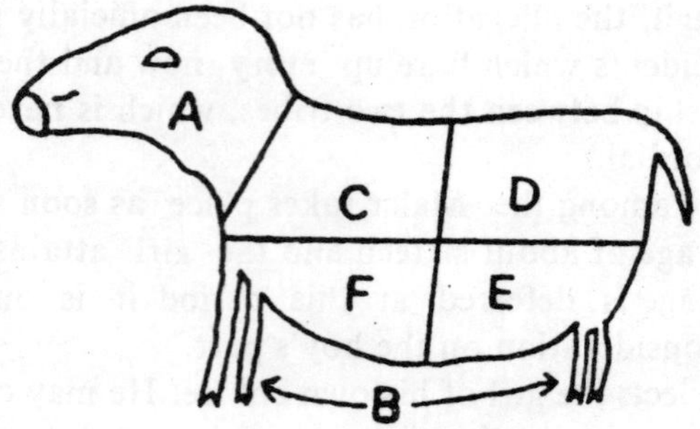

Piece A — for Barat.
,, B — Wages for clearing and cutting the pig.
,, C—E & F—Girl's side.

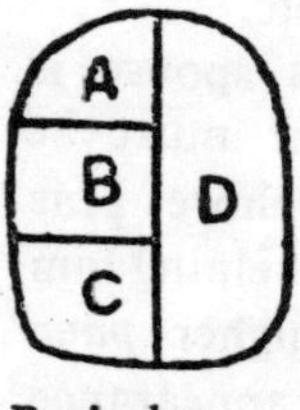

A, B and C—The three sittos (two on boy's side one from girl's side)

D—Boy's family.

Boy's share

The meat of the share of the girl's side will be cut into fifteen equal pieces and distributed in the following way. The head is offered to the Barat when it returns to the boy's village, and is cooked in the boy's house.

The girl's share's distribution

Father	Mother	Brother(s)	Sister(s)
Uncle(s)	M. Uncle(s)	Grandfather (to father, if dead)	Grandmother (to mother, if dead)
Uncle (wages for killing)	M. Uncle (wages for killing)		Sitto

————————————To be given to relatives (Gotias/on father's side)

Usually, the marriage is of two types.

(1) Pelvede (2) Sada (Simple).

The Pelvede involves a lot of time and money and the Barat accompanies it. This form is more honourable and resorted to by those who are well off and when the marriage takes place outside the village.

The Sada marriage is less expensive and can be concluded within a few hours. The Barat is not needed. Even the payment of paun and pig can be deferred. This method is commonly used by the poor and in intra-village marriages.

Divorce among the Maler is very easy and frequent, and taken as a matter of course. Either spouse can repudiate the other and no justification is needed. The grounds for divorce may vary from laziness and adultery on the wife's part to carelessness on the boy's part. Rather, it is difficult to find a Maler (not a single in Bendri) beyond the age of 25-30 years, who has not married twice or even three times.

In Bendri, a girl named Chandi has married for the third time and she is still in her teens. The first time she married in the same village (paun Rs. 100) but left the boy because he did not buy a single piece of cloth for her in the course of one year. Of course, she had to return the bride price. Then she married a boy in the neighbouring village (paun Rs. 60) but divorced him within three months because he refused to enter the hut where her mother was lying seriously ill. Now she has married a boy in the same village (paun Rs. 40) and plans to divorce him too because he has not given the pig yet.

If the boy divorces the girl for adultery and such other reasonable causes, he gets the bride price refunded. If the girl divorces she has to refund the bride price. If by that time her parents are dead, her brother or nearest relative or any of those who shared the meat of the pig during her marriage, are responsible for the return of the bride price. If a girl marries again without returning the bride price, the amount is doubled.

The Maler male and female are so engrossed in their work to supplement their food supply, and to rise above the level of mere subsistence, that they rarely find any leisure time. Whatever time they get is used for taking rest after a really hard and long day.

But, they do find some time to repel the monotony of day to day life. Drinking and dancing are usual ways of recreation, in addition to folk-songs and folk-tales, puzzles and riddles.

But the latter two are not that much in vogue.

Singing and dancing are also not part of every day life or even regular affairs. These are resorted to only during the Bandana festival and marriages, when they sing and dance for hours together.

Story-telling is also not much in use. The older women do not spend time with children. The latter play with their own age and sex groups.

Their songs are one-lined and represent their attitudes and social norms.

The children play different types of games involving two to eight persons. Usually all their free time is spent in play.

Except for the Bandana festival and marriages, their life is monotonous and dull.

An average Maler suffers from poor health and malnutrition. His life is very very hard. He has to undergo much rigours since his very childhood. Grazing cattle on the hills, collection of roots, fruits and firewood, ascending and descending the hills every day, and most of all, the Kurwa process of cultivation saps his energy to a great extent. And he cannot take nutritious food, simply because he cannot afford it. He cannot even fill his belly for one whole year. His food lacks even in quantity, not to talk of quality. Sometimes he has to remain without food for days together. He has to live on only two meals a day, while he sees the Santhal eating at least three times and the Dikus (the non-tribals) four times a day.

The environment around him is also not very conducive to good health. He lives in the same room where all household chores are performed. His animals live nearby. His hut and village are rarely if ever neat and clean, because he can never find the time for cleaning it.

The water he drinks is full of viruses. He gets water from natural springs on the hills, which never flows but seeps. This water is exposed to all kinds of malignant elements, very often causing malaria, goitre, typhoid etc. Every Maler falls ill at least twice a year, which also goes a long way in sapping his physical energy.

He husbands cows and fowl, but neither drinks any milk nor eats eggs. He is usually not aware of the advantage, and, if he does, then his concern for the life of the calves, for increasing his chicken forbids him to consume them.

These are certain reasons due to which the death rate is very high, and infant mortality specially is horrible. Every Maler suffers a loss of at least three or four children. The children mostly die of malaria and typhoid. The Maler is not always rich enough to get the services of a doctor, though he is conscious of his superiority over the traditional village Guru. The charges of doctors are really very restrictive.

The Government is proposing to open Nutritive Food Centres in Paharia areas, but, so far, only a few have been started, none within the reach of the Pahariyas. The dispensaries for Pahariyas are also few and far between.

The Maler are very much conscious of the advantages of education. Almost every person wants his children to study and get a government job. But educational facilities are insufficient.

There are only six Pahariya Primary Schools in the whole Borio Block, (where there are 149 Pahariya villages) and only one residential High School at Banjhi. The Primary School serves only the village in which it is established and in a few cases, one or two neighbouring villages. Each boy is given *khichri* worth Rs. 0.50 every day. The rice, pulse and salt are supplied from the block, but only half of it reaches the schools. The block officials and the teachers of schools sell the commodity in the black market.

The schools are so few that a large number of children never get the opportunity to study. The seats in the High School at Banjhi are limited and this is insufficient in catering to the needs of the Maler.

Until 1966, there was a school in Bendri village, but the teacher at that time wrote to the authorities that the school at Bendri was unnecessary because only five or six students attended it. This was not true. The fact was that he found the life on the hill top very hard, more so in Bendri, because this is the highest inhabited hill in Santhal Parganas.

Anyway, he got the school shifted from Bendri—and the villagers were deprived of the benefits. They have tried to contact the Block officials but to no avail. The result is that only a few persons who could study before 1966 can read and write.

Only two persons have studied up to 10th class. One boy who got admitted in Banjhi is due to appear at the Matriculation Examination this year.

Opening of many more schools in Pahariya village is needed urgently. The consciousness is there, but not the agency to use it well.

So far, Banjhi High School has produced only one Pahariya Matriculate named Mahesh Malto of Bhatbhanga village, a few miles east of Bendri in Taljhari block. Twenty-four students are due to appear for the examination this year.

The role and structure of the traditional Panchayat has changed considerably, due to the introduction of the modern democratic village Panchayat. The influence of Manjhiye is lessening every day, while the elected Mukhiya is trying to usurp the powers of the former.

In village Bendri, the structure of the village Panchayat has also changed to a large extent. The Manjhiye is still the head but there are no panches. Whenever there is any matter to judge and discuss, the whole village sits and discusses it together. The judgement does not come from the Manjhiye either, but is arrived at by consensus.

The fine imposed is distributed equally among all those who were present, and the Manjhiye has no special share.

Moreover, not everybody reports to the Manjhiye every time. Very often they go directly to the Mukhiya (who in that Panchayat is a Maler) or even to the police first.

Politically, the Maler are becoming more and more conscious gradually. Modern democratic institutions have caused this awareness.

They do vote in the elections for the Mukhiya, the Legislative Assembly and Parliament. There are at present, six male Mukhiyas in Borio Block, out of twenty five, and four Sarpanches. These Mukhiyas are trying hard to bring the Maler out so that he may learn the ways of the life of the outside world.

The Maler, or for that matter, the Mal Pahariya, are traditional supporters of the Congress. This is the only party which has deep roots among them, and, in fact except for a few educated Maler who have greater contact with non-tribals, they do not know the names of other political parties, barring the Jharkhand. This latter party is so well recognised as the Santhal Party that they never vote for it, because, they fear, that it will oust them from the hills and kill them.

But an average Maler does not understand the implication of these elections, except that it shall help Indira Gandhi, the only leader they know. They do not have a clear conception of nation or State. Mrs Gandhi is a queen who must be having thousands of maunds of maize and paddy, and unlimited money, because the rent they pay goes to her. She was ousted by some people, a few years ago, but by the will of the people she has come back.

Some educated Pahariyas, both Maler and Mal, have formed a united front called Pahariya Samaj Uthan Samiti on district level with its General Secretary Sri Sheolal Mankhi, a clerk at the Sahibganj Railway Station and a Mal Pahariya. Every Maler is conscious of this, and believes that the Manjhi will do something good for them. In fact, thousands and thousands of Pahariyas went to Deoghar under his leadership in June, 1980, and demonstrated against Sri Gauri Shankar Dalmia, the Secretary of Santhal Paharia Seva Mandal—a voluntary organisation—and demanded that all official help to the Mandal be stopped forthwith because it benefits only the Santhal and not the Pahariya.

THE SPIRIT

The Maler believe in supernatural spirits called Gossaiyan. Their religion is essentially animistic and necessitates a blood sacrifice at every sacred performance.

From earlier studies, it appears that the Maler are very God fearing and every moment of their lives is guided and controlled by Gossaiyan. It seemed then that different spirits played a major role in deciding his mode of life and his destiny.

The situation now is at a little variance. They do believe in Gossaiyan, no doubt, but these are not so paramount. No one person worships all Gossaiyan, nor does he remember the names of more than one or two Gossaiyan.

People are not as afraid of spirits as they used to be. Individual worship is on the decline. The only occasions when a man is supposed to worship are during Kurwa and Attu

Gossaiyan, and also at the time of death. But not all worship even then. This year four persons did not offer fowl before reaping the maize on the ground that the yield was very poor. They said that they would offer a small pig at the time of reaping the millet, if the yield was good—not necessarily if it was not. Many persons do not worship even Attu Gossaiyan. One villager, Potio Surja, who does not offer Kuriva for want of resources does not worship any Gossaiyan at all, and claims that he is not affected by spirits.

SACRED CENTRES

Certain stones, trees and springs are the sacred spots of the Maler, some are permanent others temporary.

There are eleven permanent sacred centres in village Bendri.

Manjhi Than or Singpate Nadu

This is the main sacred centre located on the eastern margin of the village settlement. This *Than* is worshipped twice—Bandana (*Taddi Baha*) and just before sewing operation of Kurwa (*Kudchake*). Every alternate year a buffalo along with some pigs are sacrificed at Bandana. A male Gossaiyan.

Gossain Adda

This is a cluster of five black stones on the western margin of village settlement. A black fowl is sacrificed by Gorait here at Bandana. A female Gossaiyan.

Bendri Nadu

A little to the west of Gossain Adda is a cluster of four stones. A pig is sacrificed by Gorait at Bandana. A female Gossaiyan.

Kaneya Nadu

About 50′ below the village level and to the south are three stones. Red he-goat and red fowl are sacrificed at Bandana. A male Gossaiyan.

Chal Gossaiyan

On the south eastern side of the village settlement at a distance of about 300 metres is a cluster of white and black stones, seven in number. Worshipped at Bandana and offered pig, vermilion, betel leaf, sweets, red fowl and every alternate year, a cow. A female Gossaiyan.

Rakshi Than
A cluster of eleven cylindrical stones about 20 metres south of Chal. Pigeon is sacrificed at Bandana by Gorrait. A male Gossaiyan.

Tunde Than
About one mile east of village, represented by a tree. This is worshipped by gorait at Bandana and when anybody suffers from small pox. A female Gossaiyan.

Mula Gossaiyan
This is also a cluster of stones a little north of Tunde. The Gorait sacrifices a he-goat at Bandana. Both male and female Gossaiyan.

Atgo
A little south of Rokshi, represented by three stones and offered a fowl at Bandana. A male.

Mahadeo Than or Punkwa Gossaiyan
This is a cluster of seven stones worshipped when somebody desires something and when fulfilled is offered a fowl, sweets, vermilion, incense sticks and flowers, striking similarity with Lord Siva of Hindus. A male.

Jhanda Gossaiyan
Represented by a bamboo pole, fixed near Manjhithan in Bandana.

In addition, many other trees and springs are supposed to be the abode of many types of malevolent and benevolent spirits.

The sacredness attached to the sacred centres is also not very strict. Usually sacred centres are regarded as pious objects and not touched or defiled. The place is also kept clean. But this is not so in Benderia. Nobody cares about the condition of these centres. The Manjhiya Than, which is the most important centre, and lies within the view of all villages, is not cared for or looked after. The children play there and even pigs defecate. The place is very dirty but not even the Manjhiye pays any attention to it. The centre will be cleaned and washed only when some sacrifices are to be made. The same is the condition of all the sacred centres.

A rough sketch of Benderi showing different permanent sacred centres

N

*Mula
*Tunde
*Masani

Village * Manjhi Than and Jhanda gossaiyan

* Benderi Nadu

* Gosain Adda

*Chal

*Kaniya

*Raksi
*Atgo.
*Mahadeo

SACRED PERFORMANCES

The sacred performances constitute killing the fowl or pigs or buffalo and pouring the blood over the sacred centre, at the same time uttering the name of gossaiyan. Egg is no longer an object of sacrifice. Minimum unit is pigeon or fowl.

As we noted earlier, most of the sacred performances are made at the time of Bandana when at least one buffalo or cow, about 8 to 10 pigs and a number of fowl are sacrificed. These are purchased by raising a subscription from the villages.

The responsibility for the sacred performances rests exclusively on the sacred specialist. A commoner does not take part in the proceedings, except in sharing the sacrificed meat. The meat of buffalo is not eaten. Its horn is preserved and the rest of the body is thrown down hill.

The women are not allowed to take part, nor even to stand where sacrifices are being made. The husbands of menstruating women are also forbidden to take part.

Individual worship is on the decline. Most of the sacred performances are collective. Except in Kurwa and Attu, nobody has to perform any worship.

Other sacred performances are made while administrating *telpartta* and *sarcli* by the Guru (diviner). This is a method of finding out the name of the gossaiyan who is believed to have attacked a person causing illness and diseases. The Saveli is a part of the divine oath and ordeal, where a man has to lick a red-hot iron to prove his innocence if accused of any guilt.

SACRED SPECIALIST

When the sacrifices are made at the family level, the head of the family himself acts as the sacred specialist. It is he who offers the sacrifice.

At the village level, there are certain sacred specialists who act on behalf of the whole village.

The chief sacred specialist is the Manjhiya, who is both sacred and secular head of the village. He performs all the religious functions of the village as well as fixing the dates of festivals. The Manjhiya sacrifices the most important of objects, the buffalo at Manjhiya-than. He is the priest of this sacred centre.

He is assisted by three or four guraits. Of them, only the eldest performs the sacrifices, while others help in general arrangement and also act as messengers. It is their duty to inform every person about the festival programmes, as well as collecting subscriptions which are deposited with Manjhiye. At most sacred centres, except the Manjhiye-than the gurrait does all the religious functions.

There is yet another type of sacred specialists. Certain gossaiyan are supposed to be appeased only if a particular individual does the sacrifices. If anybody else, including Manjhiye and gurrait performs the sacrifices, the gossaiyan is not satisfied.

The choice of the individual by the gossaiyan is conveyed through Demano and if he dies, his eldest son will perform the sacrifices. Thus at present in Bendri, chal gossaiyan is worshipped by one chalawe Rama, Kaneya gossaiyan by Jado Surja, Atgo gossaiyan by Labu Rama and Mahadeo-than by Shyam Malto. If anybody wants to worship these thans, he shall have to contact these persons, who will perform all the sacrifices on behalf of the worshipper.

The Demano is a person who is possessed by the spirit during Bandana. Usually the same person is possessed each year, but it is not necessary. Anybody can become Demano.

When he is possessed, he looks half-asleep and his body begins swinging. He then begs us to speak, which are supposed to be the wishes of gossaiyan and listened attentively by the villagers. He commands as to how a particular gossaiyan is to be worshipped. During this Shamanistic influence he can even change the Manjhiye.

The Guru is yet another sacred specialist. He applies Telpatta when somebody falls ill and tells the person as to which gossaiyan is to be worshipped and what sacrifices are to be made. Usually, a guru takes the training from other partriya or Santhal guru.

The Maler call themselves Hindus and react sharply if suggested otherwise. If it is pointed out that Hindus do not eat beef, which the Maler do, they will retort that many Hindus in Berio Market eat beef and are recognised as Hindus, so, why should they not be ?

IV

An examination of the present situation of the Maler of Santhal Parganas reveals that they have undergone many changes in the last twenty-five years, involving every aspect of their life and culture.

An important change in their economic mentality is a shift from Khallu to settled cultivation. They would prefer to raise paddy, because it entails less money and labour and can be used both as staple food and cash crop. Another important turn around is their will to go down and settle on the plains, if their rights to the forests are not forfeited. This is very significant because not very long ago, they were quite averse, and even hostile, to any suggestions of leaving the hills. Even now they will not wish to part with the forests altogether, though they want it to be supplementary and not the primary basis of their economy.

Hunting among the Maler is also declining. Nobody seems to be interested in hunting. A few people accompany the Santhals when they go out for their ceremonial hunting in March-April.

The Maler himself has changed considerably. He is conscious of his "primitiveness" and wants to shed it. For this he wants education, which is not all that easy to get. He is conscious of government's efforts for his development and knows that there is a special Paharia Welfare Department. He wants proper medical facilities because he does not want to die early. He knows that his habitat is not conducive to good health, but cannot help it. He likes to treat illness with medicines but cannot afford to buy them.

Politically, too, he has become more conscious. He takes part in elections and votes for Congress. He votes for a Paharia if one stands for the post of Mukhia. His faith in the traditional village Panchayat is decreasing because he has come to know that the village Manjhiye has no real authority, while the elected Mukhia does have it.

These changes have brought about inevitable changes in his religious beliefs also. He is not as afraid of the gossaiyan as he used to be. Though he still performs worship, it is more because of tradition than devotion. He usually does not remember the names of all the gossaiyan nor does he worship all of them. Even worship is sometimes differed or put off altogether without any regard to the gossaiyan or their wrath.

V

An attempt has, thus, been made to study the Nature-Man-Spirit Complex of a hill tribe in the context of its changing situation. It has been found that though there are changes in every aspect, the complex as such has not changed nor can it ever change. The ecology of the Maler has not changed and the people are as much dependent upon it as they ever were.

While their life is now not as much woven around spirits as of yore their importance cannot be totally denied. They still have their role to play in shaping the life of the Maler.

So, the Nature and the Spirits still guide and, to a certain extent, control the life of the Maler and determine their style of life.

We can thus sum up by saying that Vidyarthi's concept of Nature-Man-Spirit Complex still holds good among the Maler.

SUGGESTED READINGS

Berreman, Gerald D. : "Ecology, Demography and Domestic Strategies in the Himalayas," *Journal of Anthropological Research*, Vol. 34, pp. 326-368, 1978.

Kroeber, A. L. : "Culture and Natural Areas of Native North America, University of California Publications," in *American Archaeology and Ethnology*, Vol. 38, 1939.

Morab, S. G. : "The Soliga" Unpublished Ph.D. Thesis submitted to Ranchi University, 1980.

Prasad, R.K. : "The Parahiyas: A Study in Cultural Ecology and Tribal Dynamics" (*Acta Ethnologica Et Linguistica* Nr. 42, Series India 8) Wien, Institute fur Volkerkunde der Universitat, 1978.

Redfield, R. : *The Little Community*. The University of Chicago Press, Chicago, 1955.

Sandhwar, A. N. : The Korwa of Palamau: A Study of their Society and Economy" (*Acta Ethnologica Et Linguistica* Nr. 44, Series India 9) Wien, Institute fur Volkerkunde der Universitat, 1978.

Sinha, R. K. : "The Pandos: A Study in Nature-Man-Spirit Complex," Unpublished Ph.D. Thesis submitted to Ranchi University, 1977.

Steward, J. : *Theory of Culture Change*, Urbana, University of Illinois Press, 1955.

Vidyarthi, L. P. : "Cultural Types in Tribal Bihar," in *Journal of Social Research*, Vol. I, Ranchi, 1958.

Vidyarthi, L.P. : *The Maler : A Study in Nature-Man-Spirit Complex of a hill tribe*, Bookland Pvt. Ltd., Allahabad, 1963.

THREE

Amitava Das Gupta

A STUDY IN NATURE-MAN-SPIRIT COMPLEX

ETHNOGRAPHERS have variously identified the Ho as pre-dravidians, Kolarians, Nisadic etc., on the basis of their physical attributes and cultural traits. However, in spite of such wide variations of classification in respect of the Ho, it is generally accepted by learned scholars that the Ho are members of the Austro-Asiatic linguistic group which also includes the Santhals, Mundas, Bhumij, Korwa, Juang, Bhil etc. Majumdar (1950 : 24) in his lengthy discussion on this linguistic group has however opined that today they prevail in the Chotanagpur plateau of Bihar. Risley (1891) in attempting to identify the ethnic affinity of the Ho has also acknowledged that :

> They belong to the same family as the Mundas and that they are the only branch of the Kols who have maintained their national appellation.

The *Preliminary appraisal of the scheduled tribe of India* (157 : 100), however, identifies the Ho as a Kolarian tribe who inhabit parts of Bihar, Orissa and West Bengal. It gives their population figures in these regions as 454,746; 43,323 and 1,075 respectively.

The present geographical concentration of the Ho is within a belt, surrounding the Singhbhum District of Bihar. Roughly therefore, the distribution of the Ho lies between latitudes 21-23° N and longitudes 84-87° E. However, the main concentration of the Ho has always been in the Singhbhum District. In particular, the *Kolhan* region of Sinhgbhum—a 15 mile belt around the district headquarter town of Chaibasa—may be identified as the home of the most orthodox Ho, both racially and culturally. In respect of the Ho surrounding Kolhan, it would be relevant here to quote Majumdar (1950 : 26), who says :

> The Ho of Saraikela whom Mr. Chatterjee measured are known to be a mixed group. They have lost their language and are more Hinduized than their brethren in Kolhan.

The relevant point that emerges from the above is that the seat of the orthodox Ho culture and religion is in the area mentioned above (*Kolhan*).

In the light of the above discussion it must be revealed here that the following data on the Nature-Man-Spirit Complex has been exclusively collected from Kolhan to eliminate the possibility of the methodological error of studying mixed groups in the present context, in which it is sought to convey the facts about the typical Ho. It is also of relevance to point out here that though the Ho have been in the focus of ethnographic study since 1821, when Major Roughsedge first attempted to study them, no attempt has hitherto been made to reveal their Nature-Man-Spirit Complex.

From the methodological point of view, it would be relevant here to discuss briefly the concept of the Nature-Man-Spirit Complex, before an appraisal of the Ho can be made in this respect. This revolutionary concept of studying a group's interaction with Nature on the one hand and the Spirit on the other, was first conceived by L. P. Vidyarthi in the course of his study of the Maler, a hill tribe of Santhal Parganas. In the course of his study Vidyarthi could identify the three important aspects of Maler culture as Nature, Man and Spirit. From the operational point of view it was a difficult task to project a tribal culture within this framework. From the methodological point of view, it meant new way of selecting and organizing meaningful data to project the culture within this framework. However, through the application of the concepts of "Cultural ecology", "functionalism" and selective presentation of data,

Vidyarthi gave a lead to future scholars, through the publication of his book *The Maler* in 1963.

In the light of the above discussion on the methodology, I shall now attempt to present the Nature-Man-Spirit Complex of the orthodox Ho of Kolhan, for the reasons specified earlier. On methodological and theoretical considerations I shall present the data in three sections: Nature, Man and Spirit.

In the first section on "Nature", I shall attempt to reveal the ecological basis of Ho culture and its influence on the different aspects of the culture itself, because the Ho culture has evolved in the lap of Nature. Nature and the Ho are so intimately connected with each other that the influence of Nature has penetrated into the very ethos and world view of the Ho.

In the second section on "Man", the Man to Man relationship has been examined through the relationship obtaining among them as members of the tribe, clan, village group and family.

In the third section on "Spirit", the various aspects of the Ho beliefs regarding the supernatural world and its influence on the life of the Ho has been discussed, to reveal their dependence on the Spirit world for their subsistence. The Ho belief system envisages that the benevolence or displeasure of the supernatural is instrumental in guiding the life and destiny of man. For such a revelation, Vidyarthi's analytical concepts of sacred geography, sacred specialists and sacred performances have been taken into consideration.

Having examined the general framework of the study, we shall proceed to examine the Nature-Man-Spirit Complex of the Ho within such a framework.

NATURE

Examining the topography, flora and fauna of the Singhbhum District and the surrounding belt, we notice that the Ho live amidst the hills, dales, plains and valleys of the mountain system which constitute the Chotanagpur plateau. A brief review of the ecological setting will therefore reveal the nature of the environment in which the Ho culture flourishes.

As mentioned earlier, the main bulk of the orthodox Ho population is concentrated within 1919 sq. miles in central Singhbhum. This region lies in the Singhbhum plateau, which is in general a hilly upland tract in which the hills alternate with valleys, steep mountains, forests and the less rugged river basins. The highest mountain ranges in the region rise to 3,000 ft. above the sea in the north west, to those ranging up to 2,500 ft. scattered lower ranges lie to the north and west. Most of the mountainous regions are covered with a thick foliage of forests, bushes, herbs, creepers, climbers etc. Flanking such steep regions, however, are the open valleys of the rivers Subarnarekha, Baitarani and the Brahmani, all of which originate in the hills of Singhbhum. Such valleys are comparatively fertile, and exhibit a higher density of population.

The climatic conditions reveal that the area experiences three main seasons in a year, the hot, rainy and the cold, all of which border on the extreme. The summers extending from March to May are extremely hot and dry, with an average temperature of 116° F around Chaibasa. The humidity is low, and hot westerly winds make the atmosphere very dry during the day. The rivers, ponds, wells and dams become almost dry, causing a great scarcity of water for man and beast alike. The onset of the rainy season is heralded in June through violent thunderstorms which render many a Ho hut-roofless and uproot large trees. In July and August the precipitation is highest, often exceeding 55 inches. However, strangely enough the rain often fails totally, causing drought and even famine conditions. The failure of the *hatia* rains collapses the agriculture based Ho economy and produces severe food scarcity as experienced in 1866, 1897, 1900, 1915-17, 1935, 1940, 1979-80. Due to the mountainous nature of the terrain, the Ho have been totally unable to conserve the rainfall during the periods of high precipitation. The few indigenous weirs and dams have proved to be as grossly inadequate as the few modern irrigation projects undertaken. The failure of the rains means the collapse of agriculture for the Ho, who then turn to the forest for bare subsistence on roots and tubers, jackfruit, *mahua* flowers, honey, fruits, etc. Due to the indiscriminate hunting in the past the edible fauna of deer, rabbits, antelope have almost disappeared from the forests of Singhbhum nowadays. Hence the Ho are reduced to dire straits bordering on starvation when Nature withholds the rain. Due to the present stringent restriction on the collection of forest products and hunting, the life of the Ho becomes pathetic at such times and malnutrition of entire population results.

Winters in Singhbhum are severe and commence from early October. However, it is the time for the winter crop of paddy, hence food supply is somewhat assured.

In spite of the stringent restrictions on hunting and collecting imposed on the Ho, they still consider the forests to be their own since they have been living within and around it and are associated with it for generations. The forest is not only the source of food, drink, house-building materials, pasture for their cattle etc., but it is also the abode of their patron spirits. Such is the attachment of the Ho for the forest that they preserve a vestigeal part of the forest in every village and assign it to be the abode of their village deity. Under no circumstances is such a grove to be cut by either the Ho or by others.

In reviewing the present state of the Ho economy which centres round the practice of highland rice cultivation, we note that the Ho is betwixt and between the forces of nature in this respect. It is noticed that the entire agricultural cycle of the Ho is conditioned by the forces of nature, be it in the selection of their plots, irrigation or crop cycle. The Ho have absolutely no control over these factors which govern their very existence. To begin with, they must follow the dictates of Nature in respect of the selection of their agricultural plots, due to the nature of the topography of their habitat. Accordingly, the Ho rice cultivation has been limited to three types of agricultural plots; the *gora*, *bera*, and the *bad*, which are again at the mercy of Nature for their irrigation, as the topography does not permit the harnessing of stored water resources in most cases. Hence the Ho cultivator is almost totally at the mercy of the seasonal rainfall for his cultivation. Reviewing the nature of the agricultural plots it is noted that the *gora* lands are upland plots of light soil which are generally located near the villages. Such plots are suitable only for the cultivation of two rice crops in a year, but such plots need extensive manuring. The *bera* rice plots lie at the bottom of the valleys and are irrigated by the torrents of rain-water which cascade down the mountain side, hence the need arises for terracing them to conserve the moisture. Without such terracing they would prove to be unproductive. The failure of rain therefore limits the effective operation of such fields. Normally such plots are used for the cultivation of the winter rice and the *khesari* pulse. The *bad* plots are situated on the hill sides above the *bera* plots and are also dependent on rainfall for their moisture. Due to the nature of the terrain, the *bera* and the *bad* plots of a village are often situated at a distance, adding to the difficulty of their operation in respect of cultivation and transportation of the produce. In the overall perspective, we note that though agriculture forms the basis of the Ho economy, they have to eke out an existence in conformity with the vagaries or bounty of Nature.

Besides its role in Ho agriculture, Nature plays a dominant role in the other aspects of Ho life as well. For example, we notice that the entire system of Ho therapeutics and its pharmacopia is dependent on the various medicinal plants, roots, tubers and leaves which Nature has provided them with, in the shape of the forest. In the social life, it is noticed that many a premarital affair blossoms at the feet of Nature, when young men and women visit the forests and fields in the course of their economic pursuits. Such affairs are of significance for they mature into marriage in most cases and thus stabilize the society, and transmit the traditions to the succeeding generations. In the matter of ritual and festivals, the Ho meticulously observe the cycle of nature and time. Important among these are the *Mage* and the *Bah* festival rituals, when the participation is en masse. The weeklong *Mage* festivities mark the end of the annual agricultural cycle. Besides this, the Ho perform innumerable rituals in connection with every phase of the natural growth of the rice plants. Such phases are marked by solemnity, sacrifices and an appreciation of the agencies of nature in the development of the rice plants. The *Bah* festival marks the flowering of the *sarjom* (shorea robusta) and the spring, a season for love and propagation among the flora and fauna of nature. Through its celebration the Ho commemorate annually the 'divine marriage' between the earth bedecked with the flowers of the *sarjom* tree and the all powerful sun which sustains all life on earth. Hence the Ho perform this festival between the blooming of the *sarjom* flowers and their falling to the ground. The ritual symbolizes for the Ho the season for love, and through it the Ho identifies himself with the procreative season of nature. From the foregoing discussion, the point therefore emerges that the Ho is very close to the forces of nature, and lives amidst it for his sustenance. Through this intimate association with Nature, the Ho not only exploits nature, but also associates himself with its various phases, whims and bounty.

MAN

The present day Ho may not conform to such descriptions as :

> The Hos were as much superior to their brethren in Chotanagpur as wild buffaloes to the village herd.

or "The early use of the bow expands the chest and sets the muscles, while yet mere boys, and their passions for chase, which they pursue over the rugged hills, brings their lower limbs into a state of training which even the best *Pahelwans* of the plains of India might envy."

as attributed to them by Major Roughsedge (1821) and Col. Tickel (1840), but today the Ho are a proud people with a long tradition of bloody struggle against the forces which have tended to alter their tradition. In their struggle against oppression the Ho had risen against the British on many an occasion including during India's first war of independence in 1857. Such spirit and fighting qualities have earned for them the name *Larka Kol* (fighting Kol) among the tribes of Chotanagpur.

In spite of such traits of character in the past, today the Ho male is a docile agriculturist who has also degenerated physically due to his isolation from the forest, his natural habitat and excessive drinking of rice beer from an early age. Coupled with this, diseases like malaria, dysentry etc. have brought havoc among the Ho. In sharp contrast to their menfolk, the Ho women exhibit a much better physique and capability for hard work.

Whatever be the factors that are responsible for their degeneration, the Ho still maintain a highly organized society, guided by strict norms, principles and belief systems. The Ho social organisation exhibits that the society is stratified into four distinct functional units; the smallest of which is the family (*oa renko*). Next in size to the family come the village local group, clan and the tribe as a whole. Though functioning social units, these have exhibited the forging of a close relationship between man and man, and the supernatural, through a set of rituals, symbolic actions and beliefs associated with each such unit. To mention a few, it is noted that besides its normal social function, the family forges a link with the supernatural at every turning point in the life of its individual members, and also during the different phases of their agricultural efforts. Such liaison is established through the performance of appropriate rituals. The village local group, consisting of members of different families and classes, seeks the protection of the spirit world from drought, crop failure, epidemic etc. through the performance of appropriate rituals with a sense of collective liability. The clans which are generally believed to be of totemistic origin, form the bulwark of the Ho social order and stability, through certain prohibitions which are believed to have supernatural sanctions behind them. For example, marriage within the class is prohibited as a rule with the belief that such would precipitate supernatural punishment for clansmen and women are considered as brothers and sisters and their union would amount to incest. Such features exhibit how even the spirit has been involved in the Ho social order and their ethos and world view. The tribe as a whole maintains the social discipline within itself and takes care to see that the spirits are duly appeased both collectively as well as on the individual plane.

It would be of relevance here to point out that though most of the Ho clans have lost much of their totemic nature, yet a few are able to identify their clan symbols which they term as *killi anka*. Such symbols are of significance, for they are mostly of natural objects like birds, trees, animals etc., thus demonstrating the close association between nature and the clan and its individual members. Objectively therefore we note that the Ho have tried to maintain their proximity to nature even at the level of their social structure. The clan's link with the supernatural world is also still observable, even though it has lost its totemic significance. The Ho permit only members of the same clan to enter the kitchen (*ading*) of a household, as it is also the abode of the shades of the deceased ancestors of the clan. This further helps the cohesion of the clan members through the involvement of the supernatural and helps to maintain the social unity.

Ho society exhibits a high level of interaction within the family, clan and the tribe as a whole. Within the family there is a close interaction based on blood relationship, mutual affection and respect between the spouses and the siblings. The children are loved by their parents, who consider them to be supernatural blessings. The Ho therefore prefer to have large families which, as a rule, originate through monogamous marriages. Such marriages are contracted through as many as seven different methods. Within the process of contracting the marriage, nature and spirit play a dominant part at different levels, though such are often covert and symbolic at the level of observation.

At the level of the tribe as a whole, the interaction is observed through the maintenance of social and spiritual discipline, brought about through the marriage regulations, propitiation of the spirits and at the collective level, celebration of festivals, the weekly market ring, ritual taking back of the children of marriages beyond the sphere of tribal endogamy etc. All such factors contribute towards the socio-political as well as religious cohesion of the tribe, through a great degree of interaction within its members. Such factors have been greatly instrumental in checking the process of religious conversion, which is rampant among the other tribes of the region. Every Ho believes that at the level of interaction within his family, village local group or clan, he is always under the watchful eye of the Creator (*Singbonga*), the village god (*Desauli*) and the ancestral spirits (*Ham Ho*) who will take offence as soon as the normative code of conduct is broken, and inflict supernatural punishment. Such involvement of the spirit at the level of the social order has been greatly responsible in stabilizing the Ho society and maintaining its traditions.

The unity of the Ho village is through the consciousness of belonging to a particular village; even though most Ho villages have extensions in the form of hamlets separated from each other by paddy lands. The village unity is strongly observable on the plane of the performance of the two chief festival rituals of the villages. During these two village level rituals, the *Mage* and the *Bah* the villagers shed all their differences in respect to clan affiliation, economic and social status etc., and participate en masse, thus generating a great deal of familiarity and interaction. The village priest (*deuri*) assumes the most significant role on such occasions and exhibits powers which are above the normal level of political authority that is held by the village headman (*Munda*). Though the ritualistic performance is the main cohesive force, the priest ensures its proper maintenance. In the case of the performance of the other five rituals at the individual plane, such cannot be performed unless the priest gives permission for their performance within the village under his jurisdiction. However, as will be observed in the next section, the Ho clearly distinguish between collective and personal liability in the performances of socio-religious rituals.

While considering the role of the Ho village in the context of its secular and sacred function, it would not be out of place here to mention the significant role played by the Ho hut in this context. The small mud hut that the Ho lives in is of much significance in the context of their Nature-Man-Spirit Complex. Firstly, the hut, which forms the basis of all social and secular exercises is very much associated with Nature on the one hand and the Spirit on the other. In tracing the association of the hut with nature, it is noted that all its components like timber, soil, colouring and roofing materials etc. are all obtained by the Ho through the exploitation of nature. In the process of its construction, it is noted that the supernatural is brought into play from the stage of the selection of the house-building site to its final consecration before occupation. Again, in the matter of painting the hut with the traditional colour bands, it is found that the three typical colours black, red and yellow play a symbolically significant role, involving the supernatural. For an appreciation of this, it is necessary to mention that the outer walls of a Ho hut are painted with bands of black, red and yellow from the plinth upwards. The black colour is believed to give supernatural protection against witchcraft; the red is the favourite colour of the village deity, hence it affords his protection. The yellow is the colour of turmeric, a highly potent purificatory agent, hence its use keeps the house in a stage of ritual purity. Though each colour is of specific supernatural efficacy, the Ho basically obtain these from the naturally occurring oxides and vegetable material, thus forging yet another link between himself and nature on the one hand and spirit on the other, through their use. In the matter of thatching his hut, the Ho does it only after propitiating the *Barbhoji* spirit, with the belief that the roof will be blown away by the first storm of the year, unless the spirit is duly appeased. Lastly as mentioned earlier, the Ho believe that the ancestral spirits reside in the hut itself, particularly in the kitchen (*ading*) so the hut assumes great spiritual significance in establishing links between the Ho and the spirit world.

Before concluding this section on Man, it would be of significance to mention here that in every walk of life, the Ho maintains a link between himself, nature and the spirit for his subsistence, social control and smooth passage of life.

SPIRIT

The brief references to the spirit in the earlier sections on Nature and Man have brought into focus the role of the spirit in some of the mentioned aspects of Ho life and culture. However, in the life of the Ho, the spirit plays a far more significant role as will be presently observed in this section.

Spiritism forms the very basis and essence of the Ho religion, guiding philosophy of life and belief system. The spirit is all pervading in the various aspects of Ho life, be it mundane, social or ethical. The intimate association of the Ho with the spirit begins even when he is a 21-day old child, for it is then that he is ritually introduced to his ancestral spirits in the *ading* of his family. As the child matures to youth and manhood, the frequent experiences of disease, death, famine, drought etc., generate in him the realization that he is very dependent on the supernatural, or the spirit world, for his survival in his hilly and forested habitat. Thus the Ho becomes conscious of his eternal bond with the spirit for his very existence. Guided by the realization, the Ho tries to seek the assistance and co-operation of the spirit to meet the various contingencies of his life and well being. From a very early age, the Ho is indoctrinated by the belief that the soul of man is immortal and survives death through its transformation into the shade. The Ho child learns that the shades of his departed ancestors live in the *ading* of his house, and that they are very benign and protective by nature. Hence the Ho develops an affectionate and respectful bond with his ancestral spirits. So close is this association that the head of every household offers the daily family meal and drink to them, before these are consumed by the family members. In other words, the Ho behave as if the departed are present in the house, and occupy the same status in the family as they did when they were alive. Thus they love and respect them, rather than fear them as spirits. The extension of this belief manifests itself at the village level also, for no village level ritual can be held without invoking the *Ham ho* (ancestral spirits) of the village first. Such considerations have led the Ho to view their supernatural world according to their ethos and world view. As a consequence, the Ho religious belief envisages that the spirits have abodes like man, though of varying types; they are endowed with the male and female sexes; they indulge in sexual union; they need food and drink; they vary in temperament and nature and so on. Such views have led to the identification of the spirits, by name and capability etc. to form a distinct belief system among them.

The Ho belief system envisages that there are three main categories of supernatural beings who are invisible but omnipotent, and omnipresent; "fluttering about everywhere as if they are not". The potency of the spirit depends on its capability to be good or destructive towards man. Accordingly, the Ho believe that their pantheon comprises the Supreme Creator (*Singbonga*) and three other categories of spirits. In the first category are the gods (*bonga*) who are capable of bounty or destruction of mortals through death. There are 21 such gods. Such spirits, by virtue of their power, are believed to be capable of affecting or influencing the life and destiny of the individual as well as the village population as a whole, when displeased. Hence such spirits are regularly propitiated through offerings and sacrifices at the collective level in the course of the annual ritual cycle, or during contingencies which adversely face the village population. In the second category are the lesser spirits (*eras*) who are capable of chastisement but not death. They may inflict ailments, cattle diseases, aches and pains, loss of social standing or even penury and destitution. There are 13 types of such spirits. The third category is formed by the ancestral spirits (*Hum ho*), who are always benign and protective towards their descendants. They are believed to send

Omens and symbolic warnings to their descendants. Understandably, the number of the *Hum ho* is countless.

The vastness of their pantheon has produced problems of identification of the abodes of their deities, the approachability to such powers, and the mode of offering prestations. The Ho have successfully surmounted such operational difficulties in their religious pattern very successfully. Firstly, they have assigned the spirits 12 sacred centres within their village. Such sacred centres are the abode or temporarily resting places of the spirits, and serve as the platforms from which the respective spirits can be approached. Such sacred centres collectively form what may be termed as the sacred geography of the village. The Ho have successfully tided over the problem of approachability by assigning seven distinct categories of persons with the task of establishing liaison with the spirit through spells, divination, omens, trance etc. Collectively such persons may be termed as the 'sacred specialists', of whom the village priest is the head. The ritual process of contacting and offering prestation in a particular way has been formulated in respect to each category of spirit. Collectively we may term these exercises as sacred performances. At a specific level, the combination of the sacred geography, sacred specialists and the sacred performances give rise to the village sacred complex. Such sacred complexes are almost uniform in respect of every Ho village.

The sacred geography of every Ho village extends in and around it and even in the sky above, for it is the abode of the Supreme Being (*Singbonga*). At the topographical level, ten out of the twelve sacred centres are of collective importance, whereas the other two assume importance at the individual level i.e., as they are at the household level. The ten sacred centres at the village level are *Desauli*, *Jaira*, *Marang Bonga akhra*, *Akhra*, *Herkersa*, *Hatu dakud*, *Barbhoji*, *Sansan*, *Uturkila* and *Pawai*.

At the house level, the *ading* (kitchen) and the *gonwa* (cattle shed) are the two sacred centres. Among the village level sacred centres, the *Desauli* is the most important, for it is the abode of the village deity *Desauli*. It is a grove of *sarjom* trees which form the vestigial part of the original forest that was cleared to establish the village. This grove is the most sacred centre of the village and its destruction in any manner is unthinkable for the Ho. The association of the *Desauli* spirit with the primeval forest often gives rise to the speculation that *Desauli* was originally a forest deity, whose abode was left untouched while establishing the village. Subsequently the deity might have been incorporated as the patron deity of the village.

The functional aspect of the sacred specialists indicates that they differ in their power and potentiality for bridging the gap between man and the spirit. Of the sacred specialists, the priest (*deuri*), the medicineman (*dewa*) and the witch (*danee*) are the most important. While the priest and the medicineman use their powers for village level rituals, therapeutics and divination respectively, the witch utilizes her potentiality for the destruction of fellow human beings through the agency of spirits under her control. The importance of the witch cannot be underrated in view of the widespread belief in witchcraft among the Ho. Witches are believed to be so powerful that even while practising countermagic against witchcraft, the medicine men are afraid of naming the witch directly even if they have determined her identity through divination.

The sacred performances of the Ho are as varied as the spirits and deities of their pantheon, because each performance is associated with a specific type of spirit under a specific condition obtaining at the time of the performance. Normally, the Ho performs 7 calendaric rituals within the span of a year. Such performances are associated with fertility, phases of rice cultivation, harvest etc. Other performances obtaining in Ho society are associated with divination; therapeutics; control of epidemics; causing rainfall; deactivating the effects of witchcraft; welfare of livestock and the various phases of the human life cycle, from birth to death and disposal of the dead; calling back of the shade of the dead to the house etc.

From an appraisal of the foregoing data presented, it becomes quite clear that the Ho have developed a style of life, culture and religion which is rather specific. Such a specific feature has emerged among the Ho through the exploitation of their ecological setting on the one hand and the supernatural world on the other, thus forming as it were a Nature-Man-Spirit Complex. The foregoing study of the Ho is therefore of much significance to action anthropologists, and administrative planners, who wish to uplift the lot of the poverty stricken Ho populations. For any developmental project to be undertaken for the Ho, by the social workers or Government, due consideration must be given to their Nature-Man-Spirit Complex, and any attempt to dissociate them from Nature and the Spirit would have disastrous consequences as for them, for they are a part of the complex.

SUGGESTED READINGS

Dalton, E.T.: *Descriptive Ethnology of Bengal*, Council of the Asiatic Society of Bengal, Calcutta, 1872.

Das Gupta, A. : "A study of Ho Rituals and Symbolism", Unpublished Ph.D. thesis, Ranchi University, Ranchi, 1980.

Majumdar, D.N.: "Ho beliefs about natural phenomenon and rituals of rainmaking", *Proceedings of the Indian Science Congress*, No. 12, 1926.

Majumdar, D.N. : "Cult of the dead among the Ho", *Proceedings of the Indian Science Congress*, No. 15, page 316, 1929.

Majumdar, D.N. : "The Spirit of Bongaism", *Proceedings of the Indian Science Congress*, No. 23; page 397, 1936.

Majumdar, D.N. : *A Tribe in Transition*, Longman Green & Co., Calcutta 1937.

Majumdar, D.N. : "Bongaism", *Essays on Anthropology Presented to Raibahadur S.C. Roy*, Maxwell & Co., Lucknow, 1942.

Majumdar, D.N. : *The Affairs of A Tribe*, Universal Publishers Ltd., Lucknow, 1950.

Registrar General : *A Preliminary Appraisal of the Scheduled Tribes of India, (Ed)* No. 57; 100.

Risley, H. : *The People of India*, Thaker Spink and Co., Calcutta, 1908.

Roy, S.C.: "Magic and Witchcraft on the Chotanagpur Plateau", *Journal of the Asiatic Society of Bengal*, Vol. 10, 1914.

Roy, S.C.: "Primitive Religions in Chotanagpur", *Journal of the Behar and Orissa Research Society*, Vol. 14, page 65, 1928.

Tickell, Col: "Memories of Hodesum", *Journal of the Asiatic Society of Bengal*, 1939.

Vidyarthi, L.P.: *The Maler*, Bookland (P) Ltd., Calcutta, 1963.

Vidyarthi, L.P.: *The Sacred Complex of Hindu Gaya*, Concept Publishing Company, New Delhi, 1961.

FOUR

R.K. Prasad

THE PARAHAIYAS
A Study in Nature-Man-Spirit-Complex

THIS paper has been based mainly on the material collected by the author for his doctoral thesis which he submitted to Ranchi University in the year 1965. The Parahaiyas are a tribe who are concentrated in the Palamau, Ranchi, Hazaribagh and Gaya districts of Bihar. Palamau, however, may be taken as the centre of their habitat spreading out into the adjoining districts even up to Mirzapur in Uttar Pradesh.

According to the 1971 Census the total population of this tribe is 14,651 out of which a large portion—11,735, reside in Palamau district. Dalton in his *Descriptive Ethnology of Bengal* writes that "The Parahaiyas, the people of Palamau so called, appear to be mere remnants of a tribe who according to their old traditions and traditions of other races in the district, once formed an important section of the population. They are one of the numerous tribes, or more correctly perhaps one of the branches of the great tribe".

The Parahaiyas dwell in three different ecological settings which determine their economic activities, their social organization and their relationship with the spirit world. Thus we have the hill dwellers, the Parahaiyas of the valley, and, finally those inhabiting the plains. Their habitat therefore varies with their environment.

ECONOMIC COMPLEX

Land ownership or tenantship varies with the three different regions. The Parahaiyas who people the hills have *gairmajurwa* land in their possession. Mostly in the foothills, this land has not been surveyed nor settled by government. In the valley region they have *ukakan* land (patches of land on the hillocks and in the valley) for cultivation and habitat owned mainly by the erstwhile estate-owners or zamindars. It is only in the plains that the Parahaiyas possess *malikbakash* (ownership of land) in their own names.

The Parahaiyas are a traditionally hunting food-gathering tribe who have changed their economic activities in stages to shifting cultivation and thence to settled agriculture finally ending up as agricultural labourers.

The basic sources of their livelihood centre round the natural resources available in their respective ecological complexes. All the year round the Parahaiyas are engaged in the collection of forest produce like roots, tubers, fruits, bamboo, lac, honey and wax, and firewood. These are their traditional activities par excellence. Dwelling as they do, in the lap of Nature, they subsist on her bounty. A Parahaiya saying embodies their philosophy : *Mana mai nahi to van mai* meaning "If he (Parahaiya) is not at home, he is in the jungle".

Every Parahaiya family possesses a *sula* (a digging stick) and the normal routine of every family is to go to the jungle and dig for edible roots and tubers and wash them in the streams and rivulets running nearby.

The collection of honey and wax is one of their chief occupations living as they do in the forests which abound in beehives. A Parahaiya will not hesitate to probe with his hands to find honey however hazardous it may be. They sell the honey thus extracted to the local traders keeping some for their own consumption.

Bamboo clumps proliferate in these forests particularly among the foothills. Bamboo is a chief source of income for the Parahaiyas who make slivers out of them for weaving baskets, winnows, nets, and fishing baskets which they offer for sale in the neighbouring markets and villages.

Lac cultivation is prevalent in a very scattered form among the hill and valley Parahaiyas.

Family farming is largely practised among the plains Parahaiyas while maize is cultivated in the hill and valley regions.

The forests provide work for the valley Parahaiyas. Wood-cutting, beedi-leaf (*tendu*) plucking and charcoal making are some of the means of support for these tribes who often work for the local forest contractors. This is a phenomenon which has resulted from the commercialization of the forests and the encroachment of erstwhile tribal land by non-tribals.

Agriculture is practised mostly by the plains Parahaiyas and on a small-scale by the valley dwellers. The hill Parahaiyas indulage very little in this occupation mainly because of the terrain. To-day most of the farm labour comes from the valley and plains Parahaiyas. The Parahaiyas also domesticate animals like goats, sheep, cows and buffaloes on a large scale. They help the plains people breed these animals and also graze them. Poultry keeping is another occupation among them except for the plains dwellers.

This survey was made on the basis of 49 families in the plains region; 29 families in the valley region; and 30 families in the hills.

From agriculture the average income in the plain regions Parahaiyas is 175-51 per annum, while it is 68-97 rip per annum in the valley region and 33-33-rip per annum to the Parahaiyas of the hill regions. The income from forest is Rs. 6.12 per cent, Rs. 17.24 per cent and Rs. 30 per cent average per annum to all the above respective regions.

The income from animal husbandry alone and from dairy products is Rs. 24.49 per cent among the plain dwellers, Rs. 13.49 per cent among valley dwellers and Rs. 23.33 per cent among the hill dwellers per annum on an average per family.

So income from the forest work is nil in the plains region while it is Rs. 72.41 per cent in the valley region due to the commercial exploitation of the forest. Lastly the average income from the forest per family of the Parahaiyas living in the hill region is also nil.

The income from lac cultivation is only found in the valley region (Rs. 55.77 per annum average) because of the abundant availability of pulse, free *ber* and *kusum* trees. The Parahaiyas in the hill region were once *kusum* lac cultivators but the restrictions on the forest have forced them to stop this traditional occupation.

As already stated, bamboo craft is the only one prevalent in the hill region. They weave *sup* (winnow), *pankha* (fan), *jharu* (broom stick), *podi* (fishing nets) and *fille* (mats). They earn an average of Rs. 50.00 per annum.

According to the total analysis of the income, it comes to Rs. 51.3 among the plain dwellers; Rs. 50.6 per cent for the valley dwellers; and Rs. 36.9 per cent for the hill dwellers.

The expenditure of the Parahaiyas usually is mainly on food, clothing soda, soap and kerosene, *khaini* and *beedi* and on liquor for drinking. The average expenditure on food and clothing is the highest among plain dwellers whereas it is lowest in the hill region. The expenses incurred on soda/soap/kerosene/*beedi* and *khaini* is nil in the hill region. The expenses incurred on drink (wine and *tari*) is only found in the valley region. The expenditure incurred for the payment of the village functions is the minimum in the hill region whereas it is highest in the plain region Parahaiya villages.

So far as the extent of indebtedness is concerned it is highest among the Parahaiyas of the plain region and the lowest in the hill region. The cause is obvious. The Parahaiyas of the plains take loans for marriages and other religious ceremonies and for agriculture whereas Parahaiyas of the hill region secure loans for food and sometimes for clothing also. Looking to the fundamental aspects of the Parahaiya economy it can be said that they have varied sources of livelihood and diversity according to the variation in the environment categorisation.

THE SOCIAL COMPLEX

The Parahaiya are sparsely distributed throughout the state of Bihar and are different from each other in their cultural setting. But the basis of the social organisation remains the common territory.

SOCIAL ORGANISATION OF THE HILL DWELLERS

The social organisation of hill dwellers runs thus :

Chata
|
Lat
|
Patti
|
Kurala

A *chata* is a unit of many *lats* (hills) which comprises agnate and cognate relatives of each *lat*. All the socio-religious relationships of the tribe within a dwelling in the *lat* are reckoned within a *chata*.

A *lat* can be defined as a particular hill range and has many *patties* (wards) and lastly it has many *kuralas* (households).

THE SOCIAL ORGANISATION OF THE VALLEY DWELLERS

Among the valley dwellers the Parahaiyas have a somewhat large framework of territorial organisation which is known as

Chatai
|
Gowhel
|
Tola
|
Chapparies

The whole territorial unit of this region is found to be more functional on the *chatai* level (region) while each village (gowhel) has a centrifugal village known as *Bara Gowhel*. The Bara Gowhel is significant as the socio-religious organisation of each village. Each village (gowhel) is further divided into many *tolas* (wards) and in it there are many *chapparies* (households).

THE SOCIAL ORGANISATION AMONG PLAIN DWELLERS

Likewise the principle of social organisation is the same among the plains Parahaiyas. The basis of the social organisation runs in the following manner :

Gawania
|
Panchgaon
|
Goar
|
Dih
|
Chulha

The limit of a *gawania* (territorial extension) is as per the erstwhile states under the Zamindari system. A *gaon* forms a *panchgaon* with the other *gaons*. Lastly, a *gaon* has many *dihs* and each *dih* has many *chulas* (literally hearths or households).

From the above description it is clear that Parahaiyas living in the three regions provide three different peculiar territorial-based social organisations. Their unique forms of social organisation pose a problem for a proper understanding of the Parahaiyas. The Parahaiyas, as a whole, do not form a single unit in the sense of an integrated territorial unit. They can be viewed as being composed of a series of villages. The village may be perceived as the largest corporate group in the traditional system. This does not mean that villages are completely independent of one another. The Parahaiyas on the whole must be taken as a unit (region) of reference for the total social system.

Each *gaon* or *Bara gowhel* or *lat* occupies a definite territory typically, whether in the hills, the valley or on the plains.

THE AUTHORITY STRUCTURE

The Parahaiyas have no clan organization. They go according to a lineage (khunt) system of a segmented nature; the segments being family, sub-lineage, lineage-group, local group at village and inter-village levels.

Actually, authority yield by lineage varies with its span. In the lineage round, which is a joint family build up, the head has complete moral and ritual powers. On the whole, the lineage itself forms three types of groups, dominant lineage (*madasth khunt*, *jeth khunt* or *jeth raiyat khunt* (the follow up lineage) and *gaon Basra* (immigrant lineage). These groups have certain solidarities among themselves and authority runs according to the status of the group.

Apart from the group solidarity, the authority is structured on the two levels viz., the village and the inter-village level. But the power and privilege in the village and inter-village council is vested according to the above mentioned status of settlement and family on grounds of lineage. Of course sometimes individual traits are taken into consideration specially in the appointment of leaders.

The council on the village level is known as *Bhaiyari* and the council at the inter-village is known as *Kara-bhaiyari*.

The level of organisation differs from one region to another.

In the hill region it combines *bugha pujar* and lineage head; in the valley region it includes *gana* (village landlord) *bygha*, *mahto* on the forest line; whereas *jethkhunt* and *dewan* on the second line along with *pradhan* and on the third line there are heads of the lineage. In the plain region it includes three lines of the authority; first, the *jethraiyaırajgagha-mahto*, second, *gorait*, and *mahato* third, are the lineage heads.

THE SOCIAL INTERACTION

The Parahaiya social set-up has also been going through a series of changes.

It is already mentioned that Parahaiyas of Bihar are distributed in the three different regions:

(i) Plain region
(ii) Valley region
(iii) Hill region

Each region has its own social ecology and has dominant cultural groups which basically affect the way of life of the Parahaiyas through interaction.

On the various occasions like on economic, social and religious events Parahaiyas of the three regions interact with the different tribes and castes according to their tradition and the norms.

THE SOCIAL ECOLOGY AND INTERACTION AMONG HILL DWELLERS

The Parahaiyas dwelling in the hill region have long and permanent association with *Bhogtas*, *Ahir* and the *Oraon*. The Parahaiyas of this region speak *sadri* and celebrate many festivals of the Oraon like *Sahrul* and *Karma* in the native manner. The next social group which comes into close proximity with the Parahaiyas are *Ahir* and *Bhogta* with whom they have not only economic relationship but also interaction in socio-religious events. They invite the Parahaiyas during marriages and serve them food and the process is vice-versa. It has also been observed that the Parahaiyas also appease the chief deities *Birkur* of the *Ahir* community and celebrate the birthday of *Mansing* a Bhogta legendary leader. Another caste that comes in close contact with the Parahaiyas is the *naua* (barber) who attends birth, marriage and death ceremonies and gives regular service for their personal cleanliness. He receives *bani* (remuneration) for his services on each occasion.

The Parahaiyas supply baskets and other bamboo articles to the Nagbansi Rajputs and Kharwars twice a year. During marriages and death ceremonies they supply green leaves. The Kharwars hire female labourers from among the Parahaiyas for work on the land during the Karma and Sahrul festivals.

SOCIAL INTERACTION IN VALLEY REGIONS

The Parahaiyas of the valley region have a close interaction with the chief Hinduised tribes like Kharwar/Chero and the exchange of agricultural implements and labour is very much prevalent between the Parahaiyas and these other tribal groups. Usually, the Parahaiyas also worship their deities like *Purabia*. The Chero and the Kharwar also regularly participate in the celebration of the Parahaiyas *Jatra* (an annual fair of village deities and parental spirits). The Parahaiyas are also invited during the marriages of Chero, Kharwar and vice-versa.

Ahir is a caste group with whom the Parahaiyas of this region interact invariably in all the socio-religious ceremonies and vice-versa. It has been observed that the Parahaiyas dwelling in this region regularly worship the chief deity of the Ahirs.

Naua (barber) is another caste, which is in close contact with the Parahaiyas and which is the media for communicating the Hindu customs and traditions during the different ceremonies, like birth, marriage and the death.

The Parahaiyas also respect the Brahmins, whom they invite for performing the marriage ceremony.

Lastly the baniyas are in close contact with them as *dukania* (shopkeepers) in the neighbouring villages of the Parahaiyas through economic exchange and such dealings.

THE SOCIAL ECOLOGY AND INTERACTION AMONG PLAIN DWELLERS

The Parahaiyas dwelling in the plain region are largely under the influence of the dominant castes of the region like the Brahmin and the Rajput.

The Parahaiyas invite Brahmins (*purohits*) on all the socio-religious occasions and pay the customary fees. There are cases where the Parahaiyas have given land to the Brahmin and also used to make the customary payment to them. On the other hand, Rajputs, Kayasthas and Brahmins are mostly their ex-landlords whom they used to pay by *begari* (free labour) on all the socio-religious ceremonies and also present them with leaves, vegetables and curds as traditional offerings. Most of the agricultural activities of these castes are managed by the Parahaiyas. They are their store-keepers (*bhandari*) in the different remote villages.

The baniyas who are in close contact and are shop keepers in the village provide articles of food through exchange and sales.

Apart from these, they are in close contact with the *Nai* (barber) Ahirs and other groups of the area.

THE SOCIAL STRATIFICATION AND PROCESS IN SOCIAL ECOLOGY

The interactional process between the Parahaiyas and others and among the Parahaiyas themselves has developed certain trends of social stratification but there are also certain marks of difference throughout the Parahaiyas region.

Among the Parahaiyas the principles of stratification basically combine the factors like the housing of ladies, sitting together, inter-dining, acceptance of water, *kachcha* and *pucca* food and admittance.

The Parahaiyas have stratified all the castes and tribes living around them into four ladders of stratification on the basis of the above principles which are given below :

Barka Jati (higher castes)
This group includes the Hindu castes like Brahmin/Rajput/Kayastha/Ahir for the plain region, Chero/Kharwar/Ahir/Brahmin/Rajput/Kayastha in the valley region and Kharwar/Oraon/Ahir/Baniyas in the hill region. The Parahaiya of each region accepts all types of food and water from them.

Bhatua Jati (own castes)
In this category the Parahaiyas include their own tribes of the region. But the Rajput and Kayastha/Ahir interdine with the Parahaiyas on all the socio-religious occasions. In the valley region the Parahaiyas dine with Chero/Kharwar and Ahir while in the hill region they interdine on such occasions only with *Bhogtas*/Ahir and the Oraon.

Loharia Jati (service castes)
Under this category the Parahaiyas of different regions list all those castes who serve them on different socio-religious occasions. Among the plain Parahaiyas are *lohar* (blacksmith), *barahi* (carpenter), *nai* (barber) and *dhobi* (washerman). In the valley region they are *loharia*, *nai* and *dhobi* whereas *nai* is the only service caste in the hill region. So far as common castes are concerned, the Parahaiyas accept only *pucca* food and water from these castes.

Narkatawa Jati (untouchable castes)
For the Parahaiyas of the plain forests and, the hill region, the *chamar*, *bhuiyas* and *dom* are the untouchables; and in the valley region the Parahaiyas treat Korwa, Oraon, Munda, *bhuiya*, *chamar* and *dom* as *narkatawa jati*.

According to their stratification, the Parahaiyas dwelling in the three regions do not interdine and do not accept water among themselves. So the levels of the social stratification differ from one region to the other.

THE SPIRIT COMPLEX

The Parahaiyas dwelling in three different regions have three different parental spirits. These parental spirits are Dootho, Chedi and Chutter. Each of their traditional units is known as Chadi Raj (hill region), Dootho Raj (valley region) and Ghut-terraj (plains). The Baigas of each of these spirits are known as Raj Bhogta.

The Parahaiyas belonging to these three regions consider their own respective spirits as their *Malik* and *Malakani*. These deities forbid them to inter-marry.

The other aspect of their religion is the *mua* (soul) worship. Each family of the lineage has to worship the soul of *Bapkur* (father) and *Aajkur* (grand-father). At the socio-religious ceremonies every family has Mua-asthan-Sira-asthan in the household.

As we have seen the social set-up of the tribe with special reference to interaction, the influence of Hinduism is obvious.

It is revealed from the study that they have adopted many gods and goddesses like Suraj Bhagwan, Shri Ram, Mahabir and Krishna due to constant contact with high Hindu groups. The process is more prominent among the plain dwellers than the hill and the valley dwellers. The impact of Hinduism remains not only up to the adoption of Hindu deities but also the adoption of the jajmani system on the various socio-religious ceremonies. It is more prominent among the Parahaiyas of the plains than the valley dwellers.

The traditional festivals of the Parahaiyas can be said to be *Sarhul*, *Phag*, *Karma*, *Jitiya*, *Dashra-Nawami*, *Chandi puja* and *Sohrai*.

But they have adopted Hindu festivals like *Chhat-brat*, *Anant varat*, *Satya Narain varat*, *Shivratari*, *Ramnaumi*, *Janmasthami*. Such Hindu festivals are mostly adopted by the plain dwellers and among the valley dwellers.

No doubt that Parahaiyas of these three regions' have their parental spirits and the ancestral souls are the basis of their religious complex but the process of Hinduisation is going on.

The analysis of the socio-cultural life of the Parahaiyas may be viewed as follows with reference to the Nature-Man-Spirit Complex.

(a) The natural environment is the main factor in the socio-cultural aspects of the Parahaiyas.

(b) The cultural background viz., spirit complex remains the same among the Parahaiyas.

(c) The variations in ecological settings of the Parahaiyas represent variations in their total cultural complex.

FIVE

R.K. Sinha

A NOTE ON THE NATURE-MAN-SPIRIT COMPLEX OF A TRIBE (PANDO)

INITIALLY, the present paper was meant to be a plain ethnographic study of the Pando, as no previous study on this tribe was available except for casual references in the various Census Reports and District Census Hand-Book of Madhya Pradesh and the volumes of Hiralal. As such, the study of the Pando provided a fascinating and unexplored field.

But when the study of the Pando had crossed the exploratory stage and was well under progress, the author was simply impressed by the isolation, primitiveness of the Pando and the large extent of their dependence on the forest. Here, an idea crossed his mind that Pando life and culture could be better, and perhaps more meaningfully understood and analysed in the theoretical framework of Nature-Man-Spirit Complex, as had been done earlier in case of the Maler, a shifting agriculturist tribe of the Santhal Pargana in Bihar by L.P. Vidyarthi (1963). While making his study of the Maler, Vidyarthi recognised three important aspects of Maler culture; Nature which is forested and hilly surroundings, Man that is the Maler themselves, and Spirit that is their Supernatural world. Further, as he proceeded with his study, he could discover close interrelationships of Nature, Man and Spirit and their mutual interactions which go to constitute a complex (Ibid. pp. 8-9). Vidyarthi has mentioned in his study that "...this way of understanding a tribal culture, though not very new theoretically, was definitely a new task to conceive operationally in describing a tribal culture, I felt tempted to describe these interactions and interrelations in so far as the Maler culture was concerned and methodologically it meant a new way of selecting and organising meaningful materials, leaving apart many details as needed for conventional ethnographic presentation. This approach conceived in terms of 'Culture ecology' and 'Functionalism' attracted me to present a rounded picture of the Maler style of life by avoiding many unnecessary ethnographic details". (Ibid p. 9) Some of these considerations also guided the present author and were uppermost in his mind when he decided to view the Pando in terms of Nature-Man-Spirit Complex.

However, K. N. Sahay (1975) thinks that the Nature-Man-Spirit Complex not only provides a conceptual model for a meaningful analysis of a primitive community flourishing in the lap of Nature and closely interacting with Nature on the one hand and the Spirit on the other, but it also serves as an index to understand the broad nature of transformations taking place in that community and determines the point on the scale of change where such a community could be fixed. Sahay says that according to the nature of the Nature-Man-Spirit interdependence as analysed in Vidyarthi's study, the Maler community stands very near to one extreme end of the scale which shows a perfect and balanced interdependence among the Nature-Man-Spirit. Such communities are very old and primitive in time perspective and represent the earliest development of human society, but as we move away from this point towards the other end of the scale, the community standing at the various points of the scale, will show a gradual weakening of the Nature-Man-Spirit Complex owing to a change in their ecological setting, habitat, and the attainments of man, which are also bound to bring about a change in their belief system and relation with the spirit world. Thus, Sahay points out that at the other end of the scale there are societies which are non-primitive and considerably advanced which have brought about tremendous changes in their surroundings, habitat and have their technologies much advanced. These attainments on the one hand, have upset the Nature-Man-Spirit interdependence and acquired a new state of balance, while on the other hand, the role of Nature and Spirit in the life of man have become either virtually ineffective or have changed beyond recognition.

In view of the above methodological and theoretical formulations of Sahay related to the Nature-Man-Spirit Complex, the present author has used this conceptual model in his study not only for the purpose of showing the working of Nature-Man-Spirit Complex in the life and culture of the Pando, as done earlier by Vidyarthi in his Maler study, but also to understand as to how the Nature-Man-Spirit interdependence has gradually started weakening in their life and culture due to modern forces of change. Thus, in spite of the fact that Nature-Man-Spirit Complex works in the life of the Pando, they stand at a point beyond where the Maler stand on the scale of change.

The Pando are a little known tribe of Madhya Pradesh, who largely live in Surguja district of Madhya Pradesh, where about 95.5 per cent of their population has been shown in the Census of India, 1961 (District Census Hand-Book of Surguja, 1961). However, the Pando population is lumped together with the Bharia-Bhumia, which according to the 1961 Census comes to be 92,369. Out of it, 26,606 are in Surguja, 31,836 are in Jabalpur and 12,041 in the Raigarh district. Rest of them are spread over in other districts of Madhya Pradesh in small numbers.

Before the 1921 Census Report, which was then known as Central Province and Berar Report did not make any clear mention of the Pando tribe. The Census Report for the first time mentions the name of the Pando tribe which was amalgamated with Bharia-Bhumia or Bhuinhar-Bhumia. While mentioning about the Pando tribe, the Census of Central Province and Berar Report, 1931, quotes the opinion of Rai Bahadur Hiralal and Shootbert. Hiralal observed that "Pandos are akin to Kawar, the descendants of *Kauravas* of *Mahabharata* whose cousins were *Pandavas*, a theory which is not supported by the notes regarding their customs". While Shootbert noticed a marked similarity between them and Korwas, the present author in course of his field-work tried his best to verify these assumptions from the Pandos and observed that they do not acknowledge any association either with Kawar, Korwa or even with Bhuinhar-Bhumia as given in the Census Report following from 1921. However, they identify themselves with and claim to be the descendants of *Pandavas* of *Mahabharata* and quote some of their myths in support of this claim.

Pando of Pal Tehsil of Surguja claim that on the border area of Madhya Pradesh and Bihar, in Madhya Pradesh they call themselves *Parahia* Pando and in Bihar, they are known by the name of *Parahiya* only. Similarly, it is reported that in the adjoining area of Mirzapur on the border of Madhya Pradesh and Uttar Pradesh, they call themselves Baiga. The Pando of Baikunthpur areas of Surguja claimed that formerly they were known as Bhuinhar but for the last fifty years or so they changed themselves to Pando community. Some of these contentions were supported by myths, a few of them being related to the *Pandava* of *Mahabharata*.

Pando are divided into two endogamous groups known as *Surgujia* Pando and *Uttaraha* Pando. The *Surgujia* consider themselves to be superior to the *Uttaraha* which the latter accept. The *Uttaraha* Pando are very small in number and that too restricted to in and around the *Bhaiyathan* of *Bhaiya-Pargana* and nearby to Bisbrampur colliery in Surajpur Tehsil. The present work is based on mainly *Surgujia section* of Pando.

Pando are half-naked irrespective of men, females and children. Their usual dress is so scanty that in the name of clothing, men wear *langoti*, a short loin cloth around the waist while rest of their body is usually nude, excepting for a few persons like *mukhia*, *baiga*, or those who can afford to wear more clothes. They wear a *dhoti*, but in the *langoti* style and a shirt or *kurta* whenever they visit some other villages or weekly markets. Elderly persons may wear a piece of cloth like a turban (*pagri*) on their head. The Pando women mostly use a white *saree* and cover the upper part of their body with the same cloth. Their children usually remain completely naked up to the age of four to six. Later on, they wear only a loin cloth, irrespective of their sex.

The Pando have been traditionally living in forested and hilly areas of Madhya Pradesh and are dependent on the forest for their sources of livelihood. Hunting and food-gathering and basket-weaving constitute the main sources of their economy. However, some life-histories of the old Pando revealed the fact that in the past, they also used to practise *lahi* (lac) cultivation and shifting cultivation. The lac was raised on *bair*, *sandan*, *kusum*, *bendo* and *palash* trees, twice in a year, which remained a source of earning cash money when sold to the traders, as is the case with the gum, still sold by the Pando. As such, the Pando considered themselves to be economically comparatively affluent in those days which for many of them was nothing less than *Ram-Raj* (ideal polity). Shifting cultivation (*beora*-cutting) is said to have been practised by them till fifty or sixty years ago. *Minjhari*, *lakra*, *betri*, *jondari*, *kurusha*, and *jawari* were some of the main crops raised through shifting cultivation. It was done through the usual slash and burn method after selecting a patch of land in the forest which was cleared and burnt.

In the light of the two occupations just mentioned, the Pando state that they were leading a nomadic life in the past. They would move from place to place in search of trees suited for lac raising and after the collection of lac they would shift to another site. Similarly, every time the Pando changed their patch of forest for shifting cultivation. Even today, few Pando families are known to be in the habit of changing their village too often.

The present note is being presented here under three major heads, viz. Nature, that is their ecological setting, habitat and their interactions, in other words forest economy; Man, which deals with Pando in relation to Nature on the one hand and Spirit on the other; and Spirit, that is the Pando's 'Supernatural world'. It is another important dimension of the Nature-Man-Spirit Complex. Here the nature and the extent of dependence of the Pando on the spirit has been dealt with.

NATURE : FOREST ECOLOGY

The traditional Pando culture appears to have flourished in the lap of nature surrounded by forest and hills. This ecological setting of the Pando habitat makes a deep impact on their life which gets adequately reflected in their economy as well as in their beliefs. The influence of forest is so deep-rooted in their life and culture that they cannot conceive of living away from the forest. It is because of this fact that they look to the forest as an amicable source of livelihood and the forest really helps them in every aspect of life.

The traditional homogenous Pando villages are situated in the dense forest and on the foot-hills. Ten to twenty households made of mud-walls, wood, leaves, grass and bamboo constitute the traditional Pando village. All the raw materials for hut-building are collected from the forest. These forest villages of the Pando merge with the natural vegetation and topography of the forest which to many of us seems incredible that it might contain any human habitation. At one spot in a Pando village one finds three to five huts clustered together. Three to five such clusters of huts, which are widely separated from one another covering an area of about one square mile constitute a village. For a village settlement, they require essentially a permanent water source, as they seem unable to dig an artificial water source. Water supply assumes such an importance among them that they worship a deity to ensure permanent and adequate supply of water from a spring.

In this situation the Pando's life and culture seem to have originated, developed and flourished in the lap of nature. They are dependent on the forest to such an extent that their whole life and economy revolves round the forest. The economic role of the forest in Pando life and culture may be appreciated from their following reply on one occasion that "they will not leave the forest at any cost as they felt more secure in the surroundings of the forest because forest provides them with food articles, shelter, drinks, raw materials for their hut-building, basketry and for such other vocations".

Thus, the economic activities of the Pando are closely interwoven with forest, and the economic utility of forest in their life can best be understood under the following heads:

FOREST AS A SOURCE OF SUPPLYING SHELTER, FOOD AND DRINK

Since the Pando have a forest based economy, they satisfy most of their requirements by exploiting the forest. Here, forest not only supplies merely a patch of land to construct a hut for shelter but also wood, bamboo, thatching grass, leaves and straws to build their dwelling with. These hut-building materials are not fetched only for their own purposes but sometimes they supply it to the neighbouring villagers against cash or foodstuff.

Food-gathering from the forest constitutes one of the major economic activities of the Pando in which both males and females take part. The Pando exploit the forest and its produce to the maximum extent to meet at least their bare necessities. In the season of *mahua*, *char* and *tendu*, they devote all their time in the collection of this forest produce. From their experience, they have a very wide and thorough knowledge of the things available in the forest for their subsistence, like edible roots, tubers, fruits, flowers, leaves, herbs, shrubs, medicinal plants and wild animals edible or otherwise. Again, they have been very expert in the proper utilization of this forest produce, as they know well how these articles can easily and best be fetched and processed for human consumption. As some of the roots, tubers and leaves are bitter, sour or even poisonous, they take all precaution and care to process them before final consumption. In this way some roots, tubers and flowers are eaten as a full meal, while some others are consumed as vegetables. Oil is also extracted from some of the seeds of forest produce, viz. *umjeni*, *keoti*, *dori*, etc. Again, sweet juice is extracted from the *dhawai* flowers and honey is collected from bee-hives.

As such, Pando collect about twenty-four different types of edible roots and tubers which are locally known as *kanda*. Mention may be made of some of them, like *bagha*, *birallu*, *bhothi*, and *seo*. These are sweet and may be eaten only after washing. *Gethia kanda* is of two types, sweet as well as bitter. The latter one is consumed only during scarcity. *Bajan kanda* is known as an intoxicating tuber. It is said to be so intoxicating that one may die if one consumes it without any processing. *Kathua* and *tepna* are known as itching tubers, so these are consumed only after processing, that too by mixing with some sour substance. Again, most of these available tubers are hard so these are fried before consumption.

As vegetables, Pando consume leaves, flowers, fruits and young shoots of about twenty-six trees. These edibles are cooked as vegetables and consumed with steamed *mahua*, tubers, cooked rice, *pej* and bread. Special mention may be made of *benia-bhaji*, *koilar-bhaji*, and *saroti-bhaji*, which are said to be very tasty and are consumed by most of the people of the region.

Again, the Pando consume fruits and flowers of about sixteen forest trees. Some of them are abundant in supply which are consumed as a full meal, both at home and in the forest. Here, mention may be made of the fruits and flowers, viz. *tendu, char, mahua, jambu, chind, bhuilotna* and *mango*. As the Pando depend on these fruits very considerably, *char, mahua, tendu, mango* and *bair* are dried and stored for future consumption in the rainy season when there has been restricted food supply from the forest. *Mahua* is one of the important forest products with multiple economic utilizations. People consume it as breakfast as soon as it is collected, dried, steamed and fried. *Mahua* is consumed as a full meal. Again, it is utilised for making liquor.

In addition to the above mentioned items of food from the forest, the Pando get a number of edible fungi (mushrooms) in the rainy season. Such fungi are sixteen in number and locally known by the name of *khukhundi*. These fungi grow in the forest near to their habitat on the plains, or on the wood or near the white ant's hills. In the rainy seasons the food supply from the forest decreases very considerably, and these fungi substitute as food and provide them some relief in their hard pressed economy.

FOREST AS A SOURCE OF GAME

Hunting has always been one of the important sources for meeting a part of their food requirement. In the past, they used to organise hunting expeditions every now and then. Now, the scope of hunting has been lessened considerably due to scarcity of game and by the imposition of forest rules. In spite of this, they do not check their temptation and go for hunting without the notice of the forest officials. But, many a time, they have to return unsuccessful even after spending hours together in the forest.

Usually, hunting is organised collectively. It may be a inter-village or intra-village group. Individual hunting with one or two friends is also in practice. If they succeed in killing a big animal (edible), it is shared equally among the participants. But its head and one share always go to the village headman. Previously, the game used to be distributed among the existing families of the village. But this practice has now disappeared.

Again, these days some of the Pando sell their share of hunted animal or exchange it for foodgrains.

FOREST AS A SOURCE OF INDIGENOUS MEDICINES

Forest not only supplies food and shelter to them but also a number of indigenous medicines. And with the help of these indigenous medicines, they keep themselves healthy and obtain cures for a number of diseases.

The Pando are aware of number of roots, tubers, creepers, herbs and shrubs which are known to possess medicinal values. These are also collected by the Pando from the surrounding forests which are of great economic as well as of essential nature in their day to day life. Usually, the experts like *Gunia*, *Baiga* and *Aulwa* are considered to have a very thorough knowledge about the best and proper utilization of medicinal plants, roots, etc. They are the only persons who can recognise and utilise these with full confidence. However, commoners have only a shallow knowledge about it and they take advantage of some of the very common indigenous medicines. Under this category the Pando know with full confidence about thirty medicinal roots, tubers and such other plants which are utilised by them for curing various diseases.

Again, a few flowers and roots of such plants are utilised as *totakha* (magical charms). These are believed to possess some supernatural powers and help them very considerably. Here, the fruits of *bhejra* and *ban-bhanta* are tied round the necks of such children as get cold and cough. It is believed that by the observance of this totakha, the suffering children return to their normal health. The root of *indbagai* is tied round the neck of those women and domesticated animals in order to mitigate their prolonged travail or difficulty in normal and safe delivery. Similarly, the thread of *kumbhi* fibre is believed to be so effective that if a child wears it round the neck, no evil spirit in the world can harm him. The root of *bara-kachma* or *kachmi* and *bansemi* if buried together near the door will prevent snakes from coming there.

Further, many plants are known to be very effective as antidotes to snake-bite. The root of *bhejri* tree is crushed to paste and is applied on the part bitten by *danda-karait* snake. The leaves of *tin-patti* tree is crushed and taken by the man who is bitten by the *jharpa* snake. The root of *ram-katai* is given to the man who is bitten by the *sugga* snake. But, in the bite of *fanik* snake (cobra) the *dudhia-jari* is said to be very useful as an antidote.

FOREST AS A SOURCE OF SUPPLYING RAW MATERIALS FOR THEIR CRAFT

The utility of the forest is also very immense in supplying raw materials (bamboo) for their basket weaving craft and helps them in procuring part of their bread. Pando are expert basket-makers. They makc baskets of different shapes and sizes. They are generally criss-cross in which the warp and weft pass over each other. They claim basketry to be their traditional job, which as they say, they inherited from their forefathers known by the name of Pandaya-Raja of the *Mahabharata* period.

Basketry may be said to be one of the important sources of earning cash money or food grains in exchange. Basketry requires only bamboo as raw material which is fetched from the neighbouring forest. They require only *ghora* and *churi* (knife) as tools for basket making. At first, bamboos are brought from the forest and strips of required length and breadth are made, depending upon the types of baskets to be prepared. They make baskets of about eleven types, *supa* (winnowing fan), *mora* (big basket), *benwa* (fan), and *daura* (basket) are common among them. *Pathia* and *jhanjhari* (special type of basket) are made only on order from the neighbouring villagers. The former is required during the marriage season, while the latter during the harvesting time *Chatai* (matress), rain-coat and *tatta* (door-cover), are made only for their own use.

Basketry job is subject to traditional norms. It is strictly made by males only and females do not render their help of any kind. Again, baskets are sold usually by females only. However, in special or unavoidable circumstances, males also sell or exchange them for other articles. These days basketry seems to be one of the important subsidiary jobs for them. They devote at least half of their time when they stay in the hut. They sell their baskets in the neighbouring non-Pando villages or at the weekly markets.

It is interesting to note that basketry is associated with *Churi-Path*, a deity or supernatural power, who is believed to be responsible for any cuts and injury from the *churi* (knife) while making baskets. This deity is appeased by the Pando for his favour and protection in this job.

Besides basketry, some of the Pando also prepare ropes from *mahulain* and *lakra* fibre of the same trees which are sold in the neighbouring village and at the weekly markets. Similarly, a few of them are involved in the collection of leaves of *sarai* (sal), *tendu*, and *mahulain*, which are sold to the local contractors at very cheap rates. Again, a few of them collect silk cotton from the forest which is sold or exchanged with the neighbouring agriculturists. Silk cotton is also used by them to light *biri* (*chongi*), with the help of *chakama* (one piece of quartz and another piece of iron).

FOREST AS A SOURCE OF MATERIAL EQUIPMENTS

From cradle to grave they are dependent on the forest for something or the other, as the forest is indispensable in the life of the Pando as a source of material equipments.

For the storage of forest and agricultural products some of the Pando construct *kotha* (granaries) with the help of wood and mud. It is constructed in two to three separate compartments for storing different commodities. In most of the villages, the village *mukhia*, *baiga* and their relatives construct this type of kotha. Again, from the bamboo's stripes Pando make a number of containers. They make containers for storing small quantities of seeds and forest produce with the help of a green hollow bamboo piece. This container is also used for the keeping of gum paste while catching birds. Usually a rope is tied at the upper end of the container by which it hangs against a wall or in the roof. Again, leaf-vessels are very popular among them. The Pando make various kinds of vessels from the mahulain leaves. For this purpose leaves are plucked along with their small stalks. They make the leaf-vessel by stitching the leaves one over lapping the other, the stalks of leaves serving as needles. It is ordinarily round and oval in shape. It is ordinarily used for storing silk cotton and pulses for a longer period of time. When it is filled with any commodity, its upper portion is covered in the same style with the leaves. When required the stored things are taken out by breaking the upper part.

For sitting, relaxing and sleeping, ordinarily the Pando make basket mats and piddas but cots are also used. Bamboo mats are very popular among them which is of several sizes. The bigger one is used for sleeping purposes while the smaller one is made for sitting. Pidda is nothing but a rectangular flat piece of wood. It is used for sitting purpose and also used as a pillow while sleeping. Cots are not very popular among them as they are not in the habit of sleeping on these. Usually, in a village they possess at least one cot for the outsiders. It is made with the help of wood and ropes of lakra and Mahulain fibre. But, the Pando of Pal Tehsil make cots without the help of any rope, as they weave the cots with bamboo stripes and by mahulain bark. As said earlier, the Pando are not in the habit of sleeping on cots so they sleep on the floor spreading just a piece of cloth and a *pidda* under the head even on winter nights but keep themselves warm by a fire with the help of forest wood.

For washing agents the Pando depend fully on the forest as they wash their clothes with the ashes of *char, dhora* and *palash* wood which are available in the forest. In addition to the ashes above mentioned, the ashes of *til* (sesamum) straw is said to be very effective as a washing agent. Firstly, such ashes are mixed with water in a vessel. The dirty clothes are put into it and the vessel is kept on a fire for boiling for about an hour. When it is fully boiled, the clothes are removed and washed in the nearest stream or pond or any other available water source. Usually, they are washed once a week. Again, for personal decoration they use *dori, deoti* and *umzeni* oils which are directly supplied from the forest. Pando of both sexes decorate themselves as much as their means allow them. They rub these oils on their body as cream with a view to adding a glaze to their body. It is mostly done during festivals, fairs on market days and during marriage.

The forest also supplies them with raw materials for the implements required for the best exploitation of forest and its produce. Here, they get all types of wood for making handles of *khanta, falsi, tabal* and *kulhari*. For hunting they get raw materials for making hunting weapons, viz. bow, arrow, *gulel*, and *balua*. For fishing Pando make fishing nets and traps like *kumani* and *bishra* and the forest helps them by supplying raw materials for this. They also collect a number of poisonous fruits, flowers, leaves, herbs and roots which are utilised for catching fish by poisoning the water. This technique is very popular among them.

For carrying equipment the Pando make *dirga*, *jhalgi*, *sikka* and *sihari* and the forest is again very helpful in supplying all the raw materials for this.

Dirga is made from the shoots of *dhora* or *aura* tree and supported at the two ends of a carrying pole. It is meant for carrying fuel from forest to home and sometimes from home to neighbouring villages. *Jhalgi* is made with bamboo strips which is round in shape and its bottom being a little hollowed. Two such baskets are hung at the two ends of a carrying pole with the help of *mahulain* and *lakara* fibres which are tied at three places in each of the baskets. *Sikka* is made with the twisted ropes of *mahulain* or *lakra* fibres. It has got multifarious utility in their society. At one time with the help of a pair of *sikka* which are tied at both ends of a carrying stick, one is capable of carrying load of about two to three maunds (1 md=40 lbs) from one place to another. It is also used for carrying pitchers full of water on special occasions. Ordinarily, pitchers of liquor *mahua* are carried on a *sikka* to the liquor shop by a Pando on hire.

The foregoing discussion reflects the important role which the forest plays in the life and culture of the Pando and the close interactions of Man with Nature on the one hand and Spirit on the other. The above facts reveal that the importance of the forest in the matter of supplying shelter, food, drinks, indigenous medicines and raw materials for their craft, is very immense. It satisfies multifarious and maximum requirements of the Pando and is of great economic value to them. Hence, the traditional Pando would never think of leaving their forest surroundings, because they have been accustomed and feel a sense of security in their life, even if it be for their bare survival.

II

MAN: MAN TO MAN RELATIONSHIPS

To understand Man in relation to Nature-Man-Spirit Complex it would be necessary to begin with the self-image and identity of the Pando. Again, it can be understood firstly, in terms of their relationship with other ethnic groups of the region and how in their own self-estimation they are different from other ethnic groups. Secondly, it would be relevant to discuss their self-estimates as members of a particular tribe, a particular sub-group of the tribe, a particular clan, a particular family and a village. Besides this it has been discussed as Individual at the Axis of Self and Regulation of village life.

THE PANDO AND OTHER ETHNIC GROUPS

The Pando identify themselves as a separate and distinct ethnic group from the other neighbouring groups, having a distinct forest based style of life and speaking a particular Pando dialect. The Pando recognise themselves to be the descendants of the *Pandavas* of *Mahabharata* who, according to them, were forest dwellers and their main weapon was the bow and arrow. In other words, the Pando refer to that phase of the Pandavas' life which was spent in the forest as a consequence of being defeated by the *Kaurava* of *Mahabharata* in the game of dice, and when they were sent into exile for fourteen years from their own kingdom. In fact, the Pando feel proud of having maintained the tradition of *Mahabharata-Pandava* as they conceive that *Pandava* had a forest based life, their main weapons were bows and arrows and they had preferred to take basketry as a profession during the period of their exile in the forest. Again, the frequent mention of *Pandava* in the Pando folk-tales and folk-songs establishes some sort of relationship between the *Mahabharata Pandava* and the present Pando.

In the regional social hierarchy the Pando consider themselves to be superior to the *chamar*, *chirka* (a musician caste) or *kuar*, *oraon*, (*dhangar*), *ghasia*, *panika*, and *agaria*, but inferior to the *gond*, *rajwar*, *binjhia*, *ahir* (*mahato*), *bargah*, (*rout*), *kumbhar*, *nai* and *cherva*. Apart from the position of the Pando in a definite regional ethnic hierarchy, they are well regarded by their neighbouring ethnic groups in general as they are hereditary *gunia* and *dewari* (magical conjurers).

Whenever an occasion arises the Pando accept water, cooked food, and tobacco from their superior groups but the latter do not accept these things from the Pando. In the same way, Pando also do not accept these things from those groups wh are inferior to them while the latter accept these things from the

Pando. Under unavoidable circumstances, Pando accept raw food from inferior groups, they cook it for themselves and take it at the latter's place. If this practice is not taken into consideration or violated, they are punished by their own council.

THE PANDO AS MEMBERS OF A TRIBE

The real unity of the Pando as a member of the Pando tribe, is to be noted in their awareness of being a Pando in every sphere of life, as for all practical purposes they considered themselves to be members of the Pando tribe. This feeling is very prominently reflected during their formal or informal gatherings, viz., during festivities, ritual performances and during distress when they share the same feelings, sometimes anxieties as one body. Their awareness of belonging to a particular ethnic group is also reflected when they are oppressed and exploited by outsiders. Such occasions make them feel united and react in the same manner and whatever decision in this regard is taken, it is followed by all of them. Even though the Pando live in different villages of a region, the above mentioned occasions bind them into an ethnic unity which cuts across sub-group, clan, family and village loyalties.

Even in their day to day routine, their ethnic solidarity is reflected when they visit a distant place on some mission. On such occasions a Pando always prefers to spend the night with a Pando. There he finds a homely atmosphere and does not feel like a stranger. In the same way, during festivals, viz. the *Karma* dance, the Pando frequently visit their neighbouring Pando villages where they enjoy all the privileges of co-villagers without any formal introduction which indicates that they belong to one ethnic group.

Ethnic solidarity of the Pando also gets reflected by their practice of tribal endogamy as also found in other ethnic groups of the region. Even when a Pando acquires a marriage partner by *udalia* (by elopement), the partner is invariably from the Pando group.

The very fact that the Pando live in forested and hilly surroundings makes them closely associated, attached and dependent on the forest and its resources, as already discussed earlier, and to a great extent it is also responsible for creating among them an attitude and values of life which are distinct from other people's and to a great extent it fosters a sense of unity among them as members of the Pando tribe.

Ethnic solidarity of the Pando is again reflected in adequate measure when local forest officials, local policemen, local *Surpunch* and such other authorities have ever to deal with a Pando offender. Under such occasions all the Pando unite as one body and try their best to see that the offender is not taken into custody unless a big contingent of police force is deputed for this purpose.

Lastly, the Pando have got a set of indigenous beliefs and practices, which they have been observing since generations and which are different from other neighbouring groups and in some ways, quite distinct from others. These also givè them a sense of unity and solidarity at the whole tribal level.

THE PANDO AS A MEMBER OF A SUB-GROUP

The Pando are divided into two endogamous groups, namely, *Surgujia* and *Uttaraha*. The former consider themselves to be superior to the latter. They also differ among themselves in terms of a few of their beliefs and practices.

The *Surgujia* Pando usually make two doors to a room, one in the front and other at its back, while adjacent to this room is an apartment known as *bhitar-ghar*. The entrance to the *bhitar-ghar* is just near the front door of the main room. The women among the *Surgujia* Pando make use of both the doors for entrance except during menses and child-birth, when they are polluted and have to use the back door only. It is because of these two doors of the main room, the *Surgujia* Pando are called as *Du-Duaria*. The *Uttaraha* Pando however have only one door in the front for all occasions and an adjacent apartment known as *bhitar-ghar* as among the *Surgujia*. Because of having only one door in their main room they are known as *Ek-Duaria*.

The *bhitar-ghar* is considered to be the abode of ancestors and clan deities. This room of the hut is not used by polluted women (a woman under menses or child-birth) and a woman of another clan, as their entry into the *bhitar-ghar* is strictly prohibited.

Previously, inter-marriage between *Surgujia* and *Uttaraha* was not practised and both the groups were endogamous. But since about fifteen years or so it is said that these two groups made a compromise and started marrying with each other, but in practice *Surgujia* Pando ordinarily accept the *Uttaraha's* girls as brides but they are reluctant to marry their daughters to *Uttaraha's* boys. Now, gradually there is a change in their outlook as well as the customs mentioned above and they are coming close to each other through marriage alliances which have removed much of the water-tight compartments in which they were living.

THE PANDO AS A MEMBER OF A CLAN

Clan, being one of the important segments of Pando social system, plays a momentous role in regulating their socio-religious life. The local name for clan is *Goti* and the members of one clan consider themselves to be descended from a common ancestor which is supported by myths. The clan constitutes one of the important functional units of the Pando social system. During important ceremonies and rituals in the family, the members of that clan living in the village or in the neighbouring villages, get the first priority of invitation and it is obligatory for them to attend such functions of their clan-men and also assist them physically or economically as far as their means allow.

The Pando are divided into a number of clans and during the author's field investigation about one hundred eleven clan names were reported so far. For a systematic and convenient understanding, these clan names may be classified into three groups. All these groups are mutually exclusive but for a few exceptions.

The first group of clans is generally based on some mythical events regarding their origin and are usually associated with some specific beliefs, usages, or qualities regarding their clan. These categories of clans are found among the *Surgujia* Pando only. These are named as Bhalwa, Bhania, Bhusar, Chamadia, Dari, Gosai, Hush, Kamaro, Machraha, Pipariha, Siraya and Shikari.

The second group of clans generally indicates their association with some territory and are named as such.

These clan names are mostly based on or associated with some important hills, villages, or some important territories. Myths relating to these clans tell us that in the beginning their forefathers were the original settlers of these places and as such their descendants in due course came to be known by these names. These clan names give that much information that such territories and village names lie under *Bhayathan* or *Bhaiya-Parganas* of Surajpur Tehsil in Surguja district. Hence, it gives a historical fact about the migration of this section of Pando in other parts of Surguja from the particular places. The category of clans are found among the *Surgujia* Pando only. These are named as Baronjha, Bhawar-khoiya, Bilamia, Deo-kholiha, Deo-khalia, Jainaihiya, Moko, Mudalia, Takaria and Totokha.

The third group of clan names are those about which the author could not get any myth during his course of field-work. However, some of them belong exclusively to the *Uttaraha* Pando, viz. Badhi, Bhusar, Chandoliha, Chaparaha, Dasputwa, Ganvaniha, Jesse, Kariyaha, Morho, Palaria, Panchvariha, Panarhi, and Umaria, while some others to *Surgujia* Pando, which are about eighty in number.

Nature and Function of Pando Clan

Though the Pando have a number of clans, there is no hierarchy of clans and all the people are considered to be equal in rank and status.

Although some of the clans as discussed earlier, have got some totemic characteristics, yet the Pando society cannot be said to be totemistic. Firstly, it does not have taboos associated with such objects. However, the Pando clans play a number of significant roles in the life of the people as discussed below.

The Pando clans are exogamous. Hence, the members of a clan do not marry within the clan and help them to regulate the marriage tie in their society. Naturally, it also helps in maintaining a sense of solidarity among the members belonging to a particular clan. This feeling gets further reinforced as the members of a clan have a common association either in terms of some mythical events, certain beliefs or usages or a common territory. Even in ordinary business of life, members of a clan maintain a feeling that they have some unknown attachment and kinship with the other, though they may not be tracing their actual or consanguineal relationship among themselves. This can be easily witnessed during ancestor worship, or worship of the clan deities or during death rituals. On all such occasions the clansmen get first priority of invitation. Again, it is obligatory for the clansmen to attend such functions even though they may be living at a great distance.

One important function of the clan is that sometimes a man is addressed by his clan name, specially in other villages, particularly in the in-laws' village. Even in the ordinary business of life one addresses each other by the clan name especially when they refer to a third person.

Clan is also interwoven with the religious life of the Pando as, generally, different clan members worship different sets of deities. It is true that some of the deities are common among some of the clans but some others vary from clan to clan. These deities are enshrined in different parts of the hut, depending on the nature, function, position and usefulness of these deities among the clan members. The nature of offerings, time and duration of worship also vary from clan to clan.

Usually, the help of clansmen are sought at both the occasions whether happy or otherwise. During happy occasions clansmen are required to attend and participate during the occasions of birth, marriage, ancestral worship and worship of clan deities. All the same, during death and disease the help of clansmen is required and every clan member extends his or her full co-operation on such occasions.

THE PANDO AS MEMBERS OF A KIN GROUP

Since the Pando are patrilocal and patrilineal, the first contact which the child develops is with his immediate consanguineal kins like parents,uncles, grand-parents and Siblings and it is only when he or she advances in age that he or she understands the difference between consanguineal and the affinal kin—who visit the family only casually, by and by he develops an awareness of the network of various types and degrees of kin around him which not only gives a feeling of familiarity but also security. The Pando kinship system is not very different from other linguistic groups of Chhatisgarh. Though the Pando under study are from different ecological settings, there is very little difference in the kinship terminologies, viz. between the *Surgujia* and *Uttaraha* Pando. The term *aja* is used for grand-father and *aji* for grand-mother including the maternal grand-father and grand-mother, among the *Uttaraha*. Whereas among the *Surgujia*, the term *dadi* or *budha* is used to refer both paternal grand-father and maternal grand-father and the term *bardai* or *burdhi* is used for denoting paternal grand-mother and maternal grand-mother. Similarly, the term *bhai* is used for referring to both elder and younger brothers among the *Uttarahas* but among the *Surgujias* the term *dada* is used for elder brother and the term *bhai* for younger brother.

The Pando kinship terms can be analysed in different ways as suggested by G.P. Murdock (1949). According to linguistic structure kinship terms may be analysed as elementary terms, derivative terms and descriptive terms. It reveals from the Pando kinship terms that most of the kinship terms are of elementary nature. As regards the derivative terms, there are only two terms, viz, *jeth-sash* and *jeth-salla*. These are used for Wi El Si and Wi El Br respectively. Again, *natin-damad* (So Da Hu, Da Da Hu), *nati-bahuria* (So So Wi, Da So Wi) and *mausi-dai* are three terms which may be taken as descriptive terms in the strict sense of the term. But for all cousins descriptive terms are used when these relatives need to be described, viz. *mosera-bhai*, (Mo Si So), *mamera-bhai* (Mo Br So), *chachera-bhai* (Fa Br So), and *phuphera-Bhai* (Fa Si So). In the same way, while describing the female cousins (*bahan*) descriptive terms are used as we have seen above in case of male cousins. In the ordinary course all male cousin brothers address their youngers by their names and youngers by the term *dada* except *baraka* (Fa El Br So senior to ego). Elder cousin sisters address their younger cousin sisters by their names or by the term *bahan* while youngers by the term *didi*, unless the relationships are to be specified. In the same way *kaka-sasur*, *mama-sasur*, *mausa-sasur*, *phupha-sasur* and *kaki-sash*, *bari-sash*, *mami-sash*, *mausi-sash*, *phua-sash*, are descriptive terms when these terms need to be described.

Again, kinship terms may be described or differentiated as denotative terms and classificatory terms according to the range of application. Some of the Pando's kinship terms may be classified as denotative terms as they stand only for one relative, viz. *dau* (Fa), *dai* (Mo), *baraka* (Fa El Br El So), *sash* (Hu Mo, Wi Mo), and *sasur* (Hu Fa, Wi Fa). Few kinship terms are denotative but stand for several other relatives of identical kinship connection. For example, though the terms *bhai*, *bahan*, *dada* and *dadi* are denotative, these are used as classificatory when they stand for all types of cousins. However, cousins are always referred to with their associated specific relatives like *mamera*, *chachera* etc. Among the Pando as it is in Hawaiian terminology, sibling terms are applied to the cousin.

By the mode of use, kinship terms may again be classified as terms of reference and the terms of address. Here, the youngers always address their elder relatives by the actual terms of reference meant for them, excluding some exception, viz. *sardu*, *jeth-salla*, *jeth-sash* as younger *sardu* address his elder *sardu* as *dada* and *jeth-sash* is addressed as *didi*. On the other hand, these elders address their younger relatives of the same category by their village name or by their clan names.

The criterion of generation is always maintained. Criterion of sex is also maintained with one exception that is with the term *Goi*. As the term *Goi* stands for a man's siblings and his cousins of the same sex and his wife's siblings and her cousins of opposite sex. Here, the relatives of both sides address each other by the term *Goi* irrespective of sex. Criterion of affinity is recognised with few exceptions as in these cases it is ignored. It is ignored in case of second ascending generation and second descending generation of the ego. They are *nati*, *natin*, and *dadi*, *bardai*. As the term *nati* stands for So So and Da So, again the term *natin* stands for both So Da and Da Da, in the same way *dadi* is used for both Fa Fa, Mo Fa and *bardai* for Fa Mo and Mo Mo. Again the criterion of collaterality is maintained but as regards the cousins, it is ignored, as all cousins are known with the same term, viz. *bhai*, *dada*, *bahan* and *didi*, unless they need to be described. The criterion of bifurcation is also recognised with few exceptions of the terms applied for grand-parents and grand-children. Criterion of polarity is maintained but is ignored between *bhai-bhai*, *bahan-bahan* and *sardu-sardu*. As in each case the term of the relation is the same. The criterion of relative age is widely taken into consideration in kinship behaviour in addressing elders and youngers. As regards the criterion of speakers sex and the criterion of decadence, they are not recognised in the Pando kinship terms.

There are no specific terms of reference for husband and wife among the Pando. The word *admi* (man) and *aurat* (woman) are used for referring one's husband or wife respectively. Usually in ordinary course of life, a new couple addresses each other by referring to their village name or clan name. In case they happened to be of the same village, the wife calls her husband as *gava* or *gavahiya* and husband addresses his wife as *gavahi* or by her clan name. Again some of the relatives are addressed by some other kinship terms in spite of their actual kinship terms, viz, Wi El Br, Wi El Si, are addressed as *dada* and *didi* respectively but the actual terms for them are *jeth-sala* and *jeth-sash*. In some other cases some of the relatives are not addressed as Pando society observes taboo to address them. They are one's husband's father, husband's elder brother and one's younger brother's wife.

Kinship Obligation and Kinship Behaviour

It is important to know how members of a society behave with consanguineal, affinal and with some distant relatives. Similarly to some extent kinship behaviour can be understood in terms of joking and avoidance relationships.

On the birth of a child, one's father's sisters are required to clean the hut ceremonially with cow dung, water and soil and to receive the new born from the *suin* (*chamain*) when the new born is bathed during *chhatti*, and she is rewarded with a *saree* and some coins. During marriage, the presence of several kin is essential. They can be named as *bhato,* (El Si Hu), El Br Wi, Fa Si and Mo Br for some certain specified services of the occasion, and in return, they are suitably rewarded according to their reach. But the role of *bhatto* is very important throughout the marriage ceremony. Similarly, in case of death, nearest relatives act as the chief mourner and he or she is supposed to perform a number of functions in this regard. It is usually one's husband and one's son who act as chief mourners. While carrying a dead body, first of all the deceased's nearest relatives lift and carry the same. At the time of burying, the nearest relatives dig the grave, keep dead body into it and cover the grave with soil. Everything is done by the chief mourner first, and then it is followed by the nearest relatives, then by others. Again, it is the chief mourner who keeps the first stone on the grave which is followed by others.

Here, the Pando maintain the norms of kinship by which they know how to behave with their different relatives. Everyone learns from the standardised mode of kinship behaviour that whom to regard, whom to joke with, who are to be avoided and with whom taboo is to be observed.

Usually, joking relations are prevalent between a man and his elder brother's wife and his wife's younger sisters. *Goi-goi* relationship is very popular for joking relationships. They may joke even vulgarly with each other. Joking relations between grand-children and grand-parents are also said to be prevalent among them.

Avoidance relationships regulate and restrict the kinship behaviour according to the traditions of the society and discourage free mixing attitude in between some relatives. In some cases relatives avoid each other to such an extent that they even hesitate to face each other. In other cases they face each other but behave in a very humble manner and maintain etiquette before each other. Avoidance is observed very strictly between the elder brother and his younger brother's wife, his wife's elder sister and her younger sister's husband, between son-in-law and mother-in-law and daughter-in-law and father-in-law.

The Pando as Members of a Family

The family is a primary and the most important unit of the Pando society. This unit may be considered as a pivot around which all their day to day activities of life revolve. Generally, a Pando family consists of parents and children, both unmarried and adopted, living in a single household. But in a few cases, it also includes married children, son-in-law, grand-parents, grand-children, siblings, married brothers and some distant relatives. The father is the supreme authority of the family. He supervises and guides every family member from time to time in most of their affairs. Lineage and descent are reckoned through father only. Property is always inherited by one's own sons only but in case of barrenness property goes to the nearest blood relatives. It may be mentioned here that the Pando use the term *ghar* to denote the family as well as their hut.

The Pando are strictly monogamous, patrilineal, and patrilocal but the system of *ghar-jamai* and polygamy, though rare, are prevalent among them. Generally after marriage, within a period of three to five years, the new couple have their separate residence. From the four studied villages it appears that a Pando village consists of 10.5 families on the average, while the size of the family in a Pando village varies from 5.1 to 5.7 members in a family. The average family size is 5.4 in all the four villages. One thing is very important that the number of females is less than the males. As regards the types of families among the Pando, 50.00 per cent comes under simple type, 40.48 per cent under extended type, 2.33 per cent under composite and 7.14 per cent under broken type.

The Pando family plays a number of roles in their cultural, social, educative, economic, political and religious life. The Pando have a forest and food-gathering economy. Such an economy requires every member of the family to actively participate in the economic activities of the family and the Pando family fulfils this role to the maximum, as everybody including the minors of the family make their own contribution to meet the family requirements. Besides, a Pando family is also a religious unit, as within a family ancestral spirits and clan deities are located in the *bhitar-ghar* of the family. Such deities are worshipped by the head of the family on festivals and such other rituals by suitable offerings and sacrifices to ensure health, happiness, and prosperity in the family.

The Pando as Members of a Village

The awareness that all of them live within the same village boundary is strong and fosters a further sense of unity among the people. Besides, there are many other characteristics of village life which also reflects the unity of a Pando village and it is but natural for the Pando to consider himself as a member of this village unit.

A Pando village is characterised by a religious centre of its own. Such a religious centre is meant for the whole village and ensures the prosperity and welfare of the whole village. Accordingly, it is the responsibility of the whole village to make contribution for the maintenance and worship of village deities. The *baiga* worships the village deities who is called as village *baiga*. Again, the unity of the Pando village is also reflected in its political organisation. It is called as Pando *darbar* and *mukhia* or *patel* is the head of the *darbar* who has a control over the whole village and villagers too have a notion that *mukhia* is the head of the village and he works for the welfare, integration and prosperity of the entire village.

Their *karma* dance is also indicative of unity of the village, as such a dance party is called by the name of a particular village. *Karma* dance, besides creating an atmosphere of co-operation and coordination among them, also helps them in forgetting their mutual differences and strengthening the village unity. Again, their gregarious character is also reflected in visiting deep forests in a group for food-gathering, hunting, and going to weekly market, where they meet the Pando of other villages of that area. It is important to note that while returning they usually also come together. Such occasions go a long way in strengthening the network of relationship at village level and maintaining cordiality and co-operation among the Pando. Lastly, the unity of the village is manifest in the observance of Pando customs, rites, festivals and ceremonies. During each such occasion all the villagers are invited to attend the same. In case of death in an individual family, the entire village is taken to be polluted. As a result, they collectively take customary shaving, cutting of hair and nails, take a ritual bath and feast and get clean along with the family members.

Individual at the Axis of Self

The Nature-Man-Spirit Complex not only works on the level of self-image and identity of the Pando but it also gets well reflected when Pando are examined at the axis itself. This portion of the paper is a lively example of Man and Spirit's interaction as it brings out several occasions of Pando life where they are interacting with the spirit world.

Conception

As soon as a woman comes to know that she is pregnant, she observes a number of taboos which are based on some superstitions. She is not allowed to visit the forest alone, especially when the period of her pregnancy is near the end of its term. Again, a pregnant woman should not cross a hoe, wooden posts and the ropes by which cattle are tied. It is believed that if these taboos are not observed, the expected child would be partially blind. It is locally known as *khutta-andhar*, which means that a child having this defect fails to see the objects lying close. In the last, she is not expected to see a dead body because it is taken to be bad and believed that she may be harmed by the spirit of the dead.

Birth

Pandos believe in the transmigration of soul, which means that all the souls of their close relatives are reborn among them after their death. With this conception, during abnormal delivery or prolonged labour pains, they sought the help of sacred specialists like *gunia*, *baiga*, and *dewar*, who try to ascertain which ancestor of the family is to be reborn in the form of the child. Thereafter, a prayer is made to the coming ancestor with a view to propitiating him/her after the safe delivery, by saying, *Ho Maharaj—come safely—We shall wash your feet with milk and liquor.*

After the safe delivery, the umbilical cord of the new born is cut and buried under the roots of some specific trees, viz. *date*, *balhi* and *chind* trees with the belief that these trees have got a much longer life, so as long as the tree will grow, the child also will live.

The *chatti* ceremony is observed on the sixth day after the removal of naval-cord. On this occasion the services of barber and *suin* are required to shave the villagers including family members of the new born. After this, the new born and the mother take ceremonial bath and the ceremony ends with a feast to the relatives and villagers. *Barhi* is observed on the twelfth day of the birth in a very simple way. Here, the new born and the mother take a ceremonial bath and her clothes are washed by the family members—*rashi* or *chulaha-chuai* is observed after a month. It is the final purificatory stage of the mother.

Till this ceremony is over, she is not allowed to cook food or to enter into the *bhitar-ghar*. On *rashi* the mother and the child take their ceremonial bath, oils the new born and enters into the *bhitar-ghar* to cook food for the feast of the occasion which is served to the villagers, relatives and friends. *Annaprashan* ceremony is performed generally either on Thursday, Wednesday or Friday, as the rest of the days are considered to be inauspicious and believed to bring bad luck to the person. Saturday and Sunday are said to be 'powerful days', good for starting magical training or for such other activities. On this occasion, the child is fed with *khichari* (a preparation of rice and pulse) by the older family member and it also ends with a feast.

Technique for the Determination of the Reborn Soul

The soul of a new born is determined maximum by the age of five. It is done by the eldest person of the family or by the sacred specialists like *baiga*, *gunia* and *aulwa*, with the common belief that the souls of their dead ancestor take rebirth. It is further reported that the souls of their ancestor may incarnate sometimes even in the form of domestic animals viz, in a new born calf, goat or dog.

For identification, the sacred specialist takes an oil lamp and a handful of rice. After naming an ancestor he moves the lamp around the heap of the handful of rice and then keeps it near the rice. Later on, some grains of the rice are picked up at random and thrown on the ground. The thrown rice is taken out in pairs. This is repeated for three times. If, every time the rice is found in pairs, it is a confirmation that the child has the soul of the named ancestor. But, if the thrown rice has an odd grain, this process is repeated in the name of another ancestor until there comes an even number of rice grains.

Sometimes, the soul of a new born of a domesticated animal may also be identified with one of the family ancestors. Such doubt ingrains in their innocent minds when its master observes that a particular animal often gets sick alongwith a particular family member or vice-versa. In this case, they identify the soul of that particular animal and associate it with one of their ancestors or a living family member.

Adolescence and Young Age

A Pando child grows freely and without any inhibition. When he or she attains the stage of adolescence sexual awareness develops early. At this stage a Pando girl is taken care of by her elders, and she has to live and behave according to the norms of the society. Of course, she is free to choose her friend of the opposite sex where her parents hardly interfere but she has to avoid free mixing with her partner openly. Usually, the village playmates are changed into sex-mates. Normally, family elders or village elders hardly interfere in such matters but they are interested in the bride-price for their daughters.

In theory they do not approve of pre-marital and extra-marital sex relations, but in practice these relations exist unhindered in their society. Such relations are not confined within the village but may be established with the neighbouring villagers. But, in most of the cases, it is confined within the ethnic boundary. Again, a sex partner should not be of the same clan. The Pando get the opportunity to mix freely and fan their love during *Karma*-dance, *Ganga-Dussehra* fair and festivals and at the weekly markets. The forested and hilly surroundings also provide a good rendezvous for such romance.

In extra-marital sex relations, the Pandos take very serious and effective steps against the offenders. Such cases are dealt with severely by the Pando Darbar. If a case is proved against the person concerned, a feast is charged from the man with a warning to break the relationship immediately. But, if, it is found that a family is ruined due to such relations and one's wife having eloped with her paramour, the *Darbar* levies a very heavy fine (*bunda-bharah*) which is three to four times higher than the total expense spent for the girl and besides a feast for the whole village.

Marriage and Adulthood

The local term for marriage is *byah*. The marriage age of a boy varies from 15 to 25 and for a girl it ranges between 12 and 20 years. Among the Pando marriage is regarded as a mechanism by which the sexual union is regularised in a healthy and socially approved manner. Pando society has certain customary rules and regulations regarding marriage. Marriage with near kin, as usual, is considered to be incestuous. Cross cousin marriage is said to be practised but marriage with parallel cousin is strictly restricted. Clan exogamy is still another important consideration for the Pando. Those who violate these rules are ex-communicated and are not readmitted unless they are separated. Marriage alliance with the village is no bar but such marriages are not preferred. Usually, marriage ties are established within a radius of ten miles although in a few cases such marriages took place beyond this radius.

Marriage by Negotiation

The standard form of marriage is *byah* in which bride-price is given to the bride's father and turmeric paste is applied to the bride and groom. The first negotiation is known as *kacha-chadai* in which groom's party return from the bride's village with their consent for the marriage. Again, they visit the bride's village with two bottles of liquor and a sum of Rs. 5 for making the negotiation final. This custom is known as *pakka-jani* and the cash for *nat-torai* to break the previous kinship relations of any degree existing between boy and the girl before they come to establish a new relation.

However, the amount of bride-price varies from Rs. 5 to Rs. 100 in cash as a compensation for taking away the bride. Besides bride-price (*sukh-dam*, *rash paseri*), twelve bottles of liquor, *purvan-chawal* (it includes three *kharies** of rice, five *tamies*** of pulse and five *tamies* of oil seeds) is given to the bride's parents for the marriage. Marriage takes place at the bride's place with the performance of *matti kodai*, *marva* or *manjha-bhat*, *haldi-tel-chadana* in which turmeric and oil are applied to the bride and groom, and *sendur-bandi* in which groom applies vermilion to the bride's forehead.

Marriage by *barokhi* is another form of acquiring a wife. It is locally known as *chinmundari-pahina-ke-lana*, which means to bring a wife by putting on a ring. After *barokhi* one gets full right over the other to lead a regular conjugal life. It is said to be the oldest standard form of getting a life partner, which varies from *byah* in many ways. In *byah*, *marva* is planted,

* One *Khari* is equal to about one maund.

** One *Tami* is equal to abou: one seer.

turmeric paste and oil are anointed to the bride and groom and a number of socio-religious rites and rituals are observed which are lacking in *barokhi*. Again, there is a social implication that if one gets a wife by *barokhi*, one cannot claim *bunda* against her but only the actual cost of expenditure for her.

Bandhwa is another form of acquiring a life partner by negotiation. It is meant for those who are unable to meet the heavy expenses of marriage. But, definitely this method is adopted after the death or divorce of his or her first spouse when one plans to get a life partner for the second or third time. So, in this case either one or both the partners are widow or widower or divorced.

Besides the settled types of acquiring a life partner, Pando also get wife by some other methods, viz. *Udalia* (marriage by elopement) and *dukku* (marriage by intrusion). In both the cases the boy and the girl have love affairs. In the former case, at one fine occasion they flee away and in the latter case, the girl intrudes into the house of the boy. Ultimately, they get the social sanction of the union by the help of village *Darbar* with throwing a communal feast to the co-villagers.

Old age and Death

In old age, Pando restrict their economic activities within the hut, as they cannot undertake hard and arduous work, and engage themselves in light manual work like basketry and looking after the children.

A Pando believes that most of the diseases, ailments and death are attributed to the evil spirits or by the wrath of deities. Again, it is believed that when all sorts of magico-religious powers of a *baiga*, *gunia*, and such specialists fail to save an ailing person then one dies. But at the same time they also recognise natural death. After death, they bury the dead body but some important personalities of the village are cremated, and one winnowing fan, dry wood of *bel*, and one bow and arrow are placed on the burial ground in the case of males but in the case of females they place a digging stick and *dindari* (a peculiar type of basket) in place of a bow and arrow. On the second day, they again go to the burial ground with milk and paddy which are sprinkled on the grave, uttering these words : "Accept food and water and be reborn with food and water". On the third day or ninth day they observe purificatory rites on which shaving of beard and cutting of hair including paring of nails are done. Thereafter, they take a purificatory bath and a feast is served to the co-villagers. After one year of the death, they perform the *barashi* rite (final purificatory rite) in which they ascertain the nature of death, calling back the deceased soul into *bhitar-ghar* and a feast to the relatives, friends and co-villagers.

The study of Man also tells us a number of occasions when humans interact on one hand with Nature and on the other with Spirits. Since, the very conception of a child, the mother comes into close contact with the spirit world which is reflected in the belief in rebirth of the ancestors, taboos observed on such occasions, the methods of expediting difficult delivery with the help of sacred specialists and the belief connected with the disposal of the umbilical cord of the new born. Again, a series of beliefs and rituals associated with death and the concept of the underworld, all show the greater extent to which the Pando interact or are dependent on the spirit world for their own well-being and that of the Pando community as such.

III

SPIRIT : THE SUPERNATURAL WORLD

Like many other primitive peoples of the world, the Pando believe in a number of supernatural powers who wield a profound influence on their life and culture by controlling and directing their day to day affairs. Most of the misfortunes, ailments, accidents, disease, death, (unnatural), abortions, unnatural labour pains, failure in hunting and failure of crops are taken to be in the hands of some evil spirits. Due to the above mentioned attribution of supernatural powers, some of them are conceived as benevolent and some others as malevolent.

PANDO CONCEPTION OF THE SUPERNATURAL WORLD

According to nature, character and function, the supernatural powers are considered either benevolent or malevolent. The former are conceived to be helpful and kind, so they are appeased by worship with numerous offerings or sacrifices. The latter are regarded as harmful to the commoners, hence they are neither regarded nor worshipped, but sometimes appeased. However, the Pando are afraid of such powers because these are taken to be the causes of sickness, death, accident and ill-luck.

Benevolent Supernatural Powers

As stated earlier, such powers are regarded as useful, kind and deities of welfare for the whole Pando community. They seek their assistance in general for prosperity and welfare in every sphere of their life. Under this category such deities will be discussed at family level, clan level, village level and such other deities as are exclusively related with their economy.

Maramua or Ancestral Spirits

At the family level, every Pando worships his own ancestors who are enshrined in the *bhitar-ghar*. It is said that if the soul of the deceased is not conducted into the *bhitar-ghar* at the appropriate time (on the *barashi-day*), the soul turns into a harmful spirit and harms the family members. Again, if there occurs any negligence in the offerings and sacrifices or any polluted person enters into the *bhitar-ghar*, the spirit harms the family members.

So, it is the duty of the head of the family to keep the ancestors pleased and favourable by worshipping them on several occasions of the year, viz. during *Nawa-Khai*, *Mahua-Khai*, *Holi-Teohar*, and *Hareli*. In other words, when they observe any festivities and happy occasions, they worship their ancestors by suitable offerings and sacrifices. Besides this, they also worship *Churi-Path*, *Nakawa-Path*, *Rakti-Path* and *Rakash-Path* on emergency demand of the individual family, although not exclusively at the family level.

Clan Deities

At the clan level, a number of deities are worshipped by the Pando which varies from clan to clan, although not necessarily in all the cases. It is because of the fact that some of the Pando deities are so popular that they are worshipped by many different clan members. Each clan member worships his own clan deities. The time and the articles of worship usually vary from clan to clan and from deity to deity. Ordinarily, during most of their festivities, clan deities are offered *sarai-lassa* (gum of *sal* tree), *arwa chawal* (unboiled rice), *sendur* (vermilion), *tel* (oil), *pani* (water), *narial* (coconut) and food specially cooked for the occasion. On such occasions clan members are invited and fed. As regards the sacrifice of animals and birds, its colour and object vary from deity to deity. Ordinarily, sacrifices are made to the deities on every third or fifth year which again varies from deity to deity. Similarly, there are some regional variations in the popularity of deities, viz. in the traditional village, rehabilitated colonies and in the village of Pal Tehsil.

Again, the place and position of different clan deities among the members of different clans may be understood by their sacred seat allotted to them. As some of the clan deities are kept in the *bhitar-ghar*, some of them in the courtyard, and some others in the cattleshed. Here, the importance and the position of the deities among the families can easily be understood from their allotted sacred seats, as the deities placed in the *bhitar-ghar* are regarded to be much more helpful and worthy in comparison to the courtyard and cattleshed.

Village Deities

In this category Pando regard a number of deities who are worshipped at the village level. Such deities may be discussed under the following heads.

MAHA-MAI OR DIHARI-MAI OR BURHI-MAI

This deity is regarded as the Goddess of the village welfare. She protects the village from sickness, epidemic and from evil spirits. She also helps the Pando in their economic pursuits. She is taken to be the head of the village; without her no village remains safe and protected. She is represented by a black stone, by the side of the stone a spear, one iron rod, and a red flag are planted. She is regarded as *Maha-Mai* towards south and *Dihari-Mai* towards north. It is said that *Maha-Mai* is also known by some other names in different regions of Madhya Pradesh. In the south west of Chirmiri she is known by the name of *Kudargarhi*, at *Hingaldeep*, a place ten miles west of Chirmiri, she is called as *Hingalait-Mai*, and she is called as *Maihar-Mai* in some other parts of Madhya Pradesh.

BARAHIYA-DEO

This deity is regarded to be the son of the *Maha-Mai* and also believed to be the village deity. He is believed to be magnanimous and good natured and one who has been pleased by the worshippers very soon but, at the same time, he becomes furious and cruel with those who do not fulfil their promises. It is believed that if *Barahiyadeo* gets angry with anyone, the man begins to suffer from fever, his hands and feet become thin. Ultimately, he becomes an invalid for hunting. He is said to hold a golden stick in the left hand and an iron club in the right hand. He is represented in the village *dewalla* by a stone, by the side an iron rod and one thick iron chain hung or placed down.

It is said that in olden times *Barahiya* was a powerful source of witches (*dains*) in harming Pando but finally the Pando overpowered him. Barahiya promised to be useful to the Pando provided they also paid regular offerings to him. Since then he became a deity of the Pando, and they became the regular worshippers of the deity. Barahiya is also known by several names, such as, *Moti-Barahiya, Jhalka-Barahiya, Babu-Barahiya, Darh-Barahiya, Jhagra-Khan, Barakadeo, Kundebagh, Chindtaria, Janeva-Deota*, *Ranbagia* and *Budda-Deo*. He is known by different names at different places in Madhya Pradesh.

BAGESHWER-DEO

This deity is believed to be the master of wild and ferocious animals. Pando worship him with the belief that as long as they worship this deity no wild animal would harm them. It is further believed that he also helps them in locating one's wife who either runs away or disappears. The Pando have so much faith in him that they claim that at any moment if their wife goes away and a request is made to him, then the deity follows the woman in the shape of a tiger and compels her to stop until her husband or guardian reaches the spot. But, if he becomes angry with any one, he appears in the shape of a tiger and harms him. He is represented by a stone of red and black colour in the village sacred centre.

Benevolent Powers Associated with Economy

Here, only such powers or deities will be described who are associated with their economic pursuits like food-gathering, hunting, basketry and agriculture. Deities associated with the forest are known as *path* and believed to control and direct the activities of Pando in the forest.

Nakava-Path is taken to be responsible for the abundant supply of forest produce, especially the edible tubers and roots and *nakava* is the name of an edible tuber. The deity is offered rice, *sarai*-gum and water during *Kuar-Dashmi*. The scarcity of edible forest produce is attributed to the wrath of this deity due to some negligence and the deity is appeased by suitable offerings. *Rakash-Path* is another deity who helps and protects the Pando when they are busy in forest cutting operation. Any cut injury of axe (*tangi*) is taken as an occurrence due to the wrath of the deity. He is believed to be residing on the *sal*, *semal* or *mahua* trees. He is offered twelve pairs of bread, twelve drops of liquor (*mahua*), and a white cock by the Pando. *Churi-Path* is regarded to be the master of basketry and any cut from the knife during basket making is attributed to the wrath of the deity. He is worshipped with coconut, *sarai*-gum, *gur* (molasses) and water during *Kuar-Dashmi*. *Churi* is the local name for the knife and the deity is appeased by the injured man. Like several other *paths*, *Semaria-Path* is associated with the forest. He is believed to keep a control over the supply of game in the forest and is worshipped for the abundant supply of game during hunting, with coconut, rice, *sarai*-gum, water and a hen sacrificed in his name. *Rakati-Path* is again worshipped for the abundant supply of deer in the hunting. He is offered the blood of the shot animal (deer) on the small branch of a *sal* tree. *Noni-Moshwasi* is another deity related with hunting and said to be residing where deer are found in large numbers. This deity is regarded as the master of bow and arrow. Repeated failure in hunting for a considerable period of time is taken to be result of some evil eye on their bow and arrow. To remove it and to get success in game, she is worshipped with thread, turmeric paste, *tendu*-wood, *sarai*-gum and a black chicken is sacrificed. The Pando worship *Mashan* owing to his help in various economic pursuits. This deity is conceived to be anthropomorphic with a big turban on his head one end of which hangs down up to his hand. He holds a *tangi* (big axe) in the right hand and a *lathi* (stick) in the left hand. He is believed to accompany the Pando and protect them when they are out hunting. He is worshipped with the offerings of twelve pairs of bread, *arwa*-rice, twelve drops of liquor, *sarai*-gum, and a white cock is sacrificed in his name during *Kuar-Dashmi*. While, the *Khara-Path* is associated with the fishing and *Kaleshwer-Path* or *Dhodi-Deo* is related with the regular supply of drinking water and worshipped with the regular supply of the same.

MALEVOLENT SUPERNATURAL BEINGS

It has been said earlier that malevolent supernatural beings are conceived as harmful and troublesome to the common masses. These are several in number and called by the name of *Papi-Mai*, *Churel*, *Pret* and *Murkhori*, which needs some elaboration for a careful analysis.

Pando recognise twenty-one different *Papi-Mai*; each one of them is responsible for causing a particular kind of disease, viz. nine of them are held to be responsible for some kind of disease; eleven of them are considered to induce different kinds of pox; and two of them are taken to be brothers of these *Papi-Mai*, who simply watch the condition of the sick man and request their sisters either to cure or kill the ailing person.

When these *Papi-Mai* are found active in harming the Pandos, they worship the *Maha-Mai*, *Burhi-Mai* and *Semalai-Mai* with the offering of coconut, oil, vermilion, *arwa*-rice and *sarai*-gum and beseech them to cure the sick man by asking their *Papi* sisters to free him. In case of cure from pox, villagers bid a farewell to the responsible *Papi-Mai* and a request is made to her to leave the village and to go to the east.

Murkhori is another female spirit found in large numbers and which harm only pregnant women. If the spirit is not driven away in the very beginning, other powerful *Murkhories* attack the woman which may lead to her death. It is believed that *Murkhories* eat away the brain and foetus of the suffering woman and ultimately she dies. They are eight in number who attack a pregnant woman one by one, leading to one kind of disease or other.

Churel are also believed to be the female evil spirits who are nine in number and attack only children leading to different kinds of diseases. In most of the cases, the head of the family tries his best to detect the responsible *Churel* and to drive her away with *mantras*, water and *arwa*-rice. But the help of sacred specialists is also sought in this regard in case of failure.

Sacred Performances

Here, the rituals observed and performed by the Pando will be discussed under two heads, viz. private rituals and public rituals. The former include the worship of ancestral spirits, clan deities and the worship of some benevolent spirits associated with economic pursuits of the Pando. While the public rituals include the annual worship of village deities, and *Kathori Puja*.

Private Rituals

As already discussed, the Pando worship their ancestors in the *bhitar-ghar* several times a year. They offer the ancestors *homa* (*sarai*-gum), rice, water, cooked food of the occasion and liquor for the welfare and protection of the family members. Some of the families make sacrifices of goats, and fowl to keep them pleased and favourable.

Again, clan deities are worshipped with the suitable sacred articles on most of their festivals with the same considerations. But, such worships are observed on a small scale and only clan members participate. The worship of clan deities which falls on every third or fifth year, in which sacrifices are made, are observed on a large scale. It is attended by all clansmen of the village and close clan relatives of other villages. Usually, all the invitees come to attend the worship with some gifts (rice, flour or pulse, etc.) and villagers extend their help by supplying fuel-wood, leaf-plate, green leaves and by fetching water.

First of all the male invitees together with the sacred specialists of the village sit together and engage themselves in pleasing and calling the clan deities through singing of various hymns and devotional songs. The singers begin to get possessed by the deities and they start looking for possibilities of evil spirits in and around the hut of the worshipper. In the same way, every family member of the worshipper is thoroughly checked by the possessed persons with the help of *singhas* (deer's horns). The method is known as *singha-phukana*. If any evil spirit is found in and around the hut or on any family member including the worshipper, it is overpowered and driven away by this method. At last the offerings and sacrifices are made to the clan deities. After the sacrifices, food and the flesh of the sacrificed animals and birds are cooked for the feast which takes place in the evening. For the non-clan members food is cooked separately for the feast but the head of the sacrificed animals and birds are strictly consumed by the clan members only.

In addition to the above mentioned rituals, some of the benevolent spirits are also worshipped on the family level, viz. *Nakava-Path*, *Churi-Path*, *Rakash-Path*, although not exclusively at the family level. Besides this, Pando observe a number of festivals which are followed with some rituals, but such are discussed under festivals.

Private Rituals

The annual worship of the village deities is performed by the villagers once in a year during *Kuar-Dashmi* (Sept.-Oct.). On this occasion villagers contribute liberally to meet the expenditure of the worship. At least one day before the schedule of the worship, the *baiga* purchases all the required articles of worship including the sacrificial animals and birds. On the *puja* day, *baiga* and *aulwa* take an early bath and fast until worship is performed. Ordinarily worship starts from the forenoon and continues for hours together. At first *Maha-Mai* is worshipped, whose presence is felt only when *baiga* or *aulwa* is possessed by her, and is followed with the offering of *sarai*-gum, *arwa*-rice, vermilion, coconut, water, bread and liquor. Sacrifices of animals and birds are always made at a considerable distance from the main *dewalla* and only the head of the sacrificed object is offered to the deity. *Barahiya-Deo*, *Bageshwer-Deo*, *Rakash-Path* and other deities of the village *dewalla* are worshipped one by one in similar fashion. The possessed *aulwa* drinks away the blood of the sacrificed objects and liquor. Ordinarily, *aulwa* is possessed by the deity and *baiga* offers sacred articles to the deities. The presence of women is forbidden during worship.

In addition to the annual worship, village deities are also worshipped on the village level by the *baiga* during several Pando festivals, viz. *Nawa-Khai*, *Hareli-Teohar*, and *Kharboj*, which has been discussed under festivals and rituals. Again, the Pando take part in *Kathori-Puja* which is observed on a large scale.

Kathori-Puja

This ritual is observed on the *Tirtiya* of *Baisakh* (April) in the *Andheria-Pakha* (*Krishna Paksha*) according to the Hindu calendar. It is related to agriculture and ceremonial ploughing and sowing are observed on this occasion. In other words, this ritual is related to ceremonial sanction of *Mahadeo* for seeking permission of ploughing and sowing. Nobody dares to plough his field and sow any seeds before the observance of this ritual. Here, God *Mahadeo* is worshipped along with the other village deities by the *baiga* with suitable sacred articles and in the end ceremonial ploughing and sowing is done by the village children.

This ritual is observed by the agricultural tribes and castes. Apparently, Pando are in touch with the ritual due to their contact with them. Again, this ritual is observed in some other agriculturist villages also and very few Pandos take active participation, although they contribute to meet the expenses.

Festivals and Rituals of the Pandos

Like many other ethnic groups of the region, Pando observe a number of festivals involving the worship of deities. These are as follows:

Kharboj-Puja

It is observed by the Pandos of rehabilitated colonies in the month of *Agrahan* (June). On this occasion village deities are worshipped by the *baiga* with the offerings of rice, vermilion, oil, *sarai*-gum and *chind* grass (a thatching grass). The *chind* grass is a special offering of the occasion. Besides this, a chicken is sacrificed to the village deities. The significance of this festival is such that without this observance they do not cut the thatching grass from the forest.

Hareli Teohar

It is an occasion for ceremonial offering of *lakra* fruits and *minjhari* grain to the village deities and thereafter they consume the same. It is observed in the month of *Sravan* (July-Aug).

Baiga takes an early bath, goes to the *lakra* and *minjhari* fields to bring some sheaves of the same. On his return, he worships the village deities with the common sacred articles including liquor and *minjhari* grains and *lakra* fruits. Thereafter, the *baiga* visits every household of the village and ties the offered *minjhari* grains and *lakra* fruits to the roof of every household and in return he gets some grain.

Mahua Teohar

This festival is related with the eating of *mahua-latta*. It is observed in the month of *Baisakh* (April-May) in which *mahua-latta* is cooked and offered to the ancestors and clan deities, as without this offering no one consumes it.

Nawa-Khai

This festival has got two-fold implications. Firstly, the new yield of the season is ceremonially offered to the village deities and secondly, the new grains are ceremonially cooked and offered to the ancestors and clan deities. This festival falls in *Bhado* month (Aug-Sept.). First of all village *baiga* offers new paddy to the village deities. Then it is observed at the family level. The head of the family offers the new grain to the ancestors and clan deities and then only it is consumed by the family members.

Cherta Festival

This festival is the eating of *chura-gur* which falls on the *Til-Sankranti* day of Hindus. On this day Pando get *chura-gur* and bread from the agriculturists. In the rehabilitated colonies, young Pando of both sexes go to play the *karma* dance in the adjacent villages and get either *chura-gur* or cash which is spent on liquor.

Holi Teohar

On the Holi festival of Hindus Pando worship their ancestors and clan deities with sacred articles and cooked food. They do not perform *holika-dahan* or play with coloured water.

Karma Festival

Pando celebrate this festival on the following day of *Nawa-Khai* in which a *karma* branch is planted near the *Mukhia's* hut by the *baiga*. *Mukhia* worships the *karma* branch and then Pando start playing *karma* dance on his door which concludes in the morning.

Dashai-Darh

This festival is observed in the month of *Kuar* (Oct-Nov). It is observed in the similar fashion as discussed in *Karma* festival excepting that here *Mukhia* entertains the dance party with liquor and breads.

Jeotia-Darh

It is observed in the month of *Kartik* (Nov.-Dec.) by the Pando of rehabilitated colonies. Here, one of the villagers voluntarily comes forward and bears the expense of *karma*-dance. So, *baiga* plants a *chilhi* branch on his door and he worships the branch. Villagers come to play the *karma* dance on his door and he offers liquor and breads.

As regards the Pando's sacred specialists they are *baiga*, *aulwa*, *gunia*, or *dewar* and *dain* or *tonahi*. The former two are alone entitled to make offerings to village deities while others are medicine-men of the village.

The foregoing analysis of the Pando's "Supernatural World" throws sufficient light that most of their economic activities are associated with some sacred performances. This suggests their close interactions and interrelationships with 'Nature' and 'Spirits'. They perform rituals with suitable offerings and sacrifices to appease the benevolent and malevolent spirits to get their favours and blessings in their economic pursuits and day to day affairs.

Change in the Traditional Position

The life and culture of the Pando so far analysed, reflect a close interdependence of Nature-Man-Spirit. However, it would not be correct to presume that firstly, every aspect of their life reflects this interdependence to the same degree, and secondly, the Pando have remained immune to the modern forces of change operating in their life in the last several decades and have maintained their interdependence on their natural surroundings as well as on the Spirit world in the same degree and with the same intensity as it was found in the past.

The first observation gets substantiated when we look at the nature of Man to Man relations dealing with self image and identity and regulation of village life, respectively as compared to other aspects of Pando life, that this aspect of Pando life is such where the working of Nature-Man-Spirit Complex in the life of the Pando has come to a minimum degree.

Coming to the second point raised above, the Pando have been, beyond doubt, exposed to certain modern forces of change which in turn have affected the working of Nature-Man-Spirit Complex in their life and weakened their interrelations, as discussed below.

Traditionally, the Pando have been dependent upon forest and food-gathering, hunting, shifting cultivation, rearing of lac, and basketry constitute their main sources of livelihood. However, the independence of the country brought in its wake an uncongenial situation for them, as forests were declared as national wealth of the country, some portions of it as reserve forests and its exploitation for shifting cultivation or for lac rearing has been banned which affected their traditional modes of living. Many of them have had to leave the forest and take shelter in the rehabilitated colonies and become dependent on wage earning.

As mentioned in the very beginning, the *Uttaraha* section of Pando who are numerically small, are restricted mostly to the colliery areas and earn their livelihood as labourers. Besides this, the *mukhias* and *baigas* of the *Surgujia* Pando possess some patches of land and practise plough cultivation. Again, plough cultivation has been introduced among the Pando at the behest of the Madhya Pradesh Government in all the Pando resettlement colonies and they have been provided with all the facilities needed for cultivation. So, it may be observed that whereas on the one hand, the dependence of the Pando on nature has grown weaker under the above mentioned circumstances, on the other hand, introduction of plough cultivation has made some of them dependent on the sources other than that of Nature. Plough cultivation involves a number of activities and depends on a number of non-forest sources, viz. on blacksmith for making or sharpening the ploughshare, spade, carpenter for making of ploughs, shepherd for grazing the cattle, traders and government sources for obtaining good seeds and manure. Thus, plough cultivation has helped to develop a new set of relations and social network which was unknown to the Pando under the traditional setting.

Not only that, some of the Pando of rehabilitated colonies were reported to have taken loans and subsequently mortgaged their cultivable land to the neighbouring Gond, Kwar, Bengalis, and Telies which has given rise to a new type of relation between Pando as debtors and those from whom they receive loans as creditors. In some cases it was found that when a Pando debtor could not repay his loan to the creditor, he or some one of his family members started working as *halwaha* (ploughman) in the field of the creditor until the loan was repaid. Some of the Pando also lease their cultivable patch of land on share-cropping to the neighbouring ethnic groups. Again, such changes in their economy and decreasing dependency on Nature, whereverr it is found, have led to a decline of their belief in the deities and spirits connected with the forest. It is of interest to mention here that *Khara-Path* was an indigenous forest deity of the Pando connected with fishing but it is now falling into disuse as fishing in the forest is on the decline. Similarly, due to plough cultivation, some of the Pando have also adopted the rituals and festivals associated with agriculture. Mention may be made of *Kathori-Puja, Nawa-Khai, Hareli* and the like. Due to urban contact and the modern forces of change, some of the Pando are becoming aware of modern medicines, Panchayati Raj Scheme and the benefits of settled agriculture.

To sum up, it may be said that the Nature-Man-Spirit Complex in the life and culture of the Pando who are living in the traditional forested and hilly setting, does not uniformly work in all aspects of their life, and the Nature-Man-Spirit interdependence in their life has weakened owing to certain historical and contemporary factors. Because of the imposition of restriction on the destruction of forests after independence, the Pando are finding their interdependence with the forest gradually weakening. Besides, the *mukhias* and *baigas* of traditional villages have taken to plough cultivation which has given rise to several new types of social network among the Pando. Not only that, they have adopted several new rituals and festivals of agriculturists. Pando of rehabilitated colonies are mostly living on wage earning.

SUMMARY AND CONCLUSION

From the foregoing discussion it may be observed that Pando are a primitive tribe of Chattisgarh in Madhya Pradesh living in the midst of forest and hills. They have been traditionally dependent upon the forest for their subsistence and have developed a belief system in harmony with their ecological setting. Taken as a whole, various aspects of Pando life and culture, viz. their economy, self-image and change in their life examined at the axis of self, and belief in the supernatural world, reflect in adequate measure the interdependence of 'Man' i.e., Pando, on the 'Nature' i.e. their forested and hilly surroundings, on the one hand, and 'Spirit' i.e. supernatural world on the other. Thus Nature-Man-Spirit Complex gets prominently reflected in the life and culture of the Pando.

The Pando look to the forest as an amicable source which provides them with shelter, food supply, drink, pasture land, indigenous medicines, hunting game, raw materials for their crafts and various material equipments. On the other hand, their belief system has been very much influenced and shaped by the spirit world where supernatural beings are believed to have control over their food supply which they collect from the forest, whether it be the supply of game, fishes, roots, tubers, or fruits, and also they protect the Pando from wild and ferocious animals or save them from any possible injury during their economic operations. Thus, Pando have to appease and propitiate a number of supernatural powers like *Nakawa-Path*, *Rakash-Path*, *Semaria-Path*, *Churi-Path*, *Mashan*, *Khara-Path*, and *Noni-Moshwasi* and the like. Not only that, a number of roots and herbs are also taken to have some magical powers and believed to serve as protective charms.

The forested and hilly surroundings of the Pando make them believe in a number of supernatural powers which play very important roles in shaping Pando life and culture. Again, their habitat cannot make them hardly non-believers in spirits. An amalgamation of the same reflect that these supernatural powers have a direct bearing on the Pando and they are in close interaction with the supernatural world.

The religious life of Pando analysed with the help of three methodological terms, viz. Sacred Centre, Sacred Specialists and Sacred Performances, if conceived together may be termed as "Sacred-Complex". The sacred centres of the Pando are located at a number of places, viz. in the *bhitar-ghar*, courtyard, cattleshed, within the settlement, outskirts of the village, and in the neighbouring forests and hills. These sacred centres or deities enshrined there, are represented by stones or rocks of different colours, trees, colourful flags, spears, iron rods, chains and trident.

Their sacred performances can be similarly categorised into those which are performed at the family level, village level, festivals, and magical performances. The sacred performances take place on various occasions in which numerous offerings and sacrifices are made to the deities and spirits. Such offerings and sacrifices are made with a view to ensuring health, happiness, prosperity and plenty of food supply to the people. Some of the propitiations are also made with a view to freeing the people from disease. It may be noted here that these offerings and sacrifices are exclusively meant for the benevolent spirits and deities only. The sacred specialists are village *baiga*, *aulwa*, *gunia*, and *dain* or *tonahi*.

However, a study of the supernatural world of the Pando not only reflects the interaction of Man with the Spirit, but in adequate measure it also shows the interaction of Man with Nature. This fact gets substantiated when we look to their deities associated with their forest based economic life. The forest economy not only creates specific situations when the Pando need the help and interference of spirits, but the forest and hills are themselves believed to be the abode of a number of spirits and deities. Again, some of the festivals and sacred performances on the one hand need certain fruits and flowers which are available only in the forest while on the other hand, these are first offered to the deities before human consumption.

Thus, it is evident that the sacred complex of the Pando village wields a profound influence in regulating Man-Nature and Man-Spirit relationships. The conception of the Pando about their supernatural powers, their series of offerings and sacrifices to keep them appeased in order to ensure health, happiness, adequate food supply and water reflect a distinct style of life.

At the same time, in spite of the fact that Nature-Man-Spirit interdependence works in the life and culture of the Pando, it does not work to the same degree and with the same intensity in every aspect of their life. This point gets substantiated when one studies self-image and identity of the Pando and the regulation of their village life.

Again, the working of Nature-Man-Spirit Complex even in the life of the traditional Pando is gradually weakening due to the working of certain historical and modern forces of change like the gradual decrease of forest resources, legislation of forest rules and the like. As a result, the Pando's traditional dependence on the forest is being replaced in many spheres of life by the dependence on non-forest resources which has brought about a corresponding change also in their supernatural beliefs.

In view of this, the Pando may be said to be standing at a point on the scale of change, which is beyond the point where the Maler, studied earlier by Vidyarthi, stands.

SUGGESTED READINGS

Burman, B.K. Roy, N.D. : A preliminary appraisal of scheduled tribes of India, Office of the Registrar General, Delhi.

Elwin, Verrier : *The Religion of an Indian Tribe*, Bombay, Geoffery, Cumberlege, Oxford University Press, 1955.

Forde, C. Daryll : *Habitat, Economy and Society* : *A Geographical Introduction to Ethnology*, University Paper Back, Methuen, London, First Published in 1934, 1950 and 1968.

Forsyth, Capt. J. : "The highlands of central India : Notes on the forest and wild tribe," Natural History and Report, 1919.

Jagath Pathi, G. Supt. of Census Operation : Census of India, Madhya Pradesh, Vol. VIII Part-V-A (ii) Special Table for Schedule Tribe, 1961. Census Hand-Book of Surgujia District, Vol. VIII, Part-X, 1961. Census Hand-Book of Raigarh, M.P. Vol. IX 1961, Central Province and Berar Report, Vol. XII, 1931.

Herskovits, M.J. : *Economic Anthropology*, New York, 1952.

Majumdar, D.N. : *The Affairs of a Tribe* : *A Study in Tribal Dynamics*, Lucknow, University Publisher Ltd., 1950.

Majumdar, D.N. : *The Fortunes of Primitive tribes*, 1944.

Nag. : *Tribal Economy* : *Economic Study of Baiga*, 1958.

Redfield, R. : *Peasant Society and Culture* : *An Anthropological Approach to Civilization*, Chicago University Press, 1958.

Roughsedge, M. : *A Report on the Sirgooja and its Dependencies Written in 1818 A.D.*, Nagpur Govt. Press, 1922.

Roy, S.C. : *The Hill Bhuiyas of Orissa*, Man-In-India office, Ranchi, Bihar, 1935.

Russel, R.V. and Hiralal : *The Tribes and Castes of Central Provinces in India*, London, Macmillan, 1916.

Sahay, K.N. : "The Nature-Man-Spirit Complex and the Study of Cultural Dynamics", MSS with the Author, 1975.

Sinha, R.K. : "Pando : A Study of Nature-Man-Spirit Complex of a tribe in Chattisgarh", Doctoral Thesis submitted in R.U., Bihar, 1976.

Saxena, R.P. : *Tribal Economy in Central India*, Firma K.L. Mukhopadhayay, Calcutta, 1964.

Vidyarthi, L.P. : *The Sacred Complex in Hindu Gaya*, Asia Publishing House, Bombay, 1961.

Vidyarthi, L.P. : *Aspects of Religion in Indian Society*, Meerut, Kedar Nath Ramnath, 1961.

Vidyarthi, L.P. : *The Maler : A Study of Nature-Man-Spirit Complex of a Hill Tribe in Bihar*, Bookland P. Ltd., Calcutta, 1963.

SIX

R.S. Mann

CULTURAL—ECOLOGICAL APPROACH TO THE STUDY OF THE BHIL

ALL DISCIPLINES including the pure sciences, social sciences and humanities are in the flux of growth. In some phases, they grow faster than the other. Major developments on the academic plane are said to have been achieved when the theoretical fronts of a discipline are enriched. It also happens when the comprehension perspective is widened. In the case of disciplines like social anthropology and Human geography, the rise of theories has a great bearing on the empirical reality. A society and its social system present a field of reality to social anthropologist. For geographers, it is the environmental and other physical conditions which provide the base. As the basis for two significantly differ, the channels of theories grew independently. But there has always been an area where interests of two disciplines do converge. And this is the one where human or social settings interact with the natural or geographical conditions. No society ever exists without this kind of interaction, and some adjustment between the two has always been there. Such aspects of academic interests remained comparatively more hidden till the subjects were studied in almost watertight compartments. But the same started coming to the surface when interest in the interdisciplinary researches caught the momentum. The situation began to be tackled even at the theoretical frontier. The social anthropologists have taken a lead in the matter by focussing non-human ecology as a very important conceptual tool in the arena of anthropological methodology. One important school of thought in social anthropology has been of those who subscribed to the view-point that the understanding of external ecology and its relationship to man is of immense value in the explanation of social and cultural phenomena.

India provides a variety of geographical features. The same holds true for multiple ethnicity and the associated social structures. In village India, the tribal and non-tribal social situations form by and large, two very distinct spheres. Pockets of tribal concentration are also, in a majority of cases, characterised by typical geographical features. Even in the case of tribes, an absolute uniformity of cultural traits does not prevail. Many times are reflected the elements and events of diversity. And some of the variations can be interpreted in the context of physical environment around. For centuries, the tribals have lived in various kinds of environments. And they have adjusted their social living accordingly. Some of the social ways and cultural patterns appear as if they are the outcome of adaptation to the immediate geographical conditions. So much so that even some of the social institutions seem to have taken birth out of adjustment or adaptation with the ecological conditions around. And the same can be better explained with this background in view than any one else. In some cases it appears that the cultural traits are conditioned by the environmental pressure, and so the latter are the determinants of the same. At other times, it appears as a simple case of adjustment and adaptation. In fact, it is this kind of equation which made social anthropologists coin concepts like cultural ecology. Initially, the relationship was explored through the study of material culture, taking it closer to geographical conditions; but it gradually led to the study of social culture after convincing links were explored in some cases. By now, the cultural ecological approach, in the explanation of social universe, is considered as one of the most important ones.

In the case of the Bhil tribe of south Rajasthan, certain cultural elements can be explained as having very close association to the imminent environmental conditions. The Bhil are widely scattered in the thickness of the Aravalli hills and forest. Their distribution goes even across the Rajasthan borders. Numerically the Bhils in Rajasthan come next to the Mina tribe.

Their major concentration is in the undulating and rocky terrain of Banswara, Dungarpur, Udaipur and Chittorgarh districts. The Bhil are said to be the original inhabitants of these areas. Historical documents support that there were Bhil kingdoms in this part of the country before the immigrant Rajputs took them over. Now the Bhils are settled agriculturists, and their fields are either in the valleys or on the hill-slopes. Instances of slash and burn cultivation are not reported. Primitive agriculture techniques continue to dominate.

The pattern of village settlement is of a unique kind. There is no concept of a compact settlement and the houses are scattered, far apart from one another. The houses are built either on the tops of hillocks or on the slopes. One would rarely come across a cluster of Bhil houses. Each is at a sufficient distance from the other. There is no rule that the house of a headman or of other important persons would be at a higher elevation than the others. Likewise, there is no procedure that such people would be settled only in a particular section of the village. A commonly found feature in the settlement is that a man would build house close to his cultivable land, and on a spot from where he can easily watch over all his fields and the crops thereof. Even in case of division in a family, the son who gets separated builds his house near the agricultural field allotted to him. Originally, whosoever cleared a part of the forest for cultivation also made it a point to stay there. As the average cultivable land holding is small, the Bhil look to other occupations. To a very large extent they depend on the forest produce and labour jobs. For a Bhil, the life is extremely difficult, and even with sustained efforts he cannot manage to get two meals a day all the year round. Everyone is supposed to work hard for existence. The social practice that a son generally gets separated from his parents, immediately after marriage, is connected, among other things, to hard conditions. The couple have to fend for themselves. This leads to the pattern of nuclear families so predominantly found among the Bhil. They cannot remain a liability to the parents, nor would the parents depend on them. They have to build their own house and manage their livelihood. A son, however, does inherit a part of the land and some other household articles as his share. Only the youngest son inherits the parental house and continues to stay in the same house with the parents. The house pattern does not differ much in various regions. The Bhil themselves make their houses and all the materials, used in house construction, is procured locally. Stones, wood, bamboo, tiles etc., are the materials used. The Bhil are expert in tile-making.

If a village is a big one, it will have a number of hamlets. The hamlet pattern is no different than the one explained above for the village. But in the context of hamlets, certain sociological features with environmental bias come in. Most of the hamlets are uni-clan ones. A large number of the clans are totemistic. And such clan names are given after the animate and inanimate objects found usually in the vicinity of the hamlet. Such names are given after the trees, hills, wild animals etc. The totemic objects are respected and never dishonoured. It may be mentioned that the clan names are also given after the ancestors, and some of them seem to be borrowed ones. Another event of social anthropological interest in Bhil culture, and which has a bearing on geographical environments is connected to a bigger social division among the Bhils. In more hilly regions, a number of Bhil villages are grouped together and the people there are referred as belonging to a Pal. The boundaries of a Pal are well recognised by its inhabitants and all express their loyalty to the Pal community. The population in a Pal is referred as Palia Bhil. Others, outside the domain of high hills and forests, are socially categorised as Kalia Bhil. In the Bhil tribe, these social divisions continue to be recognised for various purposes. Palia Bhil would preferably marry among themselves. They have a feeling of social superiority over others. Most of them express their identity as Ujle or pure Bhil. The Bhil who settled down with non-tribal population in mixed village, after leaving their original moorings in hills and forest, are looked upon as slightly inferior by their own brethren. The Palias boast of their liberty, independence and non-submissive nature. Though scattered, the community feeling among the Bhil villagers, especially of Pals, is of a very strong nature. In spite of the households being far apart, people gather in no time when messages are sent through drum-beats. The highest elevations on the hill tops, which are inhabited, are known to the

Bhil as centres of any kind of warning. The latter is conveyed through the beat of a drum whose sound is heard by all the inhabitants. If it is to be conveyed to the neighbouring villages, the drum beats would be repeated at other hill tops, quite familiar to the Bhil.

Certain aspects of the institution of marriage, among the Bhil, are explained in terms of some requirements of external ecology. Most of the marriages are monogamous in nature. Such a pattern is explained more in the light of hard conditions of existence. Ordinarily the Bhil cannot afford to maintain more than one wife. Though a wife is more hardworking than her husband, keeping more wives becomes unmanageable under the difficult economic conditions posed by limited agriculture, forest and other resources. This is made still harder because of drought and famine conditions which mark Bhil habitations of south Rajasthan very frequently. In the absence of adequate rain, and because of the slopy fields, the Bhil, in a majority of cases, fail to grow winter crops, and irrigation facilities acutely lack in most of the areas. Ordinarily a Bhil would express preference for an additional wife. But such a wish is fulfilled only in the case of those who have more cultivable land, or are otherwise comparatively more well-to-do to maintain an additional wife/s. The more the wives, more would be the work output. But then everyone cannot acquire more wives because of the constraint of bride price. The value of bride price is fairly high, and a majority of the Bhil cannot themselves afford to pay it even for getting one wife. They borrow money from the money-lenders and, thus, get into debt. The custom of bride price, among the Bhil, is not the result of scarcity of women. Their number, in proportion to the males, is sufficiently high, though it is not higher than the men. A wife is valued for her industriousness. It is chiefly the women who bring wood from the forest. They also collect various kinds of other forest produce. Their contribution in agriculture activities is no less than the men. The wife looks after the livestock and their grazing. For all these considerations, a Bhil is very possessive of his wife. Ordinarily, he would not leave her alone. In order that a wife may stay with her husband, the customary laws of the Bhil have a provision of heavy penalty if she runs away or divorces the husband. The amount to be paid by the new husband, in the event of her remarrying, is almost double the value of bride price. But since the women are in demand, such cases are frequently reported, though the practice makes the Bhil highly indebted. Even the living pattern of wives, in the case of polygynous unions, is devised as per the ecological condition. Normally a man, owning more acreage of cultivable land keeps more than one wife. And this is true in a large number of cases that each wife stays separately in an independent house built adjoining one of the agricultural fields belonging to the common husband. Each looks after the fields assigned to her, as also after the interest of the common husband who rotates whenever needed. Sometimes the wives even stay together, more so if they happen to be sisters.

The Bhils are immensely religion dominated. Their animistic faith is of a superb order. The impact of developed religions like Hinduism and Christianity is not ruled out. Some of the gods and goddesses of these wider religions have been adopted by the Bhil, though their relevant interpretations may not be properly understood by most of them. In spite of all these trends, the Bhil continue to depend, in practical life, far more on their traditional animistic faith. And their religious attributes are chiefly coined and revolve round the same. They are not of as broad a nature as found in the case of developed religions. A Bhil's dependence on the supernatural continues to a very large degree uninterrupted even in the wake of certain new religious elements. Out of all the aspects, it is the religious organisation of the Bhil which has experienced less influence of acculturation. The gods, goddesses, spirits and ghosts have established a close relationship with the physical environments around. The same holds true for religious places like the Deora and Bhomia which are always built on the slightly higher elevation. These may even be on smaller hillocks. The idea is to have them at slightly more secured place, where the religious sanctity, according to the Bhil is better maintained. By keeping them aloof, and on raised ground, the religious elements feel honoured. They feel disgraced at lower elevations because of the fear of all kinds of pollution there. Religious sanctity can be maintained in a slightly secluded place which is provided by the hill tops, especially the places which are accessible too. As the life in high hills and thick forests is generally risky, the Bhil try to overcome it with the help of the supernatural. The abode of the latter are hills, forest, sky etc. For such reasons, the symbolic representations of the supernatural are often met with on hill tops and in forests. The Bhil identify various deities, located in such places, which ensure them protection against natural wrath, wild animals, etc., and which also help grow forest and other resource. For safety and other favours, such deities, are occasionally worshipped and kept happy. Even the identification of hills and forest areas is often linked with the deities or ghosts and spirits associated with them. All inhabitants of the village know of such locations. At times, even some taboos are associated with the use of such spots and the resource thereof. For fear of supernatural, the Bhil do not even traverse such areas at sunset. In order that the people may remain aware of the existence of supernatural forces at certain places, there exist definite taboos in Bhil culture. Like the hills and forests, even the agricultural fields are not spared of the deity association. There are images of deities near the fields and their propitiation provides for better crops and their safety. Thus, the natural as well as the man-made resources are, as per a Bhil's mind, governed by supernatural forces. And the man is able to derive benefit from them by appeasing the supernatural beings. And the man, through various means, has learnt to adjust to the malevolent as well as benevolent supernatural beings.

Like the social and religious perspectives, some of the economic relations, too, are ecology-based. The Bhil fully realise it and they have shaped the relationships as part of the adjustment. A relationship of reciprocity and co-operation is specially exhibited among the Bhil who live in more undulating areas, and where the level of agricultural fields sharply differs. An agricultural field, at a higher elevation gets ready for ploughing and sowing, earlier than one at a lower elevation where rain water takes more time to dry up. One man alone, with his pair of bullocks and plough, may not be able to manage ploughing and sowing of his slopy fields which get dry at a rapid speed. Under such a situation, he is joined by other cultivators of his neighbourhood or kinship sphere, who bring their respective ploughs and bullocks to help in timely ploughing of the land. As a consequence, one would see a number of ploughs operating simultaneously in the same field. The man who is helped in ploughing and sowing of his fields provides food to all the helpers. With such a joint economic effort, the timely sowing is assured. When the fields of the next man get sufficiently dried up, to the extent where ploughing is possible, the same fleet of ploughs would be operated upon there too. The operation continues till the fields of all the men in the fleet are ploughed and sown. An economic system of this kind grew out of the necessity of adjusting to the typical kind of terrain found here. Those involved in an operation are under an obligation to render help to one another. The help remains at the labour level as the produce is not shared and it goes as per the ownership of land. But where the pressure of ecology is not hard, the Bhil believe in individual efforts, and enjoy the outcome independent of one another. This holds true in the collection of forest produce. Wood, gum, honey, tendu leaves, medicinal herbs etc., are collected independently. Its returns also go to the individuals. Another example of the Bhil's adaptation with the environmental conditions is noted in case of their traditional irrigation wells. By and large they are dug near some perennial or seasonal streams of water. And they are mainly the places at the lowest elevation in the valleys where the water table is high, and the water supply is better. The Persian wheel and the buckets carrying water from the well are all locally made. The entire mechanical arrangement of the wheel is of wood, and many Bhil themselves design it. For such a thing and for digging of wells, the Bhil depend on mutual co-operation. As the Bhil's comprehension of the environment is limited, and as the latter is quite imposing, they have, in many cases, no option but to co-operate. Such a condition has even curtailed the rise of economic competition.

It may, however, be mentioned that the acculturative influences have had some impact in the relationship of culture and ecological conditions. A little change has begun to appear on certain fronts. But most of it is heading towards the reframing of relationships rather than breaking them up. At the same time, in a majority of events, the persistence of the traditional relationship is kept intact. And the empirical details, given above, do certify to some of the following derivations:

1. Even in the areas of social culture, man does not seem to react in isolation of the physical environments. Man-to-Man interaction, in a number of instances, seems to be intervened by one or the other of environmental conditions.

2. Many of the cultural elements, and quite a few of the institutions in the social structure, find feet in the environment. These may have additional social reasoning, but still seem to be more environment-based.

3. Certain kinds of social relationships are an outcome of man's adjustment and adaptability with the environmental conditions. They are coined to accept the challenge of pressure posed by the latter.

4. At times, particular kinds of human relationships, and the customs holding them up, grow out of the fear of the unknown that pervades the environment.

5. An understanding of natural phenomena is helpful in describing some elements of cultural matrix. This is better revealed with some knowledge of environmental features.

6. Formation of some social groups and the special nature of human interaction thereof are explained in the background of non-human conditions marking the local environment.

7. Cultural constancy, in certain respects, is largely maintained in the event of environmental. rigidity. When there is a shake-up in the latter, it has its repercussions on the former.

In many other situations, the man-nature relationship has been explored by social anthropologists. Exponents of the cultural ecology approach have repeatedly established the importance of external ecology in social and cultural explanations. The links are very obvious and direct in many of the material objects. In social culture, often one has to search for indirect relationships. But certainly the search for relationship between physical environment and human social and cultural system provides a very important methodological tool to social anthropologists for understanding the reality in social phenomena. This, however, cannot be interpreted to mean that the other tools are unimportant or ineffective. They have their own place in the exploration of social reality. In comparatively more remote areas, inhabited by tribals and where modern innovations have not made much of an impact, the approach of cultural ecology proves more effective and useful in the analysis of the social network prevalent there. It does not, however, mean that the method forfeits its claim to usefulness in the case of changing social orders. What is needed more is the further sharpening of this tool by grasping, to a fair degree, the existing and changing geographical perspective marking a human setting. An anthropologist, alone, has limitations in the matter. The specialist, in this aspect, is the geographer. But he, too is handicapped by his limited insight into the elements of social structure. The best exploration of social situations, under the circumstances, is more feasible through interdisciplinary efforts. Such researches can make an added contribution to the understanding of human social and cultural systems, on the one hand, and in boosting academic growth, on the other. India provides a very fertile field for such academic exercises.

SUGGESTED READINGS

Anderson, James N. : "Ecological Anthropology and Anthropological Ecology", In *Handbook of Social and Cultural Anthropology*, ed.. John J. Honigmann Chicago, Rand McNally and Company, 1937.

Barth, Fredrik : "Ecologic Relationships of Ethnic Groups in Swat, North Pakistan", *American Anthropologist*, Vol. 58, 1956.

Harris, Marvin : "The cultural ecology of India's Sacred Cattle", *Current Anthropology*, No. 7, 1966.

Helm, Jane: "The Ecological Approach in Anthropology", *The American Journal of Sociology*, 1962.

Mann, R.S. : "Eco-system and Society in Ladakh", *Journal of Social Research*, Vol XXI, No. 1, March, 1978.

Mann, R.S. : *Rajasthan Bhils*, Tribal Research and Training Institute, Udaipur, (Ed.), 1978.

Mann, R.S. : "Anthropo-Geography : A Methodological Issue", *Man in India*, Vol. 59, No. 3, 1979.

Steward, Julian : "The Economic and Social Basis of Primitive Bands", In *Essays in Honour of A.L. Kroeber*, ed. Robert H. Lowie, Berkeley, University of California Press, 1936.

Steward, Julian : "Cultural Ecology", In International Encyclopaedia of Social Sciences, 1968.

Vidyarthi, L.P. : *The Maler : A Study in Nature-Man-Spirit Complex of a Hill tribe*, Calcutta, Bookland Private Ltd., 1963.

White, Leslie A.: *The Evolution of Culture*, New York, McGraw-Hill Book Co., 1959.

SEVEN

S. G. Morab

THE SOLIGA
A Study in Ecology, Society and Religion of a Hill Tribe in South India

INTRODUCTION

THERE ARE a large number of studies in India on tribal cultures but studies with some theoretical perspective in describing a tribal culture are few and far between. One such study that has attracted the attention of anthropologists is that of Vidyarthi (1963) on the Maler tribe in Bihar wherein he developed the pioneering concept of Nature-Man-Spirit Complex. Precisely, the concept states that Nature, i.e., forest economy, *khallu* (shifting) cultivation, Man (social system), and Spirit (gossaiyan) all form a complex and are mutually interrelated with each other. Following the concept, a few students of Vidyarthi in Ranchi University undertook studies on different tribal cultures chiefly in Bihar.

The author felt that the concept of Nature-Man-Spirit Complex needed closer scrutiny from other tribal areas. Therefore, a tribal culture in South India was chosen by the author for his doctoral work on the specific subject under the guidance of Professor Vidyarthi. The tribe studied is the Soliga. The first phase of the field work was done during 1965, but intensive field work was done during 1976. The thesis entitled, "The Soliga: A Study in Ecology, Economy, Society, and Religion of a Hill Tribe" was submitted to the Ranchi University in September, 1978 and the Ph.D. Degree was awarded in April, 1980. In this study, the author had examined mainly the concept of Vidyarthi on the Nature-Man-Spirit Complex and also of the Sacred Complex with reference to the Soliga tribe. The thesis runs into 453 pages besides 64 pages of Appendices. Although it is not possible to present the material on the subject in this brief paper, an attempt is made to bring into relief the main gist and the principal findings contained in the doctoral study. The author wishes to state that due to limitations of space here, tables, diagrams, cases and biographies are not given.

The objectives

In order to examine the theoretical concept of the Nature-Man-Spirit Complex, the following objectives are spelled out in the study :

1. To study the nature of the ecological system and its economic organization;
2. To describe the salient features of the social system in its interaction with ecological features;
3. To highlight the religious aspects in the specific eco-system; and also to present the sacred complex.

Area of study

The author chose the Soliga tribe because of their close similarity to the Maler studied by Vidyarthi; the natural physical environment is also similar. The Soliga live mainly in the hilly and forested areas of the Western Ghats that extend eastwards in southern Karnataka bordering north-west of Tamil Nadu.

The author did intensive field work in a settlement known as Yarakanagadde in the Biligiri Rangana Hills. The study chiefly concerns this area. Besides, the tribal settlements in an adjoining Bedaguli forest area with the same ecological background, are covered. A Soliga village, named Ponnachi which in course of time has become multi-caste due to the immigration of non-tribal population is also covered. All these three areas are situated in Mysore district of Karnataka. The selection of the area was done keeping in view the specific objectives of the study.

The materials in the various chapters were presented in such a way that the aspects of Nature-Man-Spirit Complex became quite evident. The chapters on ecological structure and economic organization explain the Nature, whereas the chapters on social structure and life cycle process delineate the Man. The chapter on religion provides the religious beliefs and practices and the sacred complex of a tribal settlement. With this brief introduction, the salient features of the Soliga culture are given.

ECOLOGICAL STRUCTURE AND ECONOMIC ORGANIZATION

Due to the existence of the age old temple of God Rangaswamy, the particular hill ranges and forest lying in a strip in the south-eastern part of Mysore district are known as Biligiri Rangana Hills (hereafter referred to as B.R. Hills). The Bedaguli forest range adjoins the B.R. Hills in its southern direction. Both the B.R. Hills and Bedaguli are reserved forests with rich timber trees and bamboo thickets. Among the fauna, the elephant is most commonly found and their menace is quite great for the tribal people. The only tribal group that inhabits this area is the Soliga. They have flourished in the lap of Nature.

The topography and natural vegetation in the hilly and forested areas of B.R. Hills and Bedaguli reveal that the Soliga have found to be in complete harmony with their physical environment. The Soliga settlements are in fact carved out in the Nature's thick vegetation, and many a time it is difficult to locate their settlements due to the thick foliage surrounding their habitats. During the mild winter months, Nature, with its greenery brings glamour not only to human beings but also to the denizens of the area. The summer months become barren due to devastation by wildfires. These are dangerous to the Soliga as sometimes they engulf their houses too. But generally the Soliga take precautions against fire by forming safe zones around their houses and shrines, and by cutting the grass in a particular way.

Habitat

The Soliga live in small dispersed settlements, known as *podu*. They are located on the hill slopes. Due to the establishment of new settlements and the abandoning of old ones, the numbers do not remain fixed. For example, the author found

9 settlements in B.R. Hills when he was studying in 1965, but the settlements numbered 12 in 1976. The Soliga in B.R. Hills and Bedaguli depend upon shifting cultivation (*podu*) and collection of forest produces and hence movement of people from one place to another becomes quite essential.

The Soliga settlements in B.R. Hills and Bedaguli are established in the interior areas and are therefore not easily approachable. Only by foot can one reach their habitats. In Ponnachi, the situation is different. At one time, the Ponnachi consisted of only Soliga settlements, but later the Soliga were outnumbered by Hindu castes, and consequently their habitats were merged into the revenue village Ponnachi.

The situation of the forest settlements in the B.R. Hills is different. Prior to the merger of the erstwhile Mysore Province with the Indian Union (1948), the Soliga had greater freedom of movement within their own traditional boundaries. But with the rigid enforcement of forest rules and regulations, the Soliga now cannot cut trees, establish settlements, and practise shifting cultivation as they like. Efforts are being made to bring them into 'agricultural colonies', but the Soliga cannot be lured to change their life-style. By and large, in the area studied, they have been living in the thick forests (except Ponnachi), and their entire life-style revolves round the particular ecological structure, that is the natural physical environment of the forest.

Economic functions of forests

The forests have certain economic functions. Broadly these fall into three categories as illustrated by Vidyarthi (1963, p.16) with reference to the Maler. They are : Forest as 1) a source of food and drink; 2) for providing shelter; and 3) for providing raw materials for cottage industries. This is also true in the case of the Soliga of B.R. Hills as may be seen from the following description.

Forest as a source of food and drink

In their natural habitat, the forests are made use of by the Soliga both for food and drink. Blots of *podu* are cut where shifting cultivation is practised and various food crops are raised. The forests in B.R. Hills provide various kinds of fruit trees. Among them mention may be made of *mango, plantain, nerilu, eechalu, geru, gotti* etc. The hilly and forest areas of Bedaguli also have these fruit trees. Most fruits are consumed by the tribals themselves. In Bedaguli, however, if the crop of *nerilu* fruit is surplus the Soliga collect them and sell them.

The wild variety of *bangi* (Indian hemp) can be cultivated although it grows wildly in the forest Though not openly disclosed, older men and women collect bangi. It is mostly used as a narcotic and in the form of smoking. It is grown in the bushes near their *podu* fields. Due to the restriction of its use by the government, the Soliga keep a stock of it hidden in some place. It is alleged that they sell the bangi to small traders in exchange for money and some goods (clothes, cheap ornaments etc). It was learnt that the Soliga are fond of bangi and use it for curing their ailments like body pain.

Besides wild fruits, there are various kinds of berries which are consumed during their wandering to the jungle. Wild tubers like *noore* and *neve* provide food for several days to the Soliga. Small animals like iguana, rat, fowl, squirrel etc. are trapped and consumed. There are several kinds of edible leaves and greens such as *ganake, honagane, hedda, keere* etc., which are collected and brought home. They are cooked in the form of soup and vegetable dishes. There are varieties of medicinal plants in the forest which are used by the Soliga for their numerous physical ailments, and during post-natal treatment for child bearing women.

Forest as source of providing shelter

Almost all the materials used for building *gudlu* (hut or houses), *chavadi* (resting places) etc., are procured from the forest. In the B.R. Hills, except for a few houses in the government tribal colony in Yarakanagadde settlement, the houses of the Soliga are built with such raw materials like bamboo, tree branches, and grasses. The houses are temporary constructions which have to be abandoned when they shift their habitat to another place.

In B.R. Hills forest area the space in a Soliga house is small and the single room in it serves both as the hearth as well as the bedroom. Before marriage when a Soliga couple elope, they spend a few nights in the forest and then return to their settlement and build a new hut for themselves.

The B.R. Hills whose altitude is above 4,000 feet is a cold place. During the rainy and winter seasons, the Soliga need constant warmth for which they keep a fire going continuously. The Soliga are fond of fire for two reasons. As stated above, the fire keeps them warm in the biting cold. Secondly, the fire protects them from wild animals which fear the fire.

The Soliga households have certain items of their material culture which are made of forest materials. All types of basketry, such as *putte* (small basket), *tombe* (big storing basket), *mora* (winnowing fan), *talemane* (wooden plank as pillow), *dasi* (digging stick) are prepared out of the forest products. Bamboo containers for keeping certain articles like salt, pulses, and others are prepared and used. The trapping net, *paje* (cage for catching birds), *kavane* (sling) are made of forest materials only.

Forest as a source of providing raw materials

The Soliga are still in the food-gathering and shifting cultivation stage. In B.R. Hills and Bedaguli areas, the Soliga have not developed any type of cottage industry although some kind of raw materials was available. In Kollegal areas, especially in Ponnachi, many a Soliga has taken to basketry. While this was so in that part of the district, the Soliga of B.R. Hills and Bedaguli have taken up collecting certain minor forest produce, such as *kakke chakke* (cassia fistula), *alalekai* (terminalia chebula) and *pache* (lichen). These are used as raw materials for leather curing and making dyes. A kind of grass known as *sabbe*, is grown in large quantities especially in Bedaguli area. In recent years, some individuals of the plains-villages had employed the Soliga to cut grass and had made attempts to send it to a small paper factory in the vicinity of Bedaguli foothill area. This had not proved economically beneficial as there was no proper know-how of the exploitation of the grass and its cultivation process and hence collection of the grass was given up after a trial.

Forest as a source of personality development

In addition to the above three important functions, one more useful function of the forest could be considered, that is, it could be a source of personality development, as the socialization process of Soliga children depends upon the forest ecology in which they are placed. The Soliga children know the various forest areas, the different ecological features, the flora and fauna and other local circumstances. They know the names and the uses of several trees, plants, creepers and herbs. The behaviour of wild animals, particularly elephants, is known to them. It was observed that whenever any outsider visited the Soliga settlements, everyone present there soon withdrew from the scene and hid in bushes. Since their childhood, the Soliga boys are used to wandering in the thickness of the jungle. During festivals and ceremonies held at different settlements they visit them with their friends. They identify places, and know the short-cut routes to places. They develop skills to keep away from the danger of being mauled by wild animals. They can climb trees of any size and height with alacrity. The ecological base of forest life thus moulds their personality and behaviour from childhood which helps them to adjust to different environs in the eco-system in later years of their life.

Nature of local communities

A brief description of the nature and composition of their local communities is given here with a view to explain the interrelationship of forest ecology with the settlement pattern. The term 'local community' is used here as a synonym to 'local group' as defined in the *Notes and Queries on Anthropology* thus: ". . . a local group—that is any aggregate of people, who inhabit a single clearly demarcated locality and who regard themselves and act as a unit in relation to other local groups" (1960, p.64).

The Soliga settlements in the B.R. Hills and Bedaguli forest areas are 'local communities' in as much as they emphasize factors of aggregateness of people inhabiting a particular demarcated area, and regard themselves and act as a unit in relation to other settlements. Due to ecological and economic conditions, local communities are formed and subsequently dissolved.

There were 12 separate Soliga settlements in the Biligiri Rangana Hills in 1976. Each settlement consists of a few clusters of *gudlu.* A Soliga settlement is known by a distinct term *podu*. The cultivation method of 'slash and burn' traditionally practised is known as *podu*. Usually when the Soliga establish a specific settlement (*podu*) a name is given to it. A boundary is recognized by demarcating a certain area where a settlement is formed. Natural surroundings such as hill-ridge, water source, rocky-surface, growth of a particular tree grove, peculiar sounds heard, mythically known places etc., identify a settlement.

Most of the Soliga settlements are situated in the interior forest areas. The only three settlements in B.R. Hills, namely, (1) Yarakanagadde, (2) Guruvinagadde, and (3) Purani are connected by a jeepable road in 1963, when tribal colonies were established by the government in Yarakanagadde and Purani. The rest can be reached only by traversing on foot. In the case of Bedaguli, none of the settlements can be approached by road as the area has not been exposed to outsiders.

The Soliga desire to go in for *takkalu* (virgin) land on hill slopes and from their settlements. The term *takkalu* is used for such a land which was not used at all at any time. Thus it is virgin land. The term *kale* is used for the field which has been cultivated more than once. It is a common experience that as years pass by, weeds grow in exuberance so much so that the selected land becomes unsuitable for any further cultivation and is therefore considered as *sodubhumi* (infertile land). This would usually take three years, and thereafter the Soliga begin to search for pastures anew.

The Soliga, both in B.R. Hills and Bedaguli forest areas do not usually prefer to return to a place if it has been cultivated once. Virgin land was preferred solely with the intent of getting more crops which was not possible if they reverted to cultivated places. Due to stricter implementation of forest laws these days, they have to revert to some such places where cultivation has once taken place. For example, Sorekaibetta, Muttugadagadde and Minnebetta (in B.R. Hills) which were cultivated about 30 years ago were taken up again in 1974. The Soliga believe that after the lapse of 10-12 years, a land becomes suitable for cultivation once again. Such land is called as *hosa bhumi* (new ground).

Whenever the Soliga of a particular settlement have to go to another place, they observe certain socio-ritual ceremonies. When a new site is selected, be it a *takkalu* or a *hosa bhumi*, the elders with their family members go there on a Thursday, preferably after the Sankranti (in January) festival is over, and settle themselves in that place. They carry with them a few household articles as they may have to stay there for about one or two months. This type of movement on the eve of establishing a new settlement is called *hudeya*. A piece of land where a particular family decides to stay is cut out, and a temporary construction is made there. Auspicious dreams are the basis on which final decisions are taken and those dreams in which mendicants, water source, or honey combs appeared are auspicious. The bad dreams like seeing dead animals, fire, wild animals, portend evil, and such places are abandoned.

When a site is selected by means of the above method, the Soliga observe another ritual known as *allu-shastra* (rite of castor seeds) in order to choose a suitable place for erecting a house. A few castor seeds are placed in five circles or as in another method, seeds are kept one over the other, in a place chosen for the purpose. The castor seeds are covered with a basket. One night is allowed to pass and then the basket is removed. The forecast is read. If there is any slight disturbance in the position of the castor seeds the omen is bad. In case they are intact, the forecast is one of well being and prosperity and in such places they build their homes.

The houses are built in the selected place after they succeed in performing their *hudeya* and *allushastra* rituals. A few families thus cluster in a certain area. Then the Soliga begin to live in the settlement as a 'local community'. The situation demands 'community life' in the native habitat. In most cases when a Soliga local community is formed, it will have members who are close kin. When marriage takes place, the number of a family swells. The membership in a local community represented in one settlement (*podu*) is not compulsory nor is it of a permanent nature. The number of families in the various Soliga settlements in an area may differ. The most usual pattern is that some related families belonging to different clans, based on social relationship and also on kinship, come to form a particular local community.

A genealogical chart of families staying in Yarakanagadde settlement shows that usually kinship plays a dominant role in forming clustered houses in dispersed groups. Because of members moving from one settlement to the other, and regrouping, 'shuffling' and 'reshuffling' of households take place in forming a new settlement. As regards 'shuffling' and 'reshuffling' of households, information based on the 1965 survey and later their movement to different places by 1976 would be an example to show precisely the type of formation of settlements.

The relevant data is tabulated. A few notable features can be observed from this data. There has been the movement of members of families to different areas. Members of nearly 38 per cent of families have moved into B. R. Hills to different settlements while about 36 per cent of families have continued to live in their previous settlements or their neighbourhoods. In the case of the settlements like Bhavihane, Doddare and Kolla (in B.R. Hills), for instance, members of families had taken up in some adjoining areas, but the name of the previous settlements had still been retained. It was noted that about 13 per cent of the members of families have moved to the neighbouring forest areas of other taluks.

The Soliga always build their settlements usually away from water sources and hill slopes. There is a saying amongst them: 'Be nearer to kinsfolk but live far away from water resources'.

Certain specific features of local communities are analysed here. When a local community is established, the tribal people live in it as one distinct social group in relation to other groups.

In a settlement, there is co-operation among members during various socio-religious occasions. In times of economic crisis, members also help each other. It may be noted that ritual impurity accrues to the community as a whole and to all the five clans which arises due to birth or death in a family. In a local community, elderly male members settle disputes concerning members of their own settlement. In case if any matter remains unsettled, then the *kula panchaiti* (tribal council) takes such cases and decides them at the level of B. R. Hills area and also in Bedaguli.

Among different local communities, there is inter-settlement co-operation. Marriages take place between members of different clans. For this purpose, the B. R. Hills is not the limit. The area of marriage distance goes up to some miles in the neighbouring areas also. In economic activities like collection of forest produce, members from different settlements co-operate with each other in sharing wages. The B. R. Hills forest area is considered as one regional unit in contradistinction to other units like Bedaguli.

Ecological features of Ponnachi

The Ponnachi is a village situated in one of the valleys of Mahadeswar Hills in Kollegal taluk. The dominant caste in the village is the Lingayat (a saivite sect) with nearly 300 households, and next to them is the Soliga, who are numerically large. There are members of other castes like potters, blacksmiths and also Adi Karnataka (scheduled caste) who are small in number. The Soliga number 690 distributed in 145 families.

The Ponnachi hill is situated at an altitude of 4,200 ft. Formerly, the present site of Ponnachi village was a forest, and the Soliga were the first settlers there. Later on, the Lingayats of the plains-villages came into the picture. They usurped vast forest land and cultivated them. Although, previously the cultivation by the Soliga was by the method of 'slash and burn', it was changed over to plough cultivation and the Soliga too took up plough cultivation when they came in contact with the former. The crops raised here are mainly *Ragi** (eleusine corocana), and pulses especially, the *avare* (phaseolus radiatus). The Lingayats command more land whereas the large number of the Soliga have small areas of land, varying between 2-5 acres on an average.

The Soliga in Ponnachi who are landless, work as agricultural labourers in the houses of the dominant Lingayats. The Soliga live in permanent houses built by them on their lands and other places. The houses of the Soliga therefore are dispersed. The Lingayat and other castes live in certain areas as compact settlements. The Soliga participate in all economic, social, religious and political activities of other castes in

*A kind of millets.

Ponnachi village, and by their constant interaction they have emerged as a peasant caste in Ponnachi.

SHIFTING CULTIVATION

In the forest ecology, the economic life of the Soliga revolves round what is known as *podu* cultivation. There are certain distinct phases in shifting cultivation which bring together interaction between Nature, Man and Spirit in a series of situations. From this context, the *podu* cultivation of the Soliga may be understood which is usually marked with the following processes, namely, 1. Selecting and cutting of forest 2. Burning and removing of woods 3. Sowing 4. Weeding 5. Watching 6. Harvesting 7. Worshipping and 8. Merry making, and this model of Vidyarthi is used for describing the *podu* cultivation of the Soliga.

SELECTING AND CUTTING OF FOREST

As pointed out in the previous section, the Soliga select sites generally on hilly slopes. In case they cannot get *takkalu* (virgin) land, they go in for a place which has been kept fallow for a long time. Now-a-days, the forest department is using fallow land for transplanting Nilgiri (eucalyptus) and silver oak. Since such work is in slow pace, there are several places of fallow land still available, for cultivation for the Soliga and to form new podu (settlements).

The construction of houses and also one or two shrines takes place only in their respective swidden field. In a specified boundary each family demarcates its patches of land depending upon its ability to work upon it. A nuclear family unit selects patches 'on eye observation' which is about 2-3 acres. There are, however, exceptions. In Bedaguli, a Soliga of Jenumane settlement had taken up four small patches, each varying between 2-3 acres.

In B.R. Hills and Bedaguli it was found that many a Soliga has knowledge of the conditions and fertility of the soil and they choose their sites accordingly. The major soil types are based on texture, stone content, taste, colour, and fertility of crops. For instance, *hittugallu bhumi* (soft stone soil) is not fertile, whereas *barikallu* (soil with pebbles) is not fertile for ragi and maize, but fertile for castor. *Karimannu* (black soil) is very fertile, and *kempumannu* (red colour soil) is fertile. There are also other varieties like *budimannu* (ash colour soil), near water sources is good for plantain, while *hulimannu* (soil with sour taste) is fertile for ragi and maize.

Cutting

In earlier days, say about 30 years ago, the Soliga would unhesitatingly 'slash' big trees. Now they cannot cut any big tree as it is a cognizable offence. Therefore, only branches of trees, undergrowth vegetations, grass, shrubs are cut soon after a new field is selected. After cutting is done, the entire material is piled up in the field in small heaps leaving some distance in between.

Burning

The cut vegetation is allowed to dry in the sun for about two months. Each household cuts a field of the size that they require for the first year. After the Ugadi (New Year March-April) festival is over, they set fire to the entire field. The heaps made in different places are known as *ugilu* by the Soliga. Once the dried material in the field is burnt the ash sets in. Then the remains of the unburnt stumps, roots etc., are dug up and formed into *kuppe* (heaps) in certain places and once again they are burnt. The 'burned field' is a swidden (*podu*).

Sowing

By the end of April rains begin to fall and the sowing operation starts. The only tool used now is the *dasi* (digging stick). For the sowing of maize no ritual offering is done. In sowing the maize, they take 3 seeds at a time in the right hand and drop them into the holes made by the *dasi* held in the left hand, and by a simultaneous operation, the dug out earth is tread upon by the right foot. Without following any specific order the seeds are dibbled randomly, but a distance of 2-3 feet counted by means of foot are maintained. Pulses like the *togari* (*dal*, pigeon pea), and *avare* are similarly planted. In the *kuppe*, seeds of pumpkin, cucumber and *hedda* are sown. Castor seeds are sown in between the middle of the maize and especially in the stony surfaces of the swidden. The Soliga wait until the maize plants grow to a height of 9-12 inches (eye measurement) and also wait for a good shower of rain. In the months of April and May, broadcasting of ragi takes place. Ragi is a ritually important crop unlike maize and hence propitiation to deities before broadcasting is necessary.

Elders of a settlement organize a ritual known as *bhumi tayi santi* (appeasing earth goddess) and pray for plentiful yield in return. The Soliga of a podu (settlement) collect contributions, and arrange the ritual. The *tammadi* (priest) in the settlement offers worship i.e., *puje*, at the local shrine. In such *puje*, vegetarian offerings like plantain, cocoanut, flowers (wild), betel leaves and nuts, *puri* (parched rice), *hurigadale* (fried gram), jaggery etc, are given. When the offering is over, the priest holding emblems of their deities, viz. a *gandu godli* (sacred ritual axe), and a *betta* (a cane stick), goes to a swidden field, selected for performing the ritual. Each household brings ragi in small baskets. A hen is sacrificed in the field in the presence of the priest and the blood of the sacrificed animal is allowed to fall on the ragi seeds, kept in a separate basket. The priest goes into a trance and pronounces oracles. A few handfuls of ragi seeds from the common basket are broadcast by the priest in the field where the ritual is observed. The priest then goes on saying lengthy prayers seeking the forest gods' (*adavi devaru*) permission to give them plentiful crops and also saving them from destruction by wild animals.

The ragi used for sowing is a special variety i.e. *Malai ragi* (hill ragi), and seeds of it are preserved in earthen vessels and protected from pests. The Soliga also grow mustard. The mustard seeds are mixed in the ragi seeds and then broadcast. Pulses like *avare*, and *togari* are kept in bamboo containers and ash is mixed with them in order to protect them from pests. The maize cobs are hung over the hearth for several days and by constant smoke, the seeds become immune from the attack of any pest (Maler also preserve maize in this way : Vidyarthi 1963, p. 38).

Weeding

When the maize plants grow to a height of about one and half feet, there is need for weeding, as by that time the ragi also sprouts. It is very necessary to protect the crops both from the vagaries of nature, wild animals, and also malevolent spirits.

In the first year of the swidden cultivation, the danger of the growth of weeds is not very much as it is experienced that the 'burned swidden' is not congenial for the growth of weeds due to the destruction of weed seeds by the fire. The common weeds in B. R. Hills are *soora sette*, *vante*, and *unni*. In Bedaguli, there are the *javana*, and also *sabbe* along with the above three varieties grown in B. R. Hills. These weeds grow in full exuberance in a very short time, and hence, their luxuriant growth has to be contained by removing them. After the end of three years, it becomes unwieldy for the Soliga to cope with removal of weeds. The lands full of weeds lose their fertility and hence become unfit for further cultivation.

While the Soliga cannot help the weed growth, they are concerned with protection of crops from pests. They invoke the spirits for protecting their crops by observing a special ritual, called as *pairu puje* (worship of plants) as soon as the first weeding is done. The ritual is done in a place selected by the local community. The priest does it by placing the offerings like cocoanut, fried gram, plantain, parched rice on the leaves of castor trees. The number of such leaves vary from one place to another. Such offerings are referred to as *ede hakuvadu* (serving ritual food) to all kinds of evil spirits, ancestral spirits etc., and also to forest gods (*adavi devaru*).

Protection and watching

Plants like maize are affected by a kind of wind, which is poisonous (*maru*) to the crop. There are no remedies for it. The Maru wind, however, does not affect the *malai ragi*. Plants and crops are prone to the threat of many kinds of birds. The birds are driven off by shouting at them, or by using a sling made out of creeper fibre. In the case of wild animals the menace is beyond control. They have certain devices to drive away wild animals such as a tool made by a hollow split bamboo operated from hut built on a tree top as a guardhouse. During the night all members of the family sleep in the guarding hut and shout at any slight noise.

Harvesting

In the month of July, the maize becomes ready for harvesting. Before reaping it, a few cobs of the maize are cut and placed on the ground of the swidden as a kind of offering to the earth goddess. Except for this no other ritual is observed. The maize does not have any value in any ritual unlike other millets, ragi and pulses and other vegetables. Because the seeds of maize were found in the excreta of a dog, maize is considered unsuitable for offering to gods. However, before eating for the first time, offering to gods is made. The stalks of the maize are severed by a sickle and are stacked in the attic of the house. The Soliga have their hearth underneath the attic. As a result of fire used for cooking, the maize cobs get dried in due course of time. When they are dried completely, maize cobs are brought out, placed on the floor and beaten with sticks to separate the grains from the sheaths. The grain is then stored in earthen vessels.

In the case of ragi, a separate hut, known as *tene kottige*, is built in the swidden field in the first year of cultivation for storing ragi. The harvest of ragi begins from the month of October which continues up to December. A threshing floor, called as *kothar* or *kala* is prepared. It is plastered with the dung of bison. In the case of the Soliga who have domesticated cattle, cattle dung is used.

Threshing of ragi begins in the month of January. Before it is done, a certain amount of ragi is beaten and the grain is collected. It is utilized for observing a ritual *hosa ragi habba* (new ragi eating festival). Another ritual observed at this time is called as *rotti para* (bread festival). The *hosa ragi habba* is done to appease the *mane devaru* (family deities), whereas the *rotti para* is performed to placate the deities of the forest gods (*adavi devaru*). The millet, i.e., ragi, forms the main ritual item in these two observances. The Soliga do not sacrifice any animal or fowl on such occasions.

The ragi ears are brought out, severed from the stalk with a small sickle. They are placed on the threshing floor, except in one swidden field of a settlement. The ears of the ragi are beaten with long sticks. The millet is cleared from the chaff by winnowing. The swidden field which is left is taken up for performing a ritual by the members of a settlement collectively. In the selected swidden field the ragi is threshed and heaped on the threshing floor. This heap is known as *rasi*. A worship is made to the *rasi*, and is therefore called as *rasi puje*. All members in a settlement contribute to the expenses. A he-goat is sacrificed and the bleeding victim is taken around the *rasi* as propitiation. Ragi flour is cooked in the form of balls (*mudde*), and the meat of the goat is cooked as a curry. The food (*ede*) is served on *muttuga* (*butea frondosa*) leaves. At the time of *rasi puje*, the ritual food is served to several deities, and spirits whose number differs from one settlement to another. After the ritual offering, the Soliga partake of the meal. The objective of the worship is to reciprocate the obligations for giving return in the form of grain. If they do not offer anything then they do not expect benevolence from the spirits existing in Nature in giving good yield in the coming years.

Merriment and leisure

When the harvest is over the Soliga get some time for merriment and leisure. During the months of January to March, the swidden fields are barren. A festival known as *rotti habba*, in honour of the local deities is observed. Men and women from different settlements attend it. On this occasion, a ritual of 'fire walking' (walking barefoot on live embers) is performed if the deity is *Jadeswamy*. At the local shrine a pandal is erected to house the people. A sacred pole is built in the middle of the pandal. Those who had earlier taken vows to their deities in times of distress find an opportunity to fulfil these, as the priests of deities from different places attend the observance. The whole night following the worship and fire walking is marked with singing and dancing. Groups of young men participate in this merriment and devotional songs. The songs revolve round Siva and are in praise of him, their forest deities, and also the trees and places with which they are familiar in the jungle. Dance is performed by young men to the accompaniment of local drums and cymbals. Summer time is the most congenial period to visit various settlements where their kinsfolk live. Now it is also time to negotiate marriages. Some elderly persons pay visits to the temple of Mahadeswar in Kollegal.

From the above description it may be seen that the whole swidden activities go on in a cycle, in the first year of the cultivation. The activities of the swidden continue almost in a similar vein for the second and third years.

In most of the Soliga settlements in B. R. Hills and Bedaguli, the situation of food production by the method of shifting cultivation is nearly the same. If there are normal yields, the maize produced may suffice for their consumption for only one month and the ragi provides them food for about two months for a family of five members. However, considering the amount labour and the days spent in cultivating, guarding and harvesting, obviously the yield is not commensurate with their efforts. In order to supplement their food they also have to depend on what they gather for subsistence, like the edible tubers, and varieties of vegetables etc.

The operation of shifting cultivation in the swidden is full of difficulties, and traditionally it was considered to be better as they could not only move to *takkalu* freely, but could axe more land. But of late the forest regulations are being made more rigid. In spite of constraints, the quest for food continues. There are ritualistic observances to compensate for the gift given by Nature, to which they are all indebted. Swidden fields are considered sacred. Menstruating women, for instance, have to stay inside their specially built hut for three days. There will be accrual of *tume* (ritual impurity) in the case of birth and death in a household, and until the purificatory rituals are observed no member may work in a swidden field. No new grain, especially ragi, is eaten before the *hosa ragi habba* is performed. The gods will not be considerate to those who violate the norms of offering worship before eating the new grain.

The produce derived from the shifting cultivation is very meagre and the Soliga suffer from acute hunger in spite of their dependence on tubers etc. The significant point made by Vidyarthi in regard to the Maler is very much true in the case of the Soliga when he says: "Hunger dominates, as it is one of the basic drives, but at times it becomes subservient to the ideology, the moral order or the tradition of a cultural group" (1963; p.64).

OTHER ECONOMIC PURSUITS

COLLECTION OF MINOR FOREST PRODUCES

The forest produce is the exclusive property of the forest department. Every year the forest produce of minor nature is auctioned to private contractors who hold the right to their collection and sale for a specified period. There are bigger contractors who keep their agents in different places of tribal settlements in the forest areas. The Soliga in B.R. Hills and Bedaguli are engaged in collecting and 'selling' them to these agents. The chief articles among the minor forest produce available in the B.R. Hills and Bedaguli forest are *kakke chakke* (*cassia fistula*), *alalekai* (*terminalia chebula*), *pache* (lichen) and honey. The cassia fistula is used in the tanning industry and the terminalia chebula are used in making chemical dyes. Hence there is greater demand for these articles by the forest contractors.

Collection of honey

Some amount of search is required as honey bees build their combs in crevices, caves, bushes etc., usually concealed. But the Soliga are adept at bringing out these concealed combs. The season of honey-collection is during the months of May and June, and October and November. There are three varieties of honey, viz., *hejjenu* (large bee), *tuduve jenu* (a local type), *kirī jenu* (small bee). The Soliga use bamboo scaffoldings, if required, to collect honey.

The other minor forest produces collected are : wax, stag hoofs, *śeege* (*acacia concinna*), *antawala* (soap nut), *nellikai* (*phyllanthus implica*), but these are available in small quantities and the income derived from them is negligible.

Before commencement of the collection of minor forest produce, the deities in their settlement are propitiated. But for each of the four major items mentioned above, worship is done at the spot in every season before the Soliga set to work. The forest contractors, however, take adequate care to finance such worship. On a chosen Friday, or Monday, the worship is conducted. There will be a ceremonial meal consisting of rice, ragi and curry which will be offered to the forest gods (*adavi devaru*). A hen or cock is sacrificed on the occasion. Since the ritual is supposed to offer food and propitiate all kinds of spirits and gods in the forest, blood offering is essential. The priests are also invited on such occasions who go into a trance and pronounce oracles.

Hunting, trapping, and fishing

The Soliga are engaged in relatively minor economic activities like trapping, fishing etc. The Soliga are not hunters of any major game. But small animals are chased and tracked. The victims in this case are wild pigs and porcupine. As regards killing birds, squirrels, rats and wild cats, they prepare traps with stones and sticks which are arranged in such a way that the victims are injured or killed when the arranged support is dislodged.

Fish is not found in abundance and hence fishing is not done in any great scale in B.R. Hills and Bedaguli. Whatever fishing is done by the Soliga, it is done in shallow water during the rainy season, by using the barks of *sokku seege*, and *karekai*. When these are put into water the fish float by the slow poisoning effect, and then they are collected.

Plough cultivation

Although the Soliga are dependent upon the traditional shifting cultivation, their constant interaction and contact with non-tribal people of the temple village (around the temple of Rangaswamy, a village has come into being), and also of the plains-villages have made some of the Soliga settlements in B. R. Hills take to plough cultivation. Some Soliga have also learnt the technique of tending the cattle and using them for cultivation.

About 30 years ago, in Ponnachi village, it was stated that the type of cultivation in the forest was mainly in the swidden form (*podu*) as the Soliga were the first settlers. Consequent upon the non-tribal 'peasants' coming into Ponnachi and acquiring land, the method of plough cultivation was introduced in due course and the Soliga too accepted the method. They also began to tend cattle, and to learn the various processes of plough cultivation.

Since 96 families of the Soliga in Ponnachi village hold lands they have adopted the pattern of agriculture of the dominant Lingayat peasants. Various ritual observances and offerings made before sowing and during harvesting are done by the Soliga in a similar way as are done by the peasants in the village. Thus the Soliga of Ponnachi have been very much influenced by the local Hindu peasant caste.

To sum up, it may be observed that it is precisely the subsistence activities of the Soliga of B.R. Hills and Bedaguli that are chiefly dependent upon the ecological structure.

The nature of their shifting cultivation provides the much needed food grains at least for some months. In spite of certain odds, they continue to follow the traditional shifting cultivation. All the activities connected with the first year and subsequent years of shifting cultivation are done in a systematic manner, wherein the local community has an important part to play. Besides their own efforts, the Soliga believe that the yield depends upon the blessings of their gods and spirits that abound in Nature. By propitiating them they overcome several handicaps which are Nature-made, like the vagaries of forest ecology, Man-made, like theft, giving gifts etc., and Spirit-made, such as wrath and curse of deities and spirits. This is also true for another important economic activity which is Nature-based, that is collection of minor forest produce. For those living in the interior of the forest, the latter activity is very important. Right from the phase of cutting the swidden field in the forest to the phase of merriment, the Soliga enjoy the whole gamut of economic activities in their own ecosystem.

It may be seen that acquiring land in places like Purani, Yarakanagadde, and Guruvinagadde in B.R. Hills by the Soliga and cultivating them by the plough has begun. The hazards of the forests are becoming increasingly more than what they were, as many restrictions have been put on them. Yet the Soliga in the interior forests are still in full control of the swidden form of agriculture. The hill slopes on which the Soliga practise *podu* cultivation are believed to be not suitable for plough cultivation. The Soliga of Ponnachi on the other hand, have left the shifting cultivation long ago and have taken to plough cultivation due to the impact of the peasants there, and they have become part of the peasant culture.

THE SOCIAL STRUCTURE AND THE LIFE CYCLES PROCESS

In this section, the net work of relationship among the Soliga who come in direct interaction with the ecology are described.

THE TRIBE, CLAN, AND LINEAGE

The Soliga are divided into 5-clan and 7-clan Soliga. They are distributed in territorial groups. In the hilly and forested areas of Chamarajanagar, Yelandur and Kollegal taluks of Mysore district the 5-clan group predominate and are called as 'Podu Soliga' as they live in *Podus*. The present study is concerned particularly with the Podu Soliga of B.R. Hills and also of Bedaguli

The Soliga identify their people by consanguineous and affinal ties. Usually such kin ties are established among those people who live in a particular geographical area. A keen sense of solidarity is felt among the members of the group, which is discrete, and identifiable, minimally, in terms of the local community. As explained in an earlier section, the family is a functional socio-economic unit, and the podu, that is, the local community, is a group of related and unrelated members acting as a kind of cohesive unit to maintain the discrete social group, within the specified period of existence until the families are shuffled and reshuffled when a settlement is abandoned and a new one is formed.

The Soliga distinguish themselves as *kadujana* (foresters) and all others as *nadavaru* (plains-people). There are no other tribal groups living in and around the B.R. Hills and Bedaguli forest areas.

Membership is gained by birth and by affinal ties. If a man takes a woman of a caste 'higher' to them, the woman is welcome to become a member. For instance, a woman of Jenumane settlement in Bedaguli belonging to Uru Kuruba (shepherd caste) was accepted in the community as she had chosen a Soliga man as her mate. Illegitimate children of tribal women are legitimized by the tribal council, by making a ritual of purification. The Soliga, however, do not accept membership if the caste of a man is 'lower' to theirs, like the Adi Karnataka, Madiga, Lambadi (scheduled castes), and also the Muslim.

Clan

There are five clans (*Kula*) among the Soliga, namely (1) Haleru (2) Shalikiri (3) Teneru (4) Belloru and (5) Suraru. Recently one more clan, namely, Baleru was added. From the explanation on their origin of clans it is suggested that the clans do not show any totemistic practice. In all probability the clans are fictitious and are not eponymous in their origin.

For the purpose of marriage no hierarchical order in clans is found. Even members of the newly found Baleru clan are not an exception. Some hierarchical order, however, was found in assigning the various roles in the traditional tribal council (*kula panchaiti*). For instance, the members of the two clans only, that is, Haleru and Shalukiri are eligible for contesting for the office of the *yejaman* (headman of the tribal council). Hence, it may be assumed that these two clans have 'higher' status compared to other clans. The other offices of the tribal council are the *pattegar*, *kolkar*, and *cheluvade*, which are held hereditarity only by the members of Teneru, Belloru, and Suraru clans respectively.

The functions of clans are mainly two-fold. Firstly, by the association of a clan, people are agnatically related. There are also lineage in a clan. The worship to family deities is done as per the family and lineage norms and these are clearly identified. The second function is to maintain clan exogamy. While clanship emphasizes such factors as descent and exogamy, there is no significance of clans in the demarcation of any specific geographical boundaries. For instance, no clan is spatially dispersed, although the non-traditional Baleru clan has members from the B.R. Hills area only due to its recent origin.

Lineage

There are lineages called *gumpu* in each clan. The depth of each lineage among the Soliga generally exists for 3 or 4 generations. Members of a lineage trace their descent through their immediate ancestors. At one time, some members may become prominent and at that time, original or remote ancestors are forgotten, but these new members are remembered.

It was noted from some of the genealogies that members of a particular lineage who are related agnatically, differentiate between members of another lineage from that of their own in a formal 'brotherhood' relationship. The family deities are inherited generally through a male descendant. The agnatic kinship bonds are tightened during annual worship of family deities and thus through lineage some kind of social cohesion is achieved.

Zone of interaction

Vidyarthi (1963:pp.60-73) has aptly recorded the various spheres of interaction of a tribal culture, as part of developing a network of relationships in terms of tribe, region, and village community. For this purpose he has discussed four important zones of interaction, in terms of rings, namely, marriage ring, festival ring, market ring, and political ring. Each tribal group is likely to have some kind of network of relationships in the larger eco-cultural milieu. It would be worthwhile to describe the various rings of interaction among the Soliga.

Marriage Ring

The geographical area where the Soliga have their settlements falls in an M-shaped hilly tract of about 24 kilometres in B.R. Hills and Chamarajanagar forest range. However, marriages are found to be taking place within the limit of about 12 kilometres. The data on the marriages taken place during last ten years, that is, between 1966-76 in different settlements, from Yarakanagadde settlement show that the area of network of marriage relationship is very much limited. There will be visits during festival occasions and harvesting seasons when exchange of mutual gifts take place. When a new swidden field is formed the services of near relatives are sometimes sought in building a house and making fields. Usually sisters' husbands exchange labour on such occasions mutually. Although the Soliga swidden cultivator has not much to give by way of gifts when such services are rendered, a symbolic gesture is shown by offering a few kilograms of ragi, a whole pumpkin and some tender maize cobs, or raw *togari* (pulse) pods depending upon the season. When relatives visit each other's settlement, it is a common practice to give gifts and show hospitality whether one has done any work or not. Offering *bangi* (Indian hemp) is an act of valued hospitality, particularly when the former is a forbidden item. At Bedaguli also, the marriage distance is limited to their traditional boundary of about 20 kilometres.

The festival ring

The *Hosa Ragi Habba* held during November and December, and the *Ratti Habba* observed during March (see the section on religion) are the two important festivals when kin from different settlements visit. Such visits from near kin are enjoyed by them. The timings in each settlement differ, thus providing the Soliga to attend these festivals held in different places. Usually the people of nearby settlements attend each other's places due to physical convenience.

The market ring

There are no weekly markets in the B.R. Hills. In the interior settlements, shops of the forest contractors provide day-to-day articles needed by them for exchange of cash or minor forest produce. In Bedaguli area, a market is held on a Sunday at a fixed place called a 'gate'. On other occasions the tribals at Bedaguli buy articles from the shops or forest contractors, for exchange of grains, forest produce, or cash.

The political ring

In the case of the Soliga of B.R. Hills a tribal headman conducts the internal affairs of the tribal people of the nearby settlements with some assistants. The jurisdiction of the tribal headman is limited, and the members living in a specific area of B. R. Hills owe allegiance to him. There is also such a headman at Bedaguli, who controls the tribal settlements of a particular area.

Thus it may be observed that interaction within the Soliga is limited to their traditional boundaries of a specified ecological, socio-economic and political spheres and the network of relationship have the function of reinforcing strong group solidarity. It was, however, observed that their interaction with outsiders has been considerably increasing.

THE FAMILY AND KINSHIP

The family

A family is the basic corporate unit in a swidden field. Members of a family live under a common shelter and jointly share the food cooked there in the common hearth. A man or a woman is born and brought up in a family. In the course of socialization, the traditions and skills of a family are learnt. While a man stays in the family of orientation, a woman would leave the family to join the family of her husband, that is the family of procreation, after marriage, or would live in a separate household established by her husband near the house of his parents. The types of families among the Soliga are : 1. Nuclear; 2. Extended (complete); 3. Unextended (incomplete); 4. Broken; 5. Nascent; and 6. Mixed.

A Nuclear family consists of a man, his wife, and unmarried children. The Extended family can be broken into two types, namely, Extended (complete) which would consist of a man, his wife and their married sons, with or without children, including also the former's unmarried children. Extended (incomplete) family would comprise one of the living parents, together with their married sons and their children, and also the former's unmarried children. A Broken category of the family includes one of the living spouses with unmarried children, and also the households having single individuals. The newly married couple with potentiality for future progeny is called Nascent. The families having members who are related in some way constitute the Mixed group.

The composition of family types in B.R. Hills, Bedaguli, and Ponnachi, when tabulated, show that in B.R. Hills, and Bedaguli the nuclear type of family predominates with 67 and 64 per cent respectively. In Ponnachi, the nuclear type is not as numerically large as in the case of the above two areas. It has only 51 per cent. In the B. R. Hills and Bedaguli, due to the ecological structure and economic pursuits, the families are broken into nuclear units in the local communities. The percentage of the extended families in these areas is only 8 each, while in Ponnachi it is 20. In the latter case the nature of the ecology and the economy of the Soliga is different and the influence of other neighbouring Hindu communities has made a dent in their social organisation.

The family is patrilineal. Descent is reckoned through the male. The father is the head of the family and on his death the eldest brother succeeds. Usually other brothers establish their own households after marriage. Respect is shown to one's elders related by consanguineal ties, and to all those near affinal kin, and also those belonging to one's *kula* (clan). Residence is patrilocal. Sometimes, a man after his marriage may go to stay with his wife's relatives, in which case the residence is uxorilocal.

Division of labour among the different sexes in the tribal society takes place through socialization and needs of subsistence. When a household is established in a Podu, and a swidden field is prepared, men, women and children have different roles to play in fulfilling various functions of a family. Since a male member is the head of the household he wields considerable authority over all members. A wife has a subordinate position with reference to the authority of her husband, and thus does all the work assigned to her. A woman has the sole responsibility of cultivating ragi in the swidden field and a man bothers mainly about the economic pursuits falling outside the swidden cultivation. A woman does the job of collecting tubers and other domestic chores. She also takes care of her children and fulfils the functions of a wife in giving sexual pleasure at night, and in the forest during day time if her husband so desires it.

It is quite easy for a Soliga man or woman to divorce or desert his/her spouse. If a woman is good looking and hardworking, other Soliga men may cast their eyes on her and there is fear of elopement with a man. The relationship between a husband and wife is informal. Cases of ill-treatment by husbands are few. One has to look after the children and do the jobs like bringing water, grinding ragi, cooking etc. if one's wife was sick or under post-natal treatment. A period of five days 'ritual impurity' (*tume*) accrues to the husband also when there is a birth in a house. So the purificatory ceremony called as *madake ikkuvadu* (keeping new earthen vessels) has to be done on the fourth or fifth day. There are also instances of husbands ill-treating wives. A husband may tolerate a wife's laziness in not attending to her work but he may not tolerate extra-marital relations and in the latter case the matter is brought before the tribal council for settlement.

Kinship terms and usages

The kinship terms used among the Soliga are no different from the local Kannada terms used by the other communities of the plains-villages. The kinship structure is classificatory. For the analysis of the terms as far as five generations are considered, namely, two in the ascending, one in the Ego, and two in the descending generations are covered. Age, sex, and generations are the guiding factors for addressing or referring to any kin.

Among the Soliga, the exogamous clan is an important feature in regulating marriage as the clan is inherited by a person through both the parents. This type of clan principle makes them refer to members of a particular clan by the consanguineous and affinal kin terms as the case may be. In case of members of one's own mother's clan, female children are treated as one's consanguineous kin. For instance, if a man's mother's clan is Belloru, female members of the Belloru clan are referred to and addressed as *avve* (mother) and therefore marital relations with her children who stand in relation to parallel cousin is not possible. In case of one's mother's brother's children, whose clan is also the same as one's own mother, and who stand in relation to one's cross-cousin, marriage is permitted. The terminological structure provides for the bilateral cross-cousin as the prescribed marriage rule, but actual occurrences of cross-cousin marriage, however, are very few.

KINSHIP BEHAVIOUR

Parent-child relationship

The father in a family uses his authority and patronage in order to control his children. When a boy is about 15 years of age, he goes to collect forest produce and also works for the forest department. Boys would accompany their fathers in honey collection or going to other settlements. A child is told about the danger of wild animals and advised not to wander alone in the forest. Whenever parents go for work elsewhere, children stay at home in the swidden fields. They learn to climb trees from childhood and they would do so in case they saw an elephant. Boys become almost independent when they attain 15 years or so, and a father's authority ceases. By then a son may cut his own piece of swidden site, near that of his father's and may build a separate *chavadi* (resting place), although he may continue to eat in his parents' house. The father helps his son in negotiating the marriage of the latter unless it is a case of the elopement.

Relationship among siblings and other relatives

The older brothers have more responsibility in taking care of their younger brothers and sisters, in case of death of the father. As the brothers grow old, they work and earn separately but live in under one roof. The Soliga men and women visit their brothers and sisters during harvest time and on festival occasions. Usually men carry gifts to their sisters. Brothers live separately after their marriage, but in the same settlement.

A woman shows her utmost reverence to her husband's elder brother. Though there is no strict avoidance, a woman does not talk to her husband's elder brother. In the case of younger brother of her husband, a woman speaks freely and addresses him by name. But no joking relationship exists between them. A man speaks to his wife's elder sister with much respect and cordiality. A man does not speak freely with his wife's younger sister if the latter is married.

The mother-in-law and daughter-in-law relationship is formal and occasionally marked by tension too. Although the married sons live separately with their spouses in swidden fields, situations of conflict may arise due to their living in the neighbourhood. A man treats his wife's father as on equal standing to that of his mother's brother, and father's sister's husband. A man seeks help and advice from his wife's father and there are cases of uxorilocal residences. A man's attitude towards his mother-in-law is one of circumspection. There is complete avoidance between a son-in-law and mother-in-law. The attitude and behaviour of various kin among the Soliga shows that the forest ecology moulds them to live independently in early age and this independence helps them to maintain good relations and less tension among different kin.

THE LIFE CYCLE PROCESS

In Nature's lap, a Soliga grows as a child, attains adulthood, makes love, and dies. Therefore, Nature, or the forest ecology, in this case, dominates in all spheres of various stages of one's life. It is realized that a person has to pass through the various phases of the life cycle, interacting as an individual self, a member of the family, and the local community, and also beyond. The Soliga fervently believe that acts of birth and death are creations of God (*devaru* or *swamy*), and therefore it is necessary to appease God.

Birth of a child

Child birth takes place in the house of the pregnant woman. The pregnant woman works till the advanced stages, and there is no wonder if she gives birth to a child in the forest while collecting tubers. It is said that a pregnant woman knows how to cut the umbilical cord by a sharp bamboo split. A pregnant woman usually does not leave her house for fear of the 'evil eye' of spirits that abound in Nature, which may do harm to the mother and child. Before childbirth, elders take a pregnant woman to their local shrines and offer worship and pray to the deities for a safe delivery. After the birth of a child, the navel cord and other matter are taken up to a distant place and are safely buried in a bamboo thicket. A woman is given a concoction, a local variety of *acacia concinna* leaves mixed in a large quantity of pepper and salt for three days continuously for speedy recovery.

The woman and her husband have to observe birth pollution (*tume*) for four or five days and then a purificatory ceremony is observed. The entire house is cleaned, plastered with earth. The old earthen vessels are thrown away and fresh ones are bought. Worship is done to the family deities. Then a name is given to the child, usually of one of their deities.

Weaning

Children are breast-fed for nearly two years. In case a woman does not have enough milk after the delivery, she is given the paste of *halusora* (a milk yielding plant) so that there would be a good flow of milk. The mother takes ample care till the child grows to one year. Occasionally a bath is given to the child by applying castor oil all over the body. Castor is grown in plenty in their own swidden fields.

As a socialization process the boys learn various activities of their fathers while wandering in the forest, collecting roots, wild fruits, honey, tracking small animals etc. Their love for forest life, and least contact with outsiders make the Soliga grow up as individuals with some sense of isolation, and therefore they largely mind their own business.

Puberty

Attaining puberty by a girl is an important event and is attended by certain rituals and ceremonies. When a girl attains puberty she is segregated for five days. A *gummi* (separate hut) is built by her prospective husband, if any, or by a man of different clan. A young girl remains with the menstruating girl during the period giving her company. A sickle (*udugilu*) is given to the woman for protection against evil spirits. The observance of puberty is known as *hosage*. When the girl returns from the pond after the bath on the fourth day of the first menstruation, she is clothed in new garments gifted by her parents. The girl is then lead to the centre of the house and young children are made to be seated on the lap of the girl and prayers to the deities are made. The girl is fed first with the ceremonial meal consisting of ragi balls, rice and chicken curry and then others partake of the food. The symbolic seating of children on the lap of the girl suggests the begetting of children.

Marriage

There are four types of selection of mates prevalent among the Soliga, namely, (1) Marriage by force ; (2) Elopement ; (3) Marriage by service ; and (4) Negotiated or arranged marriage. For all the three areas, the tabulated data for the marriages which were held within a period of 10 years (1966-1976) shows that the incidence of marriage by elopement is high in the two hilly and forested areas (B. R. Hills and Bedaguli) while the negotiated marriage dominates the scene in Ponnachi village. In the forest environment, the Soliga boys and girls come in contact with each other, and without much difficulty they can enter into matrimony on their own volition and later, such marriages are 'ratified' by a feast to the community.

Divorce and desertion

A woman is deserted on the ground of unfaithfulness generally.

Death and Funerary Rites

Death is a shocking event for the entire community, although the individual families are affected severely. The Soliga believe that ritual impurity (*tume*) will result on account of death (as also in the case of birth). The (*tume*) will not only affect the members of a family where the death has occurred but also to the entire community of 5-clan Soliga. If the death is due to old age, and physical causes like diseases, the Soliga take it as natural phenomena. When a person is dead, all close kin and elders of the tribal council are informed about it, and when they arrive, various ceremonies are observed and the dead body is interned in the forest grave (*sagga*), usually a fixed place. In the event of unnatural death like being trade upon by an elephant, or fall from a tree, which do occur occasionally, a specific ritual known as *ravu kattuvadu* (binding the spirit) is observed. An earthen image of an elephant is made if the death has occurred due to elephant's trading, and the image is smashed on the spot, where the person had been killed by the animal. A chicken is sacrificed at the spot. All the food articles, including the meat of the chicken are placed near the mishap.

A ritual known as *hinde kulu* is done on the 6th, 9th or 12th day. This is observed in order to remove the ritual impurity. If it is not done within the specified time, the spirit of the dead is supposed to haunt the place of death. The observance of the ritual takes place near a water source close to the settlement where the death has occurred. At least one member from each of the five clans participates. The area where the ritual is performed, is cleared of the bushes, and the ritual meal consisting of rice, ragi balls, and chicken curry are cooked. Samples of each item are kept in a basket for offering to the spirit of the dead. Around the basket five leaves with leafcups containing ritual food are also placed. Meanwhile one of the elders prepares the 'stone image' (*kallugombe*), which symbolizes the spirit of the dead. Certain ceremonies follow when the chief mourner holds the stone image he goes into trance as a mark of possession of the spirit of the dead. When he returns to normalcy, the ritual meal is offered to the spirit of the dead. Later the meal is served to all assembled. The stone image is kept in a hollow of a tree. It is taken ceremonially to the ancestral shrine (*kallu gudi*) where the final ritual of placing it is done.

In brief, the rites of passage of the Soliga are inter-related with Nature, Man and beliefs of the Supernatural. The childhood environment helps them adjust to the ecological structure, and their adulthood with their subsistence activities. While the social structure provides them to strengthen solidarity in their family and kinship behaviour, their socialization process help them maintain a close inter-relationship with natural surroundings and human endeavour. The Soliga lead a life in the forests most of the time and this affects them in their day-to-day life. Their marriage which is mostly in the form of elopement does not bring any unnecessary strain on their sex life. When boys and girls come of age, they choose their own mates and begin to live independently. From birth to death, various rituals are observed in order to appease gods and spirits. Thus the Soliga have to make adjustment with the norms and values of their culture interacting with Nature.

RELIGION

In the hilly and forested ecological setting the Soliga are exclusively dependent upon the supernatural world. In their various activities such as selecting a new site for a *podu* cultivation, setting up a hut there, cultivation, or in life cycle ceremonies, the belief in the supernatural and the spirit-world is prominently seen. The supernatural beings can be broadly classified into two categories ; viz., I. Benevolent, and II. Malevolent. The first category includes : 1. Gods 2. Adavi Devaru 3. Mane Devaru 4. Melu Devaru 5. Mother Goddess 6. Karayya Swamy and 7. Ancestral spirits. The malevolent spirits include, 1. Deyya and Deyti and 2. Mariamma, and Masanamma.

The Gods

The generic word *devaru* (*swamy*) is used for the gods. The idea of belief in gods takes deep root in their socialization process. At every action, reference to the gods is made and the priests not only speak of gods, but also possession of gods in their person. Since everyone takes part in each ritual function, singing and dancing in some way, the faith that the gods are protectors of human beings in all calamities is irrevocable. The priest (*tammadi*) is considered as god-incarnate when he is in a trance and gives divine oracles and cures diseases and wards off evil influences of malefic spirits through the benevolence of the gods.

Adavi Devaru

While *Devaru* is a generic term, there are certain specific gods. These gods are supposed to live in forests, exclusively, and hence they are referred to as *Adavi Devaru* very frequently. These are, namely, Madeswar, Basaveswar, Kumbeswar, Jadeswamy and Kete Devaru. Various stone-representations in the forest are recognized as one or the other form of the gods named above. As legend has it, god Siva is believed to have been born as Madeswar Swamy, killed a demon named Sravan, and brought peace to the gods and human beings. Madeswar Swamy had adopted two sons of a Soliga couple of which one was Karayya. The latter is considered to be the ancestor of the Soliga, and Madeswar Swamy is revered as the God of the Soliga.

There are also other forms of god Siva, such as Basava (bull), Kumba (place name) etc. and they are also deified by the Soliga. Jadeswamy is the most important god who is conceptualized as the son of god Siva with 101 *jade* (lock of hair on the head) and is a powerful deity. In his honour the fire walking ceremony is observed at the time of *Rotti Habba* when the priest has to observe certain taboos like fasting, abstinence etc. Any lapse on his part may make him get burnt during the fire walking ceremony.

The Ketedevaru is stated to be the god who protects the Soliga from any calamity coming from outside. This god is conceived as a human being, seated on a white horse, dressed in trousers. The human form wears long boots, cap on the head, and holds a loaded musket, on the shoulder. In many settlements shrines for this god are built and various rituals are observed by the priests.

Mane Devaru

In some Soliga houses there are deities (inherited) which are referred to as *mane devaru* (family deities) and are enshrined in a corner of the house. The sacred objects used in the ritual worship of these deities are kept in a cane basket, which is known as *hadagu* and these are 1. female figurines made of bronze 2. spine of a boa 3. conch shell 4. gong 5. some vessels 6. stone *linga* (phallisimbol) etc. The feminine figurines have no names, but these are also included among the family deities. Worshipping of the family deities is compulsory at the time of the *Hosa Ragi Habba*. The entire lineage members are involved during such worship. Failure to perform worship bring harm to members of the family who keep the family deities. Vows (*harake*) are made to them for redressal of any difficulties. If the vows are not fulfilled the family deities are supposed to do harm. The family deities can also bring harm to enemy, either by inflicting physical harm, or causing death, if the ritual of 'burning incence' is done as stated earlier.

Melu Devaru

There are a few gods and goddesses which are worshipped by the neighbouring Hindu communities. The Soliga also worship them. They, however, refer to these gods as *melu devaru* i.e. superior gods. They often make reference to these gods in their invocation prayers to their deities. God Siva is worshipped in the form of Linga, a Saiva, (phallic) symbol, with *Trisul*—a trident spear. The Soliga pantheon consists of forms of god Siva, such as Nanjundeswara, Mallikarjuno, whose temples are found in the plains-villages like Nanjangud, Mudukutore etc. God Rangaswamy at the Temple village is considered as an incarnation of Vishnu. But for the Soliga He is the *bhuva* (brother-in-law) as He was supposed to have eloped with a Soliga woman. The Soliga consider Rangaswamy also as a forest god and when they observe any ritual in their own habitats they offer non-vegetarian food. But when they go to the temple in B.R. Hills they offer only the vegetarian articles of food, like cocoanut and fruits and return home with the *prasad* (consecrated articles) given at the temple by the Brahmin priest.

Mother Goddess

The earth is considered as mother and worshipped as mother earth (*bhumi tayi*). During sowing operations in a swidden field, prayers are made to the deity and a blood offering is made for plentiful yield.

Karayya swamy

As Karayya had helped god Madeswar to kill Sravana, the latter had ordained that the first worship was reserved for Karayya before He was worshipped. Since then Karayya has also become a hero. There are several shrines dedicated to him in Madeswar Hills, B.R. Hills and Bedaguli. Celebration to these shrines takes place in April every year. Only vegetarian offerings are made. Karayya Swamy is also considered as a forest god, but he has a special role as an ancestor. The Soliga proudly call themselves as his children.

Ancestral spirits

The dead are forgotten when their stone images (*kallu gombe*) are placed ceremoniously in the *kallugudi*. But they are remembered as a group of spirits. They consider it necessary to offer these spirits some food when certain ceremonies in a house are performed. The ancestral spirits are generally regarded as benevolent. They may, however, turn malevolent, if they are not offered food. As a form of appeasing ancestral spirits a handful of rice, ragi balls are thrown outside the house, on every ritual and festive occasion and a prayer is uttered, thus : 'let the ancestral spirits who might have come be satisfied with our offerings'.

Malevolent spirits

The spirits which are evil in character and do harm to human beings on malicious whims are termed as the *deyya* (male) and *deyti* (female). While the deyya and deyti are so powerful that they might kill human beings, there are also spirits of lesser evil, called as *peede* and *pichach*. The ancestral spirits, which cause disease and death are described by the term *gali*, i.e., wind. The wind spirits are supposed to dwell in the *sagga* (grave-yard) or in the *kallugudi* shrine.

In almost all parts of mountains and forests some kind of malefic spirits are believed to exist. Therefore they are propitiated at the time of *pairu puje* (worship of plants). On giant trees like mango, *sorevu*, the spirits are known by the term *muni* or *muneswar*. These spirits are supposed to be invisible and they cause diseases or death if any one unknowingly passes by such a tree alone. In water sources, spirits of water, i.e. *neerubhut* exist, but they are less harmful. Evil influences of spirits and *muni* can be treated by a priest-diviner (*tammadi*) by divination and worship.

Mariamma and masanamma

There are twin spirits, viz., Mariamma and Masanamma which are defined by all communities in southern Mysore, including the areas where the Soliga live. Both these spirits have the reputation of creating harm to human beings, if they are not properly propitiated. Mariamma is the spirit controlling small pox and cholera diseases, while Masanamma, who is supposed to be present in grave-yards and to cause diseases of all kinds. In order to prevent occurrence of diseases, the Soliga observe a festival, *marihabba* every year, or alternatively once in three years, and offer animal sacrifice. If the Soliga want to remove the evil effects of Masanamma, propitiation is done to her by offering an animal sacrifice.

MAGIC, WITCHCRAFT AND SORCERY

The Soliga believe in the occult power of magical experts and its harmful effects on non-tribal human beings and other tribal people (like the Kurumba). There are no witches or magicians among the Soliga. They, however, know of some supernatural power causing harm. This power is supposed to be existing in the family deities. If a ritual of 'burning the incense' to the family deities with a prayer to cause harm to enemies is performed, there are sure effects of the victim suffering disease or death. Recourse to such action is taken only when a particular Soliga has stolen ragi or other articles of another Soliga. Such cases are very few.

The religious beliefs of the Soliga presented above are based on the Supernatural Spirit World. A term 'Spiritism' is used by Vidyarthi (1963; p.140) for those beliefs which are embedded in the existence of deities and spirits of different forms which are existing in Nature. The spirits require constant appeasement in almost every walk of life, and thus the intensive interaction of the spirits with Nature and Society determines the particular way of life of the Soliga.

SACRED COMPLEX

In this section it would be interesting to examine the concept of the 'sacred complex' proposed by Vidyarthi (1963) as constituting Sacred Geography, Sacred Performances, and Sacred Specialists. The Yarakanagadde settlement in B.R. Hills forms the basis for the present description.

Sacred geography

There are two sacred centres in Yarakanagadde settlement—one in the northern and the other in the southern end. In the sketch map of the settlement, prepared for the study, all the details are shown. The shrines are called as *gudi*. The first one is the Ketedevara Gudi and the second one is the Basaveswarana Gudi. A hut is built with bamboo and thatched with *bane* grass. Inside the shrine, a raised platform is made, on which sacred objects like canestick, with silver rings, wooden footwear with iron spikes are kept. There are also other articles, like stone Linga, brass plate, bell, images of the sacred bull, elephant, some sacred ash, trident-spear etc. The shrines are built at some distance from the cluster of houses. In front of the Basaveswarana Gudi, a *tare* (beleric myrobalan) tree stands, and beneath it a few sacred objects like tridents, a black stone Linga daubed with vermilion marks are enshrined, which represent god Saniswar. Normally when the settlements are shifted from one place to another, the Soliga take their deities and build shrines for them afresh. The deities in shrines are worshipped on every Monday by the priests.

At some 200 yards in the south-eastern direction in Yarakanagadde there is a place near a pond where the Soliga dead are buried. This is called as the *sagga* which is considered to be the abode of spirits. A place situated at some 300 yards from the burial ground, is specially earmarked for keeping the stone images of the dead. This is the place of *kallu gudi*, where the stone images of the dead belonging to a lineage of the Belloru clan are placed. The Soliga go to this place only when they have to place the stone image of a dead ancestor and on no other occasion do they visit the area for fear of spirits.

A certain place is earmarked where a festival of Mariamma is observed every year. The place is situated in the eastern end near the pond. The Soliga of Yarakanagadde observe the festival by making contributions from its members annually.

In the east-west direction there is a big pond, called Someswarana Kere. The metalled deputies of god Rangaswamy with his two consorts are taken in procession once a year to the pond, in a bamboo float prepared by the Soliga. There is a stone pavilion, *mantapa,* where the deputies are enshrined. The festival is called *teppotsava.* The Soliga attend in large numbers drawn from different settlements. Whenever a headman is to be selected, it is done here. The mantapa was in earlier days used as a "sitting place" (*katte*) for the tribals to have their meetings and consider any auspicious matter, such as fixation of dates for festivals, or for marriage.

There is another place near the pond situated in the western end known as Lingayyana Katte. It was built long ago, with a view to provide drinking water to wild animals by the former landlord of the area. Near the pond, there is a *katte* (sitting place), where in earlier days, the Soliga elders used to have their meetings. This was a particularly important place, for they used to decide cases which came under the category of inauspicious matters, like ostracising a person, deciding dates for observance of funerary rituals etc.

In so far as Yarakanagadde settlement of the Soliga was concerned, the above items constitute its 'sacred geography'. But in B.R. Hills forest area, there are also other sacred centres. For example, there are shrines of different forest gods (*adavi devaru*) in different settlements, such as Jodeswamy in Purani, Guruvinagadde and Doddare and huge champaca tree near Doddare. In these shrines, a sacred performance, known as 'fire walking' ceremony is a special feature, which is held every year. There are shrines of Basaveswar in two places in which the deities are invoked to get rains in case of drought in the area. There is a hillock near Doddare settlement, known by the name of Karrayya swamy. A priest offers worship twice a year during the *Hosa Ragi Habba* and *Rotti Para* celebrations. There are other places in B.R. Hills where spirits are supposed to dwell. During 'worship of plants' offerings to all kinds of spirits are made which also include spirits of these places. The place Guruvinagadde is considered to be the sacred place of god

Madeswar where he had stayed. Another version is that god Rangaswamy had eloped with a Soliga girl from this place and hence it is a sacred place.

Sacred performances

The spirits of all kinds are invoked and propitiated by performing several rituals like worship, prayer, making vows, and offering vegetarian and non-vegetarian food etc. These various rituals can be considered as 'sacred performances'. The objectives of such sacred performances are clear. That the gods and deities give their blessings if they are appeased by elaborate rituals. Spirits are to be satiated. Failure to do so leads to harmful effects by their wrath. For example, the benevolent spirits may not do much harm if one is not able to perform a particular ritual but in the case of evil spirits, if they were not satiated, disease or death are likely effects for the defaulters. So sacred performances are essential.

The sacred performances take place at five different levels, namely, 1. individual 2. family and lineage 3. settlement (podu) 4. the B.R. Hills (a sacred area) and 5. outside the area. A person makes vows to a particular god or deity and offers prayers to overcome difficulties. In such cases the gods invoked are Madeswar, Ketedevaru, and Jadeswamy. A person afflicted with any difficulties, approaches a priest (*tammadi*). Mondays, Fridays and Saturdays are the days when the priests perform *puje* (worship) for fulfilling the 'vows' of an individual. Individuals are 'devotees (*bhakta*)' of the gods. The devotees offer vegetarian food to the above deities.

Hosa Ragi Habba

At the family and lineage level, the sacred performance observed in however of the family deities (*mane devaru*) is called *hosa ragi habba*, i.e., new ragi eating festival. When ragi is ripe for cutting, the stalks are cut and stacked in a store house. The head of the family having family deities decides a date for observing the ceremony. He consults a priest in the settlement. All agnatic kin from different settlements are invited to attend the ceremony. It is customary for one and all to keep some share of their grain to give to their family deities. Some quantity of new ragi grown in their swidden fields is threshed and flour is made.

As part of the celebration, old earthen pots etc. in the house where the performance takes place are thrown away and new ones are bought. The house is plastered with mud or cowdung. The male members get a clean shave by a barber, or one Soliga might shave another, if the barber is not available. On the occasion a ritual bath with hot water, applying castor oil on their body is invariably taken. New clothes are worn. Women also take a bath and wear new clothes. The performer and his wife have to remain on fast till the ritual is over. They cannot take meat on the previous night. The couple have also to observe abstinence on the previous night.

The ritual meal consisting of vegetarian food such as *hittu* (cooked ragi flour), *avare*, curry mixed with pumpkin and jack fruit is prepared. Men cook the meal. When the meal is ready, the chief worshipper performs an elaborate ritual for the family deities and when this is over he calls upon all the members of his lineage to pray to their family deities. The chief worshipper goes into trance several times and utters some words which are taken as oracles. At that time, those who do not belong to the lineage also can pray and can seek blessings of the deities. When the worship is over, the meal is offered to the deities, and then all the people are fed with the ritual meal. After this, there will be singing by men and women during the whole night. This is done in some cases as per the tradition. It was observed that at every interval of one or two hours the chief worshipper went into trance and uttered oracles when devotees seek redressal for their numerous troubles. When the day breaks the chief worshipper sees the Sun God and announces the end of the ceremony.

After the ceremony, the new ragi can be eaten by all. The ceremony is very important because the Soliga for the first time offer food to deities in gratitude after completion of the swidden cultivation. It is also the ritual to pray to the deities to give them good yield of ragi, which would be harvested a month later.

Rotti Habba

Members in each of the Soliga settlements join together to a celebration known as the *rotti habba* (offering of bread). It is held in the months of March and April. The local sacred shrines are the venue. Usually a few elders in a settlement visit different Soliga settlements and ask devotees to give some ragi for the ceremony. Each family usually keeps a certain quantity of ragi earmarked for each deity like Ketedevaru, Jadeswamy, Madeswara which is given on such occasions. In all shrines, except Jadeswamy, the ritual celebration constitutes only the *puje* (worship) but in the Jadeswamy shrine, there will be a 'fire walking' ceremony which is a special feature. The priests of all settlements in B.R. Hills are invited. The priests attend the celebration with the ritual insignia of deities, like umbrella, sacred axe, saffron coloured flag, sacred ash, cymbals etc.

A pandal with five poles out of which one will be in the centre is built in front of the shrine. The prominent feature of the sacred performance is the baking of *rotti* (unleavened bread) in the ritual fire. At some distance, a fire is made in which flat breads (*rotti*) made out of the ragi flour are pressed onto the leaves of Muttuga or Kooge tree and roasted in the fire. These breads are made in a state of ritual purity, i.e., after taking a bath and wearing washed clothes and being untouched by anybody. When a 'fire walking' ceremony is observed a fire 18′ in length, 3′ in breadth, and 1′ in height is made. In other places, where no such 'fire walking' ceremony is observed the fire made is only a small heap where breads can be roasted. A separate fire is made for cooking other items of the ritual meal, like rice, vegetable curry etc. A Lingayat priest (Jangama Guru) from a plains-village is invited to perform certain initial rites such as enshrining a copper pot. (This is the influence of the Lingayat sect.) Later the pot is installed in the sanctum sanctorum of the Soliga shrine and then worship is made to all the sacred objects of the deity enshrined in the place. After the worship the priest goes into trance, and walks on the embers of the fire made for the occasion. The Lingayat Guru also follows him and so also a few courageous devotees. The ritual meal is offered on Muttuga leaves to the gods, including Adavi Devaru, Melu Devaru, Karayya Swamy and others. There will be offerings of cocoanut, and plantains by devotees. The priest comes out and places a curtain in front of the deities. This marks the taking of food by the deities, not to be seen by mortals. There will be another round of worship, when the priest goes into trance and reveals the divine oracles to devotees, about how they conducted the worship, whether it was held properly or not, and also promises ample harvest for the next year, and the well being of all the people who had gone there to attend. After this the ritual meal is served to all.

The next part of the ritual is to invoke the gods by singing prayers and by dancing. It is also an occasion of merriment as the Soliga get some leisure now. While older people, both men and women, sit on vantage points to watch the dancing the young boys dance on the occasion. Girls do not join in the dancing, but give a chorus. During the course of dancing boys joke with the girls. The occasion provides opportunity for the young boys and girls to know each other which may ultimately culminate in elopement and marriage. This goes on throughout the night. There are intermittent interruptions by the priests who suddenly go into trance and pronounce divine oracles. The ritual ends at sunrise.

Other sacred performances

In the hilly and forested areas the Soliga sometimes face droughts and at other times excessive rainfall. Both are harmful to their subsistence activities. Therefore, there are certain performances which help 'make-rains' and 'stop-rains'. For 'making-rains', it is necessary that the forest god, Basaveswar whose shrines are situated in the forest as said earlier, is to be worshipped. When the Soliga feel that there were signs of drought, they decide to observe the ritual. It is done by applying plenty of honey (which they collect in the forest) on the Linga. They pray to God so that He should bless them with rains within a period of three to eight days. If the god blesses with rains, then they go there and offer the usual worship, and remove the honey. Otherwise they would never go that way which would imply that the god would suffer from the ant bites due to the application of the honey.

In the case of 'stopping' excessive rains, a Soliga priest or any elder can act as a functionary. The person who conducts the ritual goes to a secluded place on top of a hill and would place the barks of a *bhootala* tree on a rock there. By means of an axe he strikes the barks severely, standing in the rains. While doing the ritual he has to be completely naked, removing even the girdle-thread and also he has to hold his breath. The rains are supposed to stop instantaneously.

A few salient features of the sacred performances of the Soliga can be analysed. The various sacred performances are done at every level right from an individual to the community in relation to their interaction with natural and social environment as well as with the spirit world. The offerings are mainly vegetarian except in some cases of agricultural operations, and rituals for evil spirits. At the community level, the expenses are shared and the ritual meals are also shared. But when an individual has to perform a propitiation ritual to his family deities, he has to meet the expenses with other members of his lineage. Irrespective of the expenses, it is obligatory on the individual to perform the worship to family deities annually without fail. Otherwise, it is believed that harm will come not only to members of his family, but also to all those who belong to his lineage.

It was noted that the sacred performances done at the community level, like the observance of *Rotti Habba*, strengthen the solidarity of the group. The welfare of the community is the sole objective of performing the celebration on a big scale and inviting people of the group from different settlements.

In the case of worship of malevolent spirits like the Deyya and Deyti, and the spirits of the dead, and also Maramma, and various spirits in Nature, fowl and goats are offered to appease them. This appeasement in the form of blood offerings is absolutely necessary to have beneficial results as these spirits are blood-thirsty. Among the vegetarian offerings, ragi forms the major item. Along with it, curry made out of *avare* pulse and pumpkin fruit are of great importance. The festivals are observed at the time when these items grow except maize, which is not included in the ritual itinerary due to its origin.

In almost all sacred performances, the priest (*tammadi*) is possessed by the gods and pronounces oracles. When a priest is in trance, he uses the sacred axe for striking his stomach several times with its blade, but no harm comes to him because the god is behind to be in his person. The priest regains consciousness after he has made forecasts to his devotees. Thus, with the help of sacred performances, the Soliga overcome the difficulties that befall them due to the creations of supernatural and human elements.

The sacred specialists

The ritual functionaries who do various sacred performances are "Sacred Specialists". Among the Soliga, the sacred specialists are found at two levels, viz. one at the family level and the other at the level of a settlement. When sacred performances are done by a family deities, the head of the family acts as the sacred specialist. There are certain taboos such as observance of strict fast on the day of the worship, and abstinence on the previous night. The sacred specialist cannot perform the function if his wife is menstruating, and also if there was accrual of ritual impurity due to death or birth in the house. The sacred specialist decides the dates of sacred performances only after considering all these factors, and also the convenience of the members of his lineage group who are co-sharers of such worship.

The other important sacred specialist is the *tammadi*, the priest. Usually each Podu, i.e., a settlement of the Soliga, will have one or two shrines of gods and also the priests for worshipping them. While the *tammadi* does the sacred performances in a shrine, he functions also as a man prophesying the future, curing diseases and warding off spirits which possess individuals, etc. There are some priests who are also diviners.

Methods of divination

There are two methods of divination practised by the sacred specialist in this area, namely (1) *kani heluvadu* and (2) *gunji shastra*. In the case of *kani heluvadu* the diviner manipulates cowries and forecasts results. Nine cowries are used for the purpose. A *tammadi* will first pray to the deity (usually Madeswar and other forest gods) of which he is the priest, and then throws the cowries on the floor three times in quick succession. The *tammadi* then counts consecutively the number of cowries falling on the floor upturned, and then forecast good or bad aspects accordingly. Another important method of divination among the Soliga is the *gunji shastra*.

The operation of *gunji shastra* is done at night. A special kind of winnowing fan, called as *gunji mora* is used for the operation of *gunji* (*obrus precatorius*) seeds. The other articles required are an earthen lamp, incense, and a kilogram of ragi grains. The *tammadi* calls his devotees who want divination inside the shrine, or house. He offers prayers to the deities, and lights a lamp. He burns incense of a wild variety. He puts three handful of *gunji* seeds in the *gunji mora*. Then he invokes the Gurus (teachers), god Siva and other gods. He begins the operation of *gunji* seeds in quick succession. The *gunji mora* is covered on all the four sides and a broad opening is made from the top. Unless the *gunji mora* is turned topsy turvy, the seeds do not fall. As the priest goes on operating the *gunji mora*, he goes on asking several questions, about the cause of the trouble. While operating the *gunji mora*, peculiar sound of the *gunji* seeds like *kolak*, *kolak* is heard, but suddenly the sound is not heard and it is supposed that the seeds stick to the *gunji mora* and won't fall even if held topsy turvy. The operation continues to the astonishment of the devotee and the seeds make no sound whatever. The *tammadi* has got the answer now. Once again, he operates the winnow. He gives his solutions like offering a *puje*, and the devotee accepts his direction. The seeds separate and the divination is over.

The sacred specialists are also supposed to take interest in the internal affairs and in the breach of customary laws of the community. The *tammadi* when necessary speaks out during the deliberations of a tribal council meeting, and his words carry weight while deciding a case, though the headman is the final authority to deal with such matters. While in Yarakanagadde the priest diviner does not bother to take active interest in the affairs of the tribe due to old age, but the priest diviner in Bedaguli plays a more dominating role in taking up issues relating to the community.

The sacred performances done by a sacred specialist are more in tune with the traditions of the cult of Madeswar. The cult of Madeswar has incorporated several Veera Saiva sectarian ideologies like worship of god Siva in various manifestations, and vegetarianism, songs, ritual objects etc. It is in a way the characteristic of "local tradition" as various ideas have greater ritual content of the "local traditions" spread by Madeswar when he systematized the religious structure of the Soliga. If we go by legendary account, their ancestor, Karayya Swamy, who was an ardent disciple of Madeswar was the main person to superimpose the traditional religious beliefs which perhaps was founded in animism. The sacred geography, sacred performances, and sacred specialists of Yarakanagadde for example show that the whole gamut of the "sacred complex", when culturally considered is of "little traditional" or "local traditional" content.

If briefly recapitulated, in the discussion given in the foregoing pages on the religious aspects, certain features emerge, preeminently. The Soliga believe in the existence of Spirits which are capable of doing both harm and good. The conception of the supreme god, doing good to human beings overrides and this factor makes them propitiate and observe several rituals to get redressal from the influence of malefic spirits. There are several sacred centres with their deities, which are systematically cared for and the deities are approached in the event of any trouble, either it is destruction of crops by wild animals, or the supernatural cause of disease. The sacred performances take full care of the difficulties, and bestow blessings to achieve personal well being, family welfare, lineage link, increase of crops, and also the community safety. The sacred specialist sing acts as the caretaker of sacred shrines, and does the sacred performances. The sacred complex of a local community, largely reflects its relationship with the physical environment (ecology), economic activities, and the supernatural beings.

SUMMARY AND CONCLUSION

From the foregoing analysis it may be stated that the attempt in this brief paper is to present a study on the Soliga covering virtually all aspects of their culture, ethnographically, and also to focus on the inter-relationship between ecology, society, and religion. This was considered to be a departure from the usual traditional tribal studies. While excessive theorizing is not attempted, certain concepts of the "Nature-Man-Spirit Complex" (Vidyarthi : 1963) and "Tribe, Caste and Peasant continua" (Sinha : 1965) were utilised in the original study.

The Soliga of B.R. Hills and Bedaguli live in a harsh environment which in this context implies ecological features such as hilly terrain, dense forest, intensive cold weather, excessive rain, terrain, lack of communication, inaccessibility of the area, flora, fauna etc. In the struggle for existence, the Soliga have to have ecological adaptation. The term ecological adaptation means that it is the interaction of certain important features of environment on human life such as subsistence activities and techniques, settlement pattern and socio-cultural arrangements.

The Soliga of B.R. Hills and Bedaguli follow the method of shifting cultivation. A new habitat is looked for mainly to secure sites for swidden cultivation. The local communities are formed and changed due to availability of such sites. The settlement pattern is largely guided by the factors of formation, shuffling and reshuffling of families. A small isolated and dispersed pattern of settlement is the characteristic of shifting cultivators. The sparse density is also one of the factors responsible for determining the settlement pattern. The activities revolve round cultivating the millets. There are many difficulties in the forest ecology, where especially they have to face the depredations of wild animals which destroy crops. The swidden fields are very small, ranging from about 2 to 3 acres. The labour input is limited as only members of one's family actively engage themselves in the swidden activities. The technology consists of a simple dibbling stick, axe and hoe. One's family members put in ample efforts in the cultivation process. During the cultivation period which will be about 6 months beginning from April to October, they are engaged in other activities. While maize is harvested in September, ragi is reaped in November, and harvested in January. But the maize and ragi become ready for consumption after their harvest. The forest ecology provides for their subsistence certain forest produce which can be collected and sold for cash or bartered in exchange for food articles, besides tubers, fruits, leaves and honey for their direct consumption.

There has been a clear cut division of labour between the sexes. Women mainly take up agricultural work, collection of tubers, looking after children, and attending to domestic work. Men do the hard jobs of working as forest labourers and collection of minor forest produce, bringing firewood, trapping small animals etc. The produce that they get from their swidden cultivation, after giving to their kin a handsome amount of grain for performing rituals for family and shrine deities, and paying credits is very meagre. The Soliga struggle hard to prevent destruction of the crops from wild animals by invoking supernatural powers.

In their social structure the basic unit of the society is a nuclear family. The family is monogamous. A house is built in the swidden field where members of one's nuclear family live. In all activities, members of one's own family participate but when some help during building a house is required, co-operation comes from members of one's patrilineage. There are clans which have certain functions. Lineage in a clan are formed with one's immediate ancestor. Usually a lineage is reckoned through 3 generations and it consists of an average of 4 to 6 nuclear families. Except while participating in ritual observances at the *Hosa Ragi Habba*, when the family deities are worshipped, and at the ceremony of placing the 'stone figure' of the dead in the *kallu gudi*, the lineage has no other functions.

The rites of passage of the Soliga have their own traditional features. The mode of selection of a mate is largely by elopement and such unions are 'ratified' by a feast. Desertions used to be more frequent in earlier times, but the Soliga couple may not like to desert now-a-days. Perhaps this is an aspect of change. Widow remarriage is common. Matri- and patrilateral cross-cousin marriage is permissible though the frequency of their occurrence is less. Uncle-niece marriage does not prevail. Polygamous marriages used to occur, but polyandrous marriages do not take place. Ritual impurity accrues during birth and death and until purificatory ceremonies are held, the whole group is affected by ritual pollution. The death rituals specifically show that they strongly believe in the existence of the spirit of the dead, and until the spirit is placed in the lineage shrine (*kallu gudi*) the members of the family where death has occurred are not free from the wrath of the spirit of the dead.

The beliefs and practices of the Soliga regarding supernatural beings shows the devotion and anxiety of the people at the level of socio-cultural integration. The religious notions with their benevolent and malevolent spirits, and the nature of the "Sacred Complex" clearly indicate that a small, and isolated tribal culture interacts deeply with Nature. All kinds of offerings are made to express their gratitude when they get beneficence from the spirits and also to those spirits which are basically malevolent. There has been greater impact of the cult of Madeswar which has come into prominence during the 14th or 15th century in their religious behaviour and in worshipping and offering of vegetarian articles. Sometimes animal sacrifice is resorted to in keeping with their traditoinal core culture.

Culture contact with other cultures has affected the Soliga. In some cases like the Soliga of Purani settlement in B.R. Hills certain changes in their economic organization and life-style have occurred. The tribals have taken up plough agriculture and peasant economy. In Yarakanagadde, the tribals were rehabilitated in a tribal colony a few years ago, and lands were given to many but the process of acculturation had not made any significant dent. Because of their deep interaction and inter-relationship with the forest ecology, the Soliga did not stay in the colony for a long time. Most of the Soliga there still depend upon shifting cultivation and collection of forest produces.

Though the Soliga have been interacting with the people of the Temple village in B.R. Hills for some time the superficial contact has not made them accept all innovations, except the school. But the latter facility did not continue as the voluntary agency for tribal education backed out. In Ponnachi, the Soliga have long become a group incorporating many features of a peasant caste. The transformation process from shifting agriculture to peasant agriculture was rapid in their case. The interaction of the Soliga with their neighbours, shows that in so far as socio-cultural integration and techno-economic levels were concerned, they have been drifting towards the ideal caste/peasant pole, proposed by Sinha (1965).

The thrust of the study is to show how a tribal culture in a particular eco-system adapts itself to the ecological structure, and similarly, the social institutions take up the challenges of ecology; what the economic situation is like under such conditions, and whether the religious structure has any part to play when it interacts with ecology, economy and social institutions.

The foregoing analysis clearly indicates that where ecology plays a dominant role in an eco-system, with the economic activities more dependent upon the ecology, then the inter-relationship to Nature-Man becomes more intimate and deep. In that case structural changes occur very slowly. To elaborate the point, the Soliga living in various interior Podu (settlements) depend completely on the forest ecology for their subsistence. But the process of acculturation, peasantization, and acceptance of innovation is slow. Let us take the case of Purani settlement situated at some distance from the Soliga concentration in B. R. Hills and in very close proximity to the peasant villages at the foot-hills. There the tribals are finding it difficult to get more areas for their *podu* (swidden) cultivation and hence, they have taken to peasant agriculture. The Soliga families like to live here permanently, and depend not only on cultivation, but also take to other activities such as agricultural labour, domestication of cattle etc. Here changes have come up in their techno-economic level and life-style though the process is slow. In Ponnachi the Soliga are no more dependent upon the forest ecology, but they have taken up peasant agriculture and peasant economy and are staying in a permanent village. They have been assimilated into their neighbouring peasant culture.

To sum up, the Soliga in their struggle for survival, interact with ecology (Nature) and there is mutual inter-relationship with the social system on the one hand, and the religion (spirit) on the other. There are differences in their interaction as well as interdependence, when the ecology or environment covary, and such situations are helpful in understanding a society, in a different ecological context. The study of the Soliga of Ponnachi village which is far removed spatially from the other areas was made where the socio-cultural environment and ecological structure are different.

It has been shown that the Soliga living in rather inaccessible areas of B. R. Hills and Bedaguli depend more intensively on the forest ecology and hence their inter-relationship and interaction with society and religion is mutual and interdependent. The Soliga have developed a particular style of life, in the type of Nature-Man-Spirit, to borrow Vidyarthi's terminology (1963, ibid, p.179), with their own ecological context, cultural experiences and ideological belief system. Thus it gives ample evidence to prove that, by and large, the concept of Nature-Man-Spirit Complex is quite relevant in the specific ecological situations of tribal cultures of relatively isolated hilly and forested areas.

ACKNOWLEDGEMENT

The author is grateful to the Director, Anthropological Survey of India, for providing necessary facilities and Dr P. K. Misra, Regional Officer, Anthropological Survey of India, Mysore, for giving all help and encouragement when the study on the Soliga tribe was undertaken. The author expresses his profound gratitude to his teacher Dr L. P. Vidyarthi, Professor and Head of Anthropology, Ranchi University, for his stimulating guidance during the author's doctoral study. The views expressed in this paper are solely the author's.

SUGGESTED READINGS

Conklin, H.C. : "An Ethno-ecological Approach to Shifting Agriculture," *Transaction of the New York*, Academy of Sciences, 1954.

Morab, S.G. : The Soliga : A study in Ecology, Economy, Society, and Religion of a Hill Tribe, Unpublished Ph. D. Thesis, 1978.

Notes and Queries in Anthropology : London, Routeledge and Kegan Paul, Reprinted, 1960.

Sinha, Surajit C. : "Tribe-caste and Tribe-peasant Continue in Central India", *Man in India*, Vol. 45, No. 1, 1965, pp. 57-83.

Vidyarthi, L. P. : *The Maler : A Study in Nature-Man-Spirit Complex of a Hill Tribe*, Calcutta, Bookland, 1963.

EIGHT

R. S. Mann

ANIMISM, ECONOMY, ECOLOGY AND CHANGE AMONG NEGRITO HUNTERS AND GATHERERS

EVEN when being in the process of their biological extinction, the Onge have forcefully continued to help persist major areas of their traditional socio-cultural system. This small Negrito group, with its unique local dialect, has failed to maintain social isolation and now finds itself with other ethnic groups, lately inhabited in certain parts of Little Andaman. As nomads, the Onge keep on traversing thick forest areas, defined for respective groups. Though being next to Great Andamanese in coming into contact with outsiders, the Onge have not liberally exposed themselves from the point of view of their culture totality. It appears that reservations of their life-ways is a matter of positive value in the Onge social system. With native traditions, they have lived in Little Andaman, a territory of about 282 square miles, for centuries. The future of hostility, so conspicuously pointed out for Andaman tribes, is no longer a trait of the Onge. Rather, because of contact, though occasional and infrequent, these natives have lately added a few things to their material way of life. Hut Bay, a place in Little Andaman, is fast on the way to becoming a cluster of non-Onge population including government officials, settlers and traders. The government functionaries and a Social Worker have planned some programmes for Onge betterment. This tribe of gatherers and hunters has developed intimate relationship between ecology, religion and economy.

The Onge, numbering 112 (1971 census), are the old inhabitants of Little Andaman. The island of Little Andaman forms a part in the chain of the Andaman group of islands, and is situated at a distance of about 60 miles southwest of Port Blair, the administrative headquarter of Bay islands. The island is nearly 80 miles northwest of Car Nicobar, the northernmost island of the Nicobar group. Little Andaman which, at one time, used to be the home of the Onge alone, is now inhabited by the people from East Pakistan (now Bangladesh). Nearly 70 Nicobarese from Car Nicobar have also, lately, been brought to Little Andaman for permanent colonisation. The non-Onge population, including government officials and labourers, is largely scattered between Hut Bay and Butler Bay, and between Hut Bay and South Bay. The Onge have already drifted away from these areas and they now lead a semi-nomadic life in areas beyond Butler Bay, along the eastern coast. The places where they stay for longer periods, and in comparatively bigger groups, are Dugong Creek and South West Bay.

Belonging to Negrito racial stock, the Onge are shining black in colour, short statured with developed posterior. The body hair growth is scanty. Their head hair is short, frizzly, woolly and spirally curved. They have fleshy nose-tips and thick lips.

A uniform pattern of clothing, once prevalent among the Onge, has undergone some change. In the past, the children remained naked, the men wore only a loin-cloth, with a small strip of cloth going over the genitals and tucked in the back into a narrow string going round the waist. The women wore tassels to hide their private parts. But these are not always, and in all cases, now, found true. The dress pattern among the Onge is not uniform. What they wear and when they wear it are determined by weather, occasion, place, use of clay, availability of clothes, outsiders' will, age, sex and other conditions created from time to time. Depending on the situation, one can come across dress of the old kind, as also see the changed part of it. An Onge can even be seen wearing the old as well as new dress simultaneously. As such the situation is interesting and varying.

The adult men in Dugong Creek and Butler Bay, their traditional settlements, were seen wearing loin cloths of the traditional kind. The same is true in the case of the South-West

Bay dwellers. The rest of the body, including the face, the Onge-men paint with white clay. A few in Dugong Creek were seen wearing half-trousers. The Onge men, while moving around in Hut Bay, or when they are brought to Port Blair, or when presented before some distinguished visitors, are observed to be wearing shirts and shorts. In Hut Bay the Onge, wearing shirts and loin cloth, can also be observed. Even in their native hutments, when they feel cold or when somebody goes there, some, if they have them, also wear shirts. Even while in Hut Bay, but inside their own hut, both men and the women wear nothing but the traditional dress. Under this situation, they remain unconcerned even when some visitor happens to be in the hut. They feel more relaxed wearing their traditional dress. While out for turtle, pig or fish hunting, or even for collection, the Onge men remain in their traditional dress. When they feel hot, they do not wear shirts or shorts and freely roam about, wearing only a loin cloth. When I met the Onge of the eastern coast in their different camps, I found them all in their traditional dresses. When asked as to why they didn't wear the clothes given to them by the welfare agencies, the answer came that when the body was painted with clay, the shirts and shorts could not be worn. It may be mentioned that the Onge are very fond of painting their bodies with thick layers of clay, and such painting is an integral part of their cultural life. To an Onge, the value of clothing does not stand higher to clay painting on the body. The significance of painting the body with clay is far more than that involved in the lately introduced clothing styles. The former is connected with various aspects of Onge life and culture while the latter is treated at the superfluous level. That is why the Onge, most of the time, do not wear the dresses provided because doing so would obstruct their clay-painting. It may be an imposition if they are suddenly asked to do away with clay-painting, which has a direct bearing on their traditional socio-cultural milieu.

The Onge women have been wearing nothing but fibrous tassels made out of fine germinal apex of a particular vegetation. The whole thing is so smooth and soft that it does not produce rash even on the soft skin over the vagina where it is worn. The tassels are strung around the waist and over the hips. The tassels are voluminous and cover the frontal secret parts of the woman. All other portions of a woman's body remain naked. Since the arrival of the Social Worker in Little Andaman, some of the Onge women have also been given sarees, blouses and petticoats. But do the Onge women voluntarily like it? The question is very doubtful. During my visit I found no woman wearing any of these dresses in the various camps from Butler Bay to Dugong Creek. Even in Hut Bay, the women were lying in their huts, wearing nothing but the traditional tassels. When they were constantly asked by the Social Worker, two women in Hut Bay, agreed to wear petticoats. The way they wore the petticoats was really an indication that the women did not understand the significance of clothing. The petticoat was worn over the tassels. The bulky tassels were bulging out oddly wrapped in the petticoat, giving a very funny look to the women. The women could not, probably, be sure that the petticoat would serve the same purpose as the tassels did. The blouse, it seems, is not at all liked by the Onge women. None of them was found wearing it. The Onge women, brought from interior and far off hutments, are suddenly made to wear sarees, prior to their presentation before the distinguished guests in Hut Bay. When they are over-clothed, in this way, they feel uncomfortable. Even when part of the saree slips down, making the breast naked, the Onge women, standing before the visitors, remain unconcerned. They do not bother to wrap it again—as perhaps that they do not know how to do it, or they feel no necessity for doing so. Their concept of modesty is different which does not seem to fit in the cross-cultural setting where such things occur. In the light of their traditional norms, regarding female sex, clothing does not seem to have any place. Before over-clothing them, the Onge women need to understand the utility of clothing. The place of clothing, in the existing Onge culture, is to be initially created. Like the men-folk, the women also paint their bodies with clay. This is for decoration and other purposes. They make various kinds of clay designs on their face and other parts of the body. If they wear clothes, the entire beauty of their art would be hidden. The clay designs have deep roots in the Onge social structure. If we do not allow the change to take place, according to their own genius and mind, it will not be easily accepted, and would rather be resisted in the event of imposition. The adjustment is to be made keeping in view the respect for the traditional art of clay-designing on the bodies of men and women. If, in the tropical climate, the clothes are worn over the clay paint, it may prove more unhygienic and may create unhealthy conditions. Here, I may make a mention of some of the clothes which I saw in Onge Korales (huts) of eastern coast. These clothes had become absolutely dark, with layers of dirt and dust on them. They were stinking. I am sure anybody wearing them would fall prey to skin diseases. One of the functions of clothing is the protection of body. But such dirty clothes would have an adverse effect. The thinking that by simply distributing clothes to the Onge is their welfare, may prove misleading under the prevalent situation.

The Onge children have either been moving around naked or wearing smaller tassels and loin-cloths. They are also not free from clay-coating. Sometime the whole body is thickly coated to bring down fever or to provide protection against the bite of mosquitoes and ticks. Lately, some garments have been distributed to the Onge children. In Dugong Creek, an Onge camp, I found two girls wearing frocks. But the rest of the children, I came across, were dressed in indigenous fashion. No foot-wear or head-gear are used by the Onge. Some of them like to wear a cloth-band on their forehead, going round the head. Other important areas of immediate concern are the position of tassels and the loin-cloth. They are used for months together without getting them cleaned. These dirty dresses keep in constant touch with the most delicate, and reproductive parts of the males and females. Even if they get wet, they are not replaced. The Onge keep on wearing them day and night. Some superstitions and taboos, in respect of tassels, prevail among the Onge. Their replacement and touch are governed by them alone.

The Onge lack cleanliness. The unclean conditions prevailing among them are the result of different factors, both human and ecological. Till very recently, none of them ever understood the usefulness of cleanliness. Lately, a few of the Onge have started taking a bath once a while. They are also persuaded to use bath and washing soap, especially when they are brought to

Hut Bay. A few of the Onge have come to know of medicinal tablets, especially for minor ailments. They do not know the names of medicines but they understand that such things provide relief. Such people may ask for the tablets while unwell.

It may, however, be mentioned that most of the Onge, in their camps or native surroundings, remain very dirty. Under the conditions the sense of hygiene is almost absent. In most of the cases, washing and cleaning are not done. The bodies of men and women remain almost perpetually covered with clay, mixed in the locally available boar or turtle fat. They just do not bother to clean it, and rather keep on giving new coatings when the old ones get removed. Because of such a procedure, their bodies keep on emitting a striking odour. In this respect Cipriani's version that more a wife loves her husband the more magnificent designs she executes on him, continues to hold true. The paintings on their bodies reach a peak every two or three days, as the Onge fear illness and death if they are not newly daubed, and the face at least must be continually painted, with at least a smear on the chest, arms and legs. Painting with clay on the body is done for various purposes including curing of disease, decoration, display of affection to the husband, mourning, menses period and for favour of pig kill. The diseases of skin are comparatively more common among the Onges. They keep on scratching their hands, feet and the lower abdomen having slightly elevated rashings. Among skin diseases, ring worm is quite common. Apart from skin, the other diseases are no less common. The weather conditions and unhygienic food have their own role in causing such diseases. Raw food material is not properly cleaned. It is made to boil in dirty water containing mud and dust. The utensil in which the food is cooked is hardly cleaned. It is used over and over again without being properly cleaned. Layers of dirt keep on accumulating on the utensils used for cooking and eating purposes. The dogs also eat the left-overs in the same containers. In an Onge camp, slightly beyond Butler Bay, I, for the first time, saw pork being cooked by the Onge. When I reached the camp, I found no Onge attending to the cooking. They were relaxing in their Korales. About two yards, from one of the corner huts, I observed an eighteen litre tin-container (without any cover), all black on the outside with accumulation of soot, stood on three small stones over a fire. The tin-container was almost full of pork pieces and water. Nothing else was added to it. As the sea breeze was blowing fast, there was enough of sand and dust particles and free leaves floating on the water inside the tin. All these were getting boiled with the pork. No Onge bothered to remove them, or to cover the tin. Sometimes the dogs would come and peep into the tin. When I talked to the Onge, they responded that this was their usual way of cooking. Soon after the pork was boiled, it would be distributed to all the members and consumed as it was. Thus, the pork along with other unwanted material, is swallowed by the Onge. Such practices ultimately cause stomach pain, dysentery and other related troubles. The large communal huts of the Onges are dark from inside and quite congested. The cooking is also done inside the hut, either near the respective bed or in the middle of the hut. Lots of bones and skulls are found hanging inside the hut. There is a great deal of smoke inside, and soot layers are often seen on the ceiling of the hut. The conditions in the hut are far from healthy.

In addition to food and personal hygiene, an Onge camp and its immediate surroundings also add to the unhealthy conditions. The animal, caught or killed, is brought to the camp and cleaned there itself. Its bones, skin and other parts not to be eaten, are thrown around the huts. Even from the cooked food, the material, not meant for eating, is thrown around. Near the current as well as the abandoned camps of the Onge, one finds bones scattered around in thick layers. Shells, not properly cleaned, other animals and shell fish in rotting condition are seen in close vicinity of the communal hut. No latrine structures are made near the Onge camp. In the near vicinity of camps, excrement is spread in a disorderly manner. Though the Onge claim to lightly cover it with leaves and sand, there is sufficient scope for flies to lay eggs on them. Gradually, the camp-surroundings become the breeding ground for flies and other insects and mosquitoes. They multiply fast and cause hazard to Onge life. Quite often, the Onge suffer from malaria. With all this, the Onge are not spared of exposure to weather variations. Sudden exposures to cold and fast wind also trouble the Onge. Chest, joint and muscular pains are often reported by them. Pulmonary diseases have also been explained. If one suffers from an infectious disease, there are favourable chances of its quick infection to others. In a Bera (communal hut), where many Onge stay together, the chances of infection are favourable. Contagious diseases also find scope especially through their system of breast-feeding the children of others. An Onge woman can, and does, breast-feed any child belonging to any Onge woman when the latter gets sick or dies. This kind of breast feeding may also pass on diseases.

Under the unhygienic and unhealthy conditions, the Onge keep on struggling with life. They try their indigenous methods of curing disease. A most common method of treatment, prevalent among the Onge, is to use clay. It is specially done in case of fever. Cipriani has also made a mention of such practice while stating that "for any kind of fever the Onges turn immediately to their stock remedy, smearing the entire body with usual mixture of ochre, turtle fat and honey. The legs, arms, chest and abdomen are then tightly bound with strips of ficus bark, which are removed and renewed from time to time. Whether the patient has pains in the abdomen or in the chest, appropriate part is given a rigorous massage by the feet of one of the bystanders". For fever, red clay is believed to have more medicinal value; white clay is meant to save the skin from insect-bite. According to the Onge, the clay, ochre, honey and turtle fat have medicinal value and are used for cure as well as prevention of disease. The clay as such, or mixed with other medical substance, is used in case of the snake bite or scorpion attack, constipation and breast infection. It is further believed that honey, too, has medicinal value and helps in healing wound. In addition to the .medicinal substances, another method of curing a patient of .wounds and pains is to expose him to hot smoke. The other method is through the religious man, who, with his power, helps cure certain diseases. It is also regarded as the chief method of prevention. Kuvera is their traditional medicine-man who helps cure the patients suffering from the influence of evil spirits. So far, no agency of health, or any other department concerned with providing medical cover to the Onge, exists in any of the Ongecamps. Even in the two major settlements, at Dugong Creek and South-West Bay, not even a compounder is posted.

Some medical facilities are available at Hut Bay, which is a far off place from the Onge hutments. Because of their traditional beliefs and the distance factor, the Onge, in general, are reluctant to visit the dispensary at Hut Bay. In fact the Onge could be better motivated to use modern drugs and medicines provided some agency could work right in their major settlement areas. Looking to the problems of biological extinction among the Onge, there is an urgent need to establish better medical facilities at least in the two major settlements. The health educator has to convince the Onge about the superiority of the modern methods of treatment. Apart from curing disease, a thorough medical check-up at regular intervals of time, of the Onge is desired. In the context of the declining number of the Onge, the health programme should be taken up on a priority basis and in right earnest. Any superfluous exercise, in this regard, would be damaging to the Onge.

In case of sickness the resulting sufferings are sometimes indirectly shared by all members of the group. In the case of a chronic ailment, and when it assumes a serious form curtailing the mobility of the patient, the community members come to the rescue. The sick man, as well as his family members are then looked after by others in the ground. Food and protection are ensured to them. The arrangement continues till the man recovers or till any other male member in the family becomes capable of securing food through traditional means. Likewise, in case of the death of a mother, or in her being seriously sick, her child, if dependent upon breast-feeding, is fed by any other woman of the group. These practices make it certain that miseries are shared among the Onge. More so, it could be because of their belief in common concepts of diseases and cures, both secular and religious. In the light of the above situation, the change-agent, in the field of health and hygiene, has to be careful of Onge attitude and reaction to the concerned innovations. Indigenous practices are not to be outrightly and suddenly discarded. The new practices, as substitutes, would be more feasible only when gradual adjustment with, and replacement of the indigenous ones is thought about. It is likely that some of the traditional cure practices are really helpful to the Onge. The diffusion of innovations can be provided an impetus by reminding the natives of their dwindling number.

RELIGIOUS ATTRIBUTES

In comparison to other major areas of Onge life-designs, the religion is less developed. The attributes and components of religion are limited. Certain features of religion are almost missing, and even those existing are not elaborate. Their religious performances, chiefly organised at the time of some threat or difficulties, are only a few. The elements of fear and protection, however, form the essential ingredients of Onge religion. The idea of daily worship is non-existent. The Onge religious performances, whatever they are, point to their being animists. The animism of the Onge can be more pointedly differentiated. The recognition of various kinds of spirits is well marked. Animism apart; the practices, imbibed from any other religion, are not at all found among the Onge. Christianity of the Nicobarese, Hinduism and Islam as prevalent in Great Andaman, have, so far, not affected the Negrito inhabitants of Little Andaman. The religious components, that characterise the Onge, are absolutely their original and fall within the framework of animism.

While writing on Onge religion, Cipriani has stated that 'there is complete absence of any form of cult, prayer, representation, or votive offering. No sacrifices of any kind are practised in the Andaman, nor is there any concept of propitiation. The taboos do not exist among the Onge. There is complete absence of any form of ritual surrounding birth, the purification of woman, initiation etc.' In this connection it may, however, be stated that some of the rituals and beliefs have been found existing among the Onge. May be that these might have not been reported in Cipriani's conversation because of mutual communication difficulties. For instance, the totems and taboos do exist among the natives of Little Andaman. They trace their descent from some of the birds. The latter are considered as sacred and are never killed and eaten. It is taboo to kill these birds. The belief is that so doing would annoy their ancestors whose spirits, in revengeful mood, might harm the people. Likewise there is a puberty rite, involving certain taboos. During the first menses, the female is segregated for 22 days. Nobody may closely see her during this period (even the husband's cohabitation is avoided). At the end, she takes bath in sea water. Her mother paints her body with clay. The propitiation of spirits also exists. One of such ways is through the wearing of human jaw, taken out from the grave, after about six months of burial. It is worn by the relatives, one after another, for many days and then reburied. The jaw is still worn by most Onge of West Bay. In Dugong Creek and among the other neighbouring groups the Onge take out a small piece of jaw, or a tooth, and wear it round their necks on a particular day, while embracing each other. It represents a deep concern, of the surviving relatives, towards the dead. The performance further conveys that the dead are to be remembered and respected. After so doing, it is believed that the spirit of the dead will not have any bad effect on the group members. The Onge recognise various types of spirits. These include both malevolent as well as benevolent ones. Some of these spirits are said to be associated with the local ecological purview. The background of their formation, as also the modus operandi, at times, differ. The Onge believe that the spirit is formed after death, and there is every chance of its returning. Another belief is that when the spirits get angry, they can cause harm, and hence the people are afraid of the same. But in spite of this, the Onge do not perform any spirit worship. Rather, they try to make them run away through magical performance. This specially applies to malevolent spirits. The offerings and prayers which form integral part of religion of many of the animals, are almost non-existent among the tribals of Little Andaman.

"Tomanje" is one of their evil spirits. The Onge hold the view that Tomanje comes out of the earth, especially from the graves which the Onge dig inside the hut. It is believed that the nearer the grave, the lesser would be the harm of Tomanje. Tomanje is believed to eat pork. The spirits can attack children as well as grown-ups, irrespective of sex. To avoid Tomanje, the Onge burn resin. Simultaneously they forcefully blow air from their mouths pointing towards the spirit. The ritual is taken as repulsive to the evil spirits. At times, the observation of the ritual is accompanied by the shouting of 'Ha-Ha-Ha'.

"Gay Boratekada" is another malevolent spirit whose abode is believed to be in the interior of the forests. The spirit takes birth when a person dies in the forest. In case of accidental death in the forest, the body is normally buried there itself. This spirit is believed to survive on crocodile flesh. Comparatively speaking, the Gay Boratekada gives more trouble to the men. A sudden death, in the forest, is believed to be caused by this spirit. One of the methods of keeping aloof, or of driving away the evil spirits, especially Gay Boratekada, is to hold a burning branch in one hand, and a broom, made of tree leaves, in the other. Then, raising both the hands, and pointing towards the spot, under the spirit influence, the Onge loudly shout some words (equivalent to "go go"). This ritual, as also the one performed to drive away Tomanje, makes it clear that fire is an important element to scare away spirits. In addition to various other uses of fire, its utility for driving away the malevolent spirits is of vital importance. The belief that fire provides protection against evil spirits is likely to be the reason, among others, why the Onge carry fire whenever they move from one camp to another, and why they always keep fire burning near their sleeping platforms. Of course, the other reasons cannot altogether be ignored. Simultaneous to fire, the force of Onge breath is of no less magnitude. They always make use of it while driving away the spirits, especially the evil ones. Although the Onge are not in a position to categorically explain this it may be presumed that the breath has some connection with the spirit. Likewise, the noisy atmosphere, created through shouting, is another integral part of the ritual meant to scare away the spirits. Such a conception might be one of the reasons why Onge usually keep quiet, or speak in very mild tones when in contact with outsiders. Even their mode of greeting stresses quietness, especially when they meet people after long intervals of time. While greeting, the Onge sit on each other's lap and keep quiet for a couple of minutes. Ritual and other symbolic expressions are, thus, indicators of multi aspects of Onge life and culture.

Another popular belief of the Onge is that some of the deaths, caused due to accidents, also result in the formation of benevolent spirits. For instance, when a person dies of falling off a tree, or as a result of stabbing, the incident gives rise to a benevolent spirit, popularly known as 'Tejawala Lange'. The sky is taken to be the abode of Tejawala Lange. This spirit survives on honey. Normally, Tejawala Lange does not assume a harmful attitude. In case it does, the Onge resort to their normal rituals of driving away evil spirits. It may be mentioned here that the symbolic representation of any of the spirits, in any of the art or object forms, is absent among the Onge. No figures of spirits are ever made. They, rather, recognise them essentially in the situation wherein their influence is felt. Interplay of man and spirit is more glaring as a situational phenomenon.

As a benevolent spirit, the major advantage of Tejawala Lange is in the context of pregnancy of a woman. The Onge feel that this spirit makes a soul enter into honey, or some other edible root or fruit, and when such an eatable is consumed by a woman, she gets pregnant. "Unless the spirit is kind enough, the woman cannot conceive", is a popular belief in the Onge belief system. In order to appease the spirits, and to get favour, the Onges, many a times, take out a part of the honey collected by them, for the spirit. Such a religious belief, in regard to the sky spirit, continues to hold uniformly true among all the Onge. There is no change in this concept of pregnancy. Ganguli and Roy also made a mention of this belief among the Onges and wrote about the sky spirits, Onkoboykwes. Sky is the abode of Onkoboykwes. They have also stated that the Onge believed that the Onkoboykwes send unborn souls of babies to Little Andaman which enter into certain food articles such as honey-comb, certain varieties of edible tubers etc. When an Onge woman eats that food, the soul enters into her womb making her pregnant. Onge are aware of the fact that sexual intercourse is a pre-requisite for conception, but they also believe that no conception is possible unless the Onkoboykwes send a soul. Occasionally, a childless couple, who desire to have children, set apart a piece of honey-comb after collecting honey and place it on a tree as an offering to Onkoboykwes.

Like birth, the death rituals too are not free of the religious consideration. Even the place of burial is governed by religious factors. The Onge accord all possible honour to their dead. Barring specific exceptions, a dead body is buried inside the hut, and under the raised platform, meant for sleeping. Such a burial is done with the intention of keeping the spirit of the dead close so that they remain appeased. The spirit living so close, is believed to provide protection. The bones of the buried dead body ever remain an attraction to the spirit and so it continues to stay around. Burial inside the hut is done in case of relatives, both agnatic and affinal, and friends. The enemies, unknown and hostile ones are cremated somewhere inside the forest, away from the Onge settlement. The spirits of such people are considered more nasty, torturous and revengeful. That is why the Onge cremate them with the idea that cremation would either completely destroy such spirits, or they would be taken far off to the sky, along with smoke. Another advantage of cremation, within the Onge belief-complex, is that it reduces all the bones to ashes and then the spirit has no chances of being attracted to the place of cremation. There is yet another way of performing the last rites. The body of a person, who dies suddenly in the forest, is not brought to the hut; it is disposed of there itself, even when he or she is a relative or friend. The burial in the forest is done because such a death is believed to be caused by the evil spirit alone. It is believed that the body is brought to the hut, the evil spirit may follow and harm other occupants too. The Onge also recognise an association between the name of a person and his/her spirit, after death. After a man dies, his name is not offered by the Onge. The fear is that if they do so, it would attract the spirit.

An interesting feature in Onge religion is a late induction. This element did not exist prior to the arrival of dogs in Little Andaman. Since the Onge started domestication of dogs, they have developed a belief that the forest spirits are afraid of the dogs as the latter can bite them. Such a consideration might probably be a strong reason why the Onge love dogs so much. The dogs share food served in the same container in which the Onge eat. In some Onge camps, the number of dogs exceeds the human population. The Onge never kill dogs. It may be mentioned here that the Onge also consider the killing of birds, except pigeon, as taboo. They consider birds as the abode of souls. Regarding them as totemic objects, the Onge express association of birds with clan-like groups. This provides another reason for their protection.

Among the Onge, witches do not exist. As such witch-doctors are unheard of. Most of the sickness is believed to be caused by malevolent spirits. However, Kuvera is a traditional medicine-man who helps relieve spirit possession. The spirit of the boar is also considered treacherous for human beings. Sometimes it overpowers a man when he is not on pig-hunting. Kuvera detects its influence and cures. Pork eating, for the affected person, is temporarily stopped. This act is supposed to quicken recovery. Kuvera, the spirit-curer, can be of either sex. The position of Kuvera is not hereditary; it is an acquired one. Kuvera is the chief religious person of the Onge, and such a position is recognised on formal occasions when a new-born is dedicated to the community. On the 22nd day after the birth of a baby, the mother gives some fish to the father of the child. He subsequently passes it on to Kuvera. From Kuvera, it is handed over to the headman who, finally, gives it back to the father. The ritual is also symbolic of sharing food, with the new-born, taking him or her as a community member, as also the community liability.

That a person gets polluted and ritually unclean, after certain happenings, is also recognised by the Onge. Such a recognition is made apparent in a few of the practices observed by them. How far the element of religion is involved in such observances is, however, not explained by the tribals. After giving birth to a child, an Onge woman does not sleep on the raised wooden platform for about a month. In normal course, she sleeps with her husband on a common platform. But in the post-delivery period, she keeps away for nearly a month. Likewise the period of ritual pollution after death is twenty-two days. The mourning, however, continues for a longer duration. It is chiefly observed on three occasions within the first year of death.

ECONOMIC ORGANISATION

Primarily, the Onge have all been collectors, and hence depending upon hunting, fishing and gathering. For such economic pursuits, the tribals have always led a nomadic life. The Onge continue to be semi-nomadic, though the group in Dugong Creek has become comparatively less mobile because of the attraction of lately provided coconut plantation to them. The entire produce of the plantation is meant for the Onge. In general, there is more intimate interplay of social life in the rainy season when many Onge families stay together in the communal hut. Because of the heavy rainfall and strong breeze, the Onge cannot manage to stay in temporary lean-to type structures. At the same time they have to come out of the interior forest as heavy rains make life difficult there. Further not much of game and products of collection are available in this season. But in the dry season, that is, from December to the middle of May, the Onge get distributed in smaller groups, mainly in their respective band groupings. Their movements are very frequent, and sufficient game and articles of collection are then available to them. As such, the Onge get enough to eat in the dry season. But they are hard pressed in the rainy season when they have to forego their meals many a time. The sea is an added source of food for the Onge. Making use of their canoes, the Onge get into the sea for fishing. This is done at individual as well as collective levels. The fishing equipment comprises bows, arrows and nets. But when the sea is rough, a common phenomenon in the rainy season, the Onge do not dare to go out to sea to fish. In such an eventuality, the fishing is done in small water sources, especially creeks, with the help of small fishing nets. On full moon nights during the dry season, the Onge resort to turtle hunting. The women in Onge society do not make any contribution to the hunting; but they are helpful in fishing. The women are specially helpful in collection pursuit. Digging stick and *dao* (chopper) are the major tools used in gathering. Commonly collected food materials include *teetkara* (aroot), *kokona* (soft cane shoot), *digi* (wild potato) and *akandar* (wild jack-fruit). The women also pray, especially to Tejawala Lange, for the safe and successful return of their husbands when the latter go on boar hunting expeditions. On this occasion, they smear white clay on their faces and sing folk songs connected with hunting, victory, forest etc. On the return of a hunter, the ladies eagerly listen to his story of success. When the men are busy in some other affairs, one can see Onge women fishing in coral reefs. Such fishing is done with small nets only. The prevalence of the above conditions, therefore, points to the fact that the forest and sea surroundings, as also the weather conditions, impose their limitations on the economic and the connected cultural life of the Onge. When these ecological conditions remain favourable, the food supply is sufficient. But under abnormal conditions the difficulties are posed and the Onge then face hard days.

Beyond the natural and geographical factors, already stated the man-made situation, lately developed in Little Andaman, is of no less importance in the context of the tribal economy. The Onge are indifferent to this kind of situation as they find it threatening to some areas of their economic life. The new situation is an outcome of non-Onge immigration to Hut Bay, and also to other neighbouring areas extending to Butler Bay and South Bay. Thousands of non-tribals have poured in; some for temporary and others for permanent stay in Little Andaman. It may be mentioned that the settlers and labourers, working in Little Andaman, go to hunt wild boar. It is being done in addition to the clearing of forest for human settlement and road construction. Under these circumstances, the Onge have started experiencing the scarcity of boar the only wild game available in Little Andaman, and their chief source of food. The hunting activities of the immigrant are on the increase because of greater influx from outside. Even some of the very interior forests of Little Andaman have been approached for the purpose. The labourers, engaged by the resin contractor, visit the remote areas for resin collection. Simultaneously, they resort to boar hunting. The Onge are indifferent to such hunting. They, however, do not openly oppose such encroachment, being afraid of the increasing strength of the outsiders. In the light of the fact that the Onge largely continue to depend on hunting and collection, the sharing of their hunting and collection resources by the non-tribals is adversely affecting them. And then giving of coconut plantation to the Onge of Dugong Creek is no adequate compensation for such kind of activities. The starting of construction works in the island has not at all been economically beneficial to the Onge. Not a single Onge is employed on any construction site, neither on daily wages nor on a regular basis.

Simultaneous to the reported economic hardship, largely believed to be caused by the non-Onge hunters, there is another trend taking shape in contradiction to Onge traditions. This is the feeling of economic dependency being created and encouraged among the Onge. It is again an outcome of Onge contact with the outsiders. Right from the early stages of contact with the Onge, the outsiders have been giving them gifts of various kinds. The gifts include clothes, tea leaves, tobacco leaves, *dao* etc. Prior to their contact with outsiders, the Onge were not aware of these items. To meet all their requirements, they depended upon the local ecology and resources. In due course, the Onge became almost habitual in using certain alien articles. For instance, tobacco and tea leaves are by now the most preferred articles which these people expect from any visitor. If their expectations are not met, they feel somewhat disappointed. This is because the visitors have almost always given them something. Often, the Onge ask for presents if they are not given the same. Even now, it has been made a point that all dignitaries, visiting Hut Bay, should carry some gifts for the Onge. As a matter of fact the Onge do not now live in Hut Bay, and their hutments are in far off places. But on the occasion of visits of important people to Little Andaman, the tribals are brought to Hut Bay to be presented before them. For this purpose the Onge are sometimes made to come to Hut Bay three to four times a month. Many a time the tribal people are made to dance before important visitors. Their photographs are taken, followed by the presentation of gifts. Such incidents not only promote the Onge attitude of dependence on others but also are, otherwise, unwanted. The parade of tribals in Hut Bay is itself unpalatable to them. When I conversed with the Onge of Dugong Creek, they expressed unhappiness over their presentation before visitors in Hut Bay. On every occasion they have to walk long distance to reach the place. Some of the informants remarked in anger that if anybody is keen to meet them, they should care to come to their hutments. But this is never done, and every time they are persuaded to come to Hut Bay. A major part of the Social Worker's time in the dry season is spent in collecting and bringing the Onge to Hut Bay. The situation is discouraging to the tribals. The way the tribal people are displayed, in altogether a new situation, is nothing short of humiliation. So long as they live in this situation, they feel uncomfortable and nervous. Sometimes they are presented before outsiders in their traditional dresses. This, too, is disturbing to them amidst hundreds of non-tribals. People stare oddly at their ladies who wear nothing but fibrous tassels to hide their frontal secret parts. This kind of parading of the Onge is done to make the visitors feel happy, as also for petty gain of gifts, some of which may not even be liked and used by the Onge. In addition to the fact that their routine is disturbed, the Onge hardly receive enough to completely bank upon it for a few days. This way of treating the Onge is seriously defective and unscientific. It goes contrary to the very basic principle of tribal welfare. The act is not of great economic value nor is it appreciated in the context of social dimensions.

The formal presentation of the Onge in Hut Bay is even psychologically damaging. It accords a feeling of depression and sense of inferiority. People gathered at Hut Bay laugh at the very sight of the Onge, and some short saying the *junglis* (the wild people) have come. It is likely that the tribals might get further shock from this kind of treatment. The trend may gear up loss of interest of life, an outcome which can prove damaging to the Onge in the context of their declining numbers and cultural living. A similar phenomenon has been reported from some other tribes of the world. The frequent bringing of the Onge to Hut Bay is further harmful from the health point of view. Lots of people come to the island by every incoming ship. It is likely that some of these may carry infectious disease, and subsequently pass it on to the Onge brought to Hut Bay. Its further extension to the remaining tribal population might prove destructive. Such incidences have already been reported from other Negrito tribes of Great Andaman which have geared up their extinction. Under the situation, for a simple desire of the dignitaries to see the Onge, the latter may have to pay a very high price. If one is to honestly look for the guided change among the Onge, the factors leading to their physical decline and social disorganisation are to be taken care of.

The outsiders have more intensively explored the eastern coast of Little Andaman, Hut Bay, Butler Bay and the areas in between have been far more exploited than those of the western coast. In fact the nomadic mobility for hunting and fishing of the Onge has largely been curtailed in these areas. The increased human habitation in the region has caused the Onge to drift further northeast. Till very recently the Onge of South and West Bay were not much affected by the immigrants in Hut Bay. But lately, the arrival of Nicobarese in the south-west territory of the island has not been happy news to the Onge of South-West Bay. In fact the area exclusively meant for the Onge for hunting and fishing, is now being shared by the Nicobarese immigrants. These Nicobarese, brought from Car Nicobar, are to be permanently settled on the island. The Nicobarese being fond of pig and fish have already started consuming a part of the food resources traditionally meant for the Onge of South West Bay. This has started contributing to the condition of food scarcity. In the light of such a trend the Onge are likely to be further cornered in their economic existence. It would be further promoted under the circumstances when the new economic pursuits do not offer much to the Onge. The systematic means for the economic betterment of the Onge are yet to be devised and brought to the forefront. The settlement of the non-Onge at the cost of the Onge is unwise. Economic development of the Onge should have been given priority in the matter.

The encroachment of outsiders on Onge territory has not only adversely reached to their economic life but has even crossed over to the social aspect of the Onge life-ways, especially their groupings. For centuries, the Onge have lived in groups occupying fixed territories. The sanctity and sentiments associated with the boundaries have never allowed the Onge to cross over to the territory of the other group, especially for hunting, fishing and collection purposes. Due respect and recognition were accorded to such territorial limits. Even within a territorial group, the still smaller social divisions have also been existing. The movements of their members, too, were guided within the defined areas. Now the areas widely traversed or occupied by others than the Onge are hardly under the Onge possession, for any of their economic pursuits. The Onge groups, originally in possession of these areas, no longer do hunting, fishing or collection there. Under the conditions the Onge of the evacuated groups adjusted themselves with the members of other Onge groups. Traditionally, and as a part of the tribal customary law, they could otherwise never do so. But the force and pressure that emanated from outsiders encroachment, made them behave in that manner. Whatever the affected ones got out of such adjustment is insufficient. Secondly, the process itself would not have been palatable because it caused a wider imposition. Any alternative as an immediate substitute was also not thought of by the outsiders. Destroying the traditional values of such non-literate groups under compulsion is disappointing to the Onge. Such happenings lead to loss of nerve, a psychological phenomenon explained by many as an important cause of population decline.

In the setting where the Onge live, there is an intimate interplay of economy, social organization and the ecological conditions. Outsiders do not realise that when they influence one aspect, the others also get affected. The deforestation, for various ends and the big population influx influenced in the case under reference, the tribal economy. This, in turn, reacted to the Onge social organization. Therefore the revelations based on holistic purview of Onge life and culture need to be utilized to make Onge-non-Onge contact planned, and to avoid disorganization in the tribe in order to avoid further disorganization and hardship to the members of this tribe, already in the process of biological extinction, the various agencies and departments in Little Andaman should understand and consider the background of Onge life and culture. In the absence of such orientation and the proper policies for their economic development, the Onge may achieve nothing but disappointment. Ultimately, they may meet the same fate as the Great Andamanese have experienced.

Domestication of animals and plants

In the Onge economic system, the domestication of animals and plants find very little place. And this, too, could generate at quite a late stage. So far the Onge have hardly domesticated any plant by themselves. The coconut plantation, at Dugong Creek was raised by government machinery. The tribals have not raised it themselves. Of course, they now collect the fruit and are also occasionally made to clean the undergrowth. But this could generate some interest in them for the domestication of plants. During the course of my visit (in 1973) to Dugong Creek, I was shown a few plants of papaya, tapioca and sweetpotato raised in a small plot of land, and the same, as reported by the Social Worker, had raised by the Onge. The Social Worker claimed that some interest in this regard has been created among the Onge. It may be pointed out that

Cipriani, during his course of long field work among the Onge, also demonstrated to the Onge the technique of vegetable-growing. Cipriani, in association with the Onges, cleared a patch of land to grow vegetables. Brinjals and beans were grown in the small plot. But after Cipriani left the island, the Onge discontinued the practice. Growing vegetables was, however, taken up again after 1970. But even now the Onge do not seem to be interested in the domestication of plants. Perhaps the occupation does not suit and attract them in the light of their traditional economy, ecology and nomadic way of life. Or, they may not be finding that much pleasure in this occupation as they have been deriving from hunting, fishing and collection pursuits. A sudden or hasty switch-over of the Onge hunters and collectors to settled agriculture does not seem to be feasible nor wise. It may take some more time to bring them to the domestication of plants. But at the same time, some other economic provisions need to be made for the Onge to gradually bring them to sedentary life fit for agriculture. The food habits of the Onge are another important factor to be considered prior to make them switch over to the domestication of plants. Except the coconut plantation, which the Onge got readymade, the rest of the plants grown by them have not been of any economic utility. The plants that I came across can hardly give them anything because they were almost dead then.

The position is no better in regard to the domestication of animals. In fact the Onge, traditionally, have never reared any bird or animal. The only animal they know of was the wild boar which they shot and used as food. Even now the Onge do not domesticate any bird or animal, except the dog. Lots of dogs can be seen in the Onge camps. When one approaches their camps, the dogs bark at strangers. One of the ways of detecting their camps in the thick forest of the island is through the spotting of dogs. The dogs normally move around in the forest adjoining an Onge camp. In addition to dogs the observance of smoke, coming out of the trees, is another indication of an Onge camp. The Onge report that the dog is not native to Little Andaman, but was introduced by the Britishers after their first friendly contact with them sometime in the sixties of the last century. Traditionally, it is not correct to say that the Onge had some special fascination for dogs and so started domesticating them. Rather, it was resorted to because of the dog being found very useful in chasing the boar and bringing the same to the spot where the hiding Onge could throw spears at them. Thus, the hunting of boar became more convenient with the help of dogs. The tribals could then kill more and that too in comparatively less time. Gradually the dogs became more domesticated and now are found eating, in a common container, with the members of an Onge family. And the Onge do not seem to mind it. By now the dogs have multiplied and their number seems to exceed what may be actually required for hunting. The extra ones are a liability to the Onge because they also have to be fed. The attachment of the Onge to their dogs is so deep that they cannot bear to see them starve, even when there is shortage of food. No milch animals or poultry birds are reared by the Onge. Even when some of the birds are considered as the totemic objects by the tribals, and when they express great respect for them, they are never reared. The absence of animal husbandry among the Onge may be attributed to the fact that they had never seen other animals, except the boar, on the island. And a boar, they might not have domesticated thinking that it was otherwise available in the surrounding forest. Even now they continued to be as much ignorant of animal husbandry as they were in the deep past. It may be mentioned that the Onge have no religious or cultural prohibition against the domestication of animals and plants. Hunting and collection continue to form the major base of Onge economy.

Trade, exchange and money

Trade and money have never found any place in the traditional economy of the Onge. Being in complete isolation from other communities, the Onge could never, for centuries, develop any kind of trade. Things were confined to the local groups alone. In the light of existing means of securing food, the chances of a flourishing trade were always minimised. The tribe as well as its sects remained self-sufficient. With everyone having similar kind of economic means, and a common ecology, nothing special was required by any one group apart from the other. The concept of private possession did not exist, and whatever was obtained, was consumed by all equally. The system provided no scope for borrowing, lending or exchange. Things required in Onge life were available with all of them. Food was a common possession. Individual recognition, in terms of economic possession, was non-existent. Under such circumstances, the system or concept of surplus never took root. Whatever collected was consumed. No value was attached to economic possession. As a result the calculations, in respect of primitive money, were not made. At the same time, its need was also not felt. It may further be pointed out that the tools, artifacts and other objects, possessed by the Onge, were found with all the families. Under such a system the life always remained corporated and co-operative. One in difficulty was helped by the members of all families of the local group. For instance, when one felt sick and was not in a position to hunt, he and his family members were provided food, without involving any element of economic obligation. The practice prevailed under the norm—beehive of Onge society. For construction of Korale, as also for Bera, people joined hands. No system of remuneration either in cash or kind existed. There has not been any restriction in the exchange of articles possessed by the Onge. One could, and still can, ask for any article from the other. No strict rules ever existed for regulating the borrowing and exchange of things. No object was given a specific exchange value. No return of the equivalent was asked for. May be that after the purpose, it served, the article was returned to the owner. There did not exist the practice of assessing the value of an object in terms of money, or other currency.

From the above analysis of the traditional Onge economic structure, it is clear that trade, exchange and money did not find sufficient scope among the Onge. Money in any form did not exist. Nothing in the name of trade survived. For exchange, there were no set rules. No Onge in need of a basket for instance would offer something of equal value to the lender. Artifacts and objects were not treated in a way as one can find in some other primitive communities where barter and exchange were made use of through fixed modes. It was related that some Onge used to beg food from those who initially came to work on the island under Reclamation and Harbour Work Department. The tribals came to the latter's house and waited quietly at the door till they were obliged with some food. Sometimes they were asked to do odd jobs and then only given a little food to eat. At times the Onge gave honey, cowries and coconuts to get some cooked rice, chapati, bidi or tea leaves from the new comers to the island. The labourers and others, thus, exploited the Onge and the process continued till the middle of 1970.

Lately, more so after the development of more frequent contact with the outsiders, the above mentioned aspects of the Onge economy have received a shake up. The change, more so in the form of addition and less as alteration, is slightly more conspicuous in the economic life-way than that in the social or spiritual life. The trade, money and exchange, are by now, not altogether unknown to the Onge; of course the intricacies and details involved in them are not understandable to most of them. Their contact with the members of other ethnic groups, temporarily or permanently settled in Little Andaman, has had some contribution in this kind of development. The outsiders, in fact, introduced the Onge to certain articles like flour, tea, tobacco, clothes, sugar, bags, torch, rice etc. Initially, such items were given as gifts. But later on some of these became additional requirements for the Onge, and could only be obtained from the non-Onge. At the same time, the arrival of outsiders in Little Andaman demanded that certain things be collected by the Onge. The greatest demand is for honey, resin and coconuts. The placement of a Social Worker in Hut Bay proved useful under the situation. Looking at the new needs of the Onge, as also the requirements of the immigrants, the Social Worker took advantage of the newly created conditions. He explained to the Onge that the resin, honey and the coconuts were in demand by the non-Onge population, and that they could meet some of their requirements from the money obtained through the sale of such products. The establishment of a Consumers' Co-operative Society in Hut Bay could prove still more useful in the matter. New things, required by the Onge, were available in the Consumers' Co-operative shop; and at the same time the Society could straightaway buy the things brought by the Onge. A resin contractor, in Hut Bay, gave further incentive to the Onge to supply resin at fixed rates.

Because of the frequent visits of Onge to Hut Bay, some became familiar with the new conditions. The occasional visits of the Onge to Port Blair, and longer sojourns of some outsiders with them, helped give them some idea about money. By now, many Onge are familiar with money, but not its details. Currency is no longer unknown to them, though they have yet to know its proper calculation. Their understanding of currency notes and coins is of a rudimentary form only. Likewise, the system of weights and measures is not understood by the Onge. However, in spite of their lack of clarity of details, the Onge have fallen into some channels of trade and exchange. A prominent change-agent, in this matter, is the Social Worker on whom the Onge depend. Being themselves unfamiliar with minimum requirements of trade, the Onge have left most of the details to the Social Worker who acts as a middleman between the seller and the buyer. The Social Worker regulates the trade with fixed rates for the commodities of trade. For instance, honey brought by an Onge, is bought at the rate of rupees three a kilogram; resin at the rate of rupee one and twenty-five paise per kilogram: coconut at the rate of forty-five paise per piece.

It may be mentioned that the Onge have to undergo a good deal of hardship to maintain this trade. Normally they live and move about in the forest areas, far away from Hut Bay. It is from these areas that they collect the honey and resin. The coconuts are collected from Dugong Creek. These articles are then carried, mostly on their backs, to Hut Bay, the place of the Social Worker. The coconuts are also transported by their small-sized outrigger canoes. The quantities carried are little because the Onge have to cover long distances. The goods are then delivered to the Social Worker, provided no one interrupts on the way to quietly bargain with them. It is then taken to the Consumers' Co-operative Store where the articles are weighed or counted. The value of the goods is then calculated in terms of money. Onge do not understand such transactions. The requirements of the Onge are then brought forward. Things are bought from the Consumers' Co-operative Store, and the money deducted from the sale amount of Onge goods. The account of balance, if any, is maintained by the Social Worker. After staying for a few days in Hut Bay, the Onge then return to their respective places of camping. The visit is repeated as and when desired by the Onge. The commodities, brought by the Onge, are fixed. But the things they ask for are of different and new kinds. Sometimes they may ask for things which are otherwise not of much utility to them. But because they have seen others using them they feel they must be valuable. Wrist-watches are one such item which a few of Onge ask for, and two have even bought them. I met these two gentlemen wearing watches. When asked of their utility or whether they could tell the time, the answer was in the negative. The watches were not even working, and probably were out of order. The two Onge men spent a good amount of money on them. To cite another example an Onge was found wearing spectacles meant for poor eye sight. When asked about it, the man said that he had got it from someone and had just started wearing them. This, he did, as he found some outsiders wearing the same. What harm these spectacles would do to his eyes he did not know. Out of sheer ignorance, the man feels that spectacles were a symbol of some superior status. The Onge often display such child-like qualities when they come in contact with alien cultures.

It may be mentioned that during the year 1971-72, the Onge sold resin, honey and coconut worth rupees 4,423 (honey for Rs. 30; coconut for Rs. 1,078 and resin for Rs. 3,315). The Onge were not given this cash, instead, they bought flour, beedi, blades, torch cells, bags, iron files, sarees, shirts, pants, turmeric, fishing hooks, onion, potato, pulses, rice, sugar, soap, tea, tobacco, shoes and milk powder. As informed by the Social Worker, most of the eatables were consumed by the Onge during the course of their stay in Hut Bay itself. Sometimes, when the Onge are to be presented before the dignitaries visiting Hut Bay, they are made to stay there for many days at a stretch. During all these days, they are fed out of the money collected from the sale of their products. Only very little is carried by them to their settlements. By now the trade among the Onge is, that way, limited to an indirect form of barter. They bring the articles, and accept the return only in kind, though the deal is not direct and one to one. Monetary value is fixed for commodities. For instance, it is not fixed that an Onge would exchange ten coconuts for a bag. But the monetary value of the two is determined. The Onge, especially those who know a little Hindi and who are frequently or occasionally brought to Hut Bay and Port Blair, know that there is something like money with which things can be bought. Sometimes, especially when they are in Port Blair, the Onge ask for money. When asked as to what would they do with it, on the spot comes the answer that they would buy something from the shops. But at the same time, the value of being a moneyed person is yet to develop among the Onge. They are not yet familiar with the details of monetary transactions.

Relevant issues

1. In spite of mounting depopulation and heavy loss of human lives among the Onge, an extreme kind of ethnocentric attitude, in various walks of life, persists uninterrupted. At the same time, no sufficiently adequate efforts, taking care of their interests, from outside, have been made. It is high time that such a psychological front is carefully tackled with dedication and genuineness of purpose. Irrelevant assumptions of native need not persist limitlessly.

2. Onge life pattern is so intricately designed that only a holistic search into the religious, economic and social life can bear fruit to cater to the designing of a proper policy for their betterment. Because of typical ecological conditions around human life is not to be seen in isolation. Some of the socio-cultural ways hint at their adaptation with prevalent ecological setting.

3. An unfortunate event has been the sudden growth of other human groups around Onge settlements. And the rise of certain problems can, to a great extent, be attributed to the non-directed interaction between the native population and the new comers. Contact seems to have lacked in helpful direction. The protection of Onge interest was given last priority.

4. Introduction of material innovations among the Onge without creating awareness and need for them, does not seem to have proved a useful exercise. Under the circumstances, only the giving end poses as active. The real purpose, otherwise, remains short of being served.

5. Onge living in two perspectives, that is, when a large number of them live together, and when they move out in smaller bands for hunting and collection pursuits, requires to be seen from slightly different angles. The description of one, in isolation of the other, provides only an incomplete picture. Related to this are the necessity of searching and respect for the ways conforming to community living and solidarity.

6. Ordinarily, the Onge religion (animism) appears undeveloped. However, the religious life, in its active form is reported when examined microscopically in reference to certain imposing and threatening situations. While facing the latter, tribals resort to a variety of religious rites. To a change-agent, there is need to identify benevolent and malevolent spirits, along with their place in Onge life and culture. Such knowledge, in consonance with their religious sentiments, can be taken advantage of in planning and creating social change. On the other hand, their outright discarding and rejection, in the light of cross-cultural ideology, may create serious confrontation and barriers for proposed innovations. Socio-economic life cannot truly be assessed in isolation of belief and value systems based on religion.

7. Likewise, the hunting and collection economy is not to be treated as disjointed from patterns of social life, including nomadic group formations. In addition, for a sound strategy of economic development, the economic aspect of Onge living is to be seen in the context of non-Onge immigrants, and the resulting constraints thereof. Taking stock of the sentiments and impositions, emerged out of the arrival of, and interaction with others, is a prerequisite for imbibing accuracy in planning for Onge economic development. In the most primitive economy, as that of the Onge, it is otherwise a forcefully challenging task to induct economic innovations. Any attempt, in this respect, is to go along the background of economic understanding of the Onge, keeping, as far as possible, the associated social life undisturbed. More stress, for this purpose, is to be laid on the development of new economic sense, without making the people more dependent on others. And non-formal education seems to be an important instrument to achieve the same. In addition, it may be further useful in explaining the rationality

of relevant intricacies of monetized economy to which some of the Onge are lately getting exposed.

8. The unwanted items or ideas which, in reality, sound almost valueless to an Onge, need to be immediately stopped from being introduced in Onge society. More appropriate would be the provision of inspiration for what is most immediately and urgently required, and for what is befitting to the existing norm-complex put forth by societal ways, at times in conjunction with the eco-system.

Note: The data and information, used in the paper, date back to the beginning of the year nineteen hundred and seventy-four.

SUGGESTED READINGS

Cipriani, Lidio : *The Andaman Islanders*, Ed, D.T. Cose and Weidenfeld and Nicolson, London, 1966.

Director of Census : Provisional Population Totals, Andaman and Nicobar, 1971.

Mann, R.S. : "Jarawas of Andaman—An Analysis of Hostility", *Man in India*, Vol. 53, No. 2, 1973.

Mann, R.S. : "Defective strategy Regarding a Negrito Tribe of the Andamans, Problems and Suggestions", *Man and Life*, Vol. 2, No. 1 & 2, 1976.

Mann, R.S. : "Depopulation among Andaman Aborigines—An Analysis", *Indian Journal of Social Research*, Vol. 7, 1976.

Mann, R.S. : "The Bay Islander", Institute of Social Research and Applied Anthropology, Calcutta, Bidisa Press and Printing, 1979.

Roy, B.C. and Ganguly, Pranab : "Some ceremonial customs in Onge life Cycle", Published in *Folklore*, Vol. II, No. 6, 1961.

NINE

Vijoy S. Sahay

THE NICOBARESE
A Study in Nature-Man-Spirit Complex

THIS study of the coconut growing Nicobarese is exactly in tune with the study of *The Maler: A Study in Nature-Man-Spirit Complex* by Professor Vidyarthi (1963). There is, of course, a great difference between the socio-ecological condition of the Maler and the Nicobarese. This has indeed necessitated quite discernible differences between the two. The Maler, living in the hilly regions of the Santhal Parganas in the state of Bihar, are no parallel to the Nicobarese, who are not only surrounded by thick forests, but are also dwelling in absolute proximity with the sea. Therefore, it is very apt to say that if the forests are on the left hand side of the Nicobarese dwellings, the sea, must be, then, on the right side, and vice versa.

Such a complete dependence of Nicobarese life and culture on the sea and the forests has resulted in the forming of quite a distinct cultural group. However, for analytical purposes, the present author has taken the liberty to draw the initial form of thought and necessary theoretical framework from his intellectual guru's masterpiece work on the Maler (Vidyarthi, 1963).

I

Off the deep south east, of the long stretched eastern coast of the Indian Peninsula, between Sumatra and the Andaman Islands, in the Bay of Bengal, lies a chain of twelve inhabited and seven uninhabited islands of various sizes, known as the Nicobar Archipelago.* The inhabitants of these twelve islands

*The situation of the islands being 8.00N & 94.00E.

namely Car Nicobar, Chowra, Teressa, Bompoka, Katchall, Kamorta, Trinket, Nancowrie, Kondul, Pulomilo, Little Nicobar and Great Nicobar constitute a sizable population of 17,874 souls (Census of India 1971) and the people are referred to as the Nicobarese.

The history of these islands dates back to a remote past. For long years the islands were dreaded and reckoned with horror and abhorrence as the 'land of the naked people' or 'paradise of the pirates'. The existence of the Archipelago was known to the world since antiquity for its characteristic location along a very ancient and major sea-trade route from India to Burma and the Far East. They have been mentioned by Ptolemy (3rd Cent. B.C.), the Chinese Buddhist Monk I 'Tsing (A.D. 672); the two Arab travellers of the 9th Century; Marcopolo (A.D. 1286); Frier Odoric (A.D. 1322); Nicolo Conti (A.D. 1430) and many others too. An inscription of the Chola dynasty of the 10th Century A.D. founded in the Tanjore district of Tamil Nadu, asserts that this Archipelago was frequently visited by the early sea-voyagers of the mainland of India.

In the seventeenth century, the Nicobar Islands began to attract the attention of the missionaries. At various times France, Denmark, Austria and Great Britain, all had more or less obscure rights to the islands. The fatal climatic condition of the region continually frustrated their zeal and they always retired from their mission. It was not until 1869 that the Danes who were the most persistent in their efforts to occupy the entire group, relinquished their claims in favour of the British, which ultimately resulted in their overall occupation by the latter, and it was now that the bountiful nature and amicability of its people were first realised. The British in 1872 formed an external territory of India by uniting the Andaman Islands and the Nicobars under one administration. Though, the missionaries tried their utmost to elevate the mental status and exalt the social plight of the poor souls, the administration concerned seldom paid any attention to the improvement of the economic condition of the people there. At this hour of crisis, there appeared a man named V. Soloman (1887), who dedicated his entire life in his effort to emancipate the people from their deep rooted magico-religious beliefs and superstitions. He picked up a bunch of young boys from Car Nicobar and sent them to Rangoon for studies. Thus, education was first introduced in this illiterate archipelago. The islands remained under the Japanese occupation from 1942-45. During this period some roads were built, notably on Car Nicobar and jetties were constructed at village Malacca (Car Nicobar) and village Kamorta (Central Nicobar). The atrocities of the Japanese during the war disrupted their peaceful life, and for the first time, physical force was exercised upon these peace loving people. Today, the Andaman and Nicobar Islands are administered by the President of the Republic of India, through a Chief Commissioner, who is advised by a local council of five members. The administrative headquarters are at Port Blair on South Andaman and a Deputy Commissioner is stationed on Car Nicobar in the Nicobar district.

The independence of India (1947) and the enactment of the Special Acts, Andaman and Nicobar Islands, Protection of Aborigines Tribes Regulation (1956), marked the advent of a new era, and have further ensured the protection and preservation of the customs and culture of the people.

The language in the Nicobars is derived from the Mon Khmer Speech Family. Five different dialects are spoken there. Car Nicobarese and Chowrians speak separate dialects. People of Teressa and Bompoka have a common dialect. A different but common dialect is spoken in the Nancowrie group of islands and the islands of the southern zone speak a separate dialect. Geographically, the Nicobar Islands are divided into three zones i.e. the Northern, the Central and the Southern. The Northern Zone consists of Car Nicobar. The Central Zone comprises the islands of Chowra, Teressa, Bompoka, Nancowrie, Katchall, Trinket and Kamorta. They are also known as the Nancowrie group of islands. The islands of Kondul, Pulomilo, Little Nicobar and Great Nicobar constitute the Southern Zone.

The Nicobarese are not divisible into tribes and, what differences are observable among the inhabitants of several islands, may be safely referred to their habitat, and the physical difficulties of communication between the islands. The Shompens are the only other tribe of the Nicobar Islands. They dwell in the interior of the thick forests of

Great Nicobar. Scanty information about them has been available hitherto. They are still known as food-gatherers and hunters. They speak a different dialect; however, inter-tribal relations between the Nicobarese and the Shompens do exist today. The inhabitants of each island of the Nicobar group have separate ideas about themselves and their lands. The inhabitants of Car Nicobar are locally though, referred to as the Nicobarese; the term, broadly applies to all the people of archipelago.

Though, the Nicobar Islands are known to the world since antiquity, the literature about them available hitherto has been very sporadic in the form of handbooks, gazetteers, settlement reports and a few ethnographic essays. The earliest reference of this tribe is found in a book by Renandot (1733). Subsequently, Yule (1871), Man (1888), Temple (1925), Kloss (1902) and a few others have given comprehensive accounts of the people. These reports contain a very naive description of the land, life and culture of the Nicobarese. Besides the works of the aforesaid scholars, a number of papers were published by several others. It is remarkable that an anthropologist of the calibre and repute of Professor Radcliffe Brown, had come to the Andaman Islands as early as in 1912. Professor Brown, however, confined his studies to the Negrito people of the Andaman Islands. In later years, he also published a monumental book *The Andaman Islanders* (1921). As Professor Radcliffe Brown confined his interest to the Negrito people of the Andaman Islands it remains a puzzle why the Nicobarese culture remained unnoticed by the trained eyes of social or physical anthropologists till a very recent period.

Of late, it has drawn the attention of the social scientists and eventually Professor Vidyarthi in 1970-71 undertook the challenging task of studying the tribes of the Andaman and Nicobar Islands. Professor Vidyarthi's articles at various times appeared in different journals in India and abroad. However, a full length monograph on the Nicobarese remains yet to be written.

I have been to the Nicobar Islands altogether on three occasions covering a total period of ten months. This enabled me to cover the entire Nicobarese area. However, for intensive data collection I confined my studies to the villages of Kinyuka (Car Nicobar), Tahila (Chowra) and Champin (Nancowrie). In the present work, though, references have been made to many of the villages of different islands, data collected from the aforesaid villages have been used to facilitate the comprehensive understanding of the Nicobarese Nature-Man-Spirit complex.

II

Besides the introduction, in our first part, we have dealt with "Nature" i.e. the ecological setting of the Nicobarese life. As we know that the forests and the sea are the two dominant themes of the Nicobarese eco-system, therefore, it has been further divided into two parts. The second part on "Man" is divided into three chapters. First we have dealt with the network of relationships of a Nicobarese as a member of his village, as a member of his family, and finally as a member of his tribe. Above all, the different "regions of contacts" of the Nicobarese have also been dealt with in this chapter. In the second chapter, pattern of relationships, the nature of family organisation and the economic, social, religious and reproductive activities of the Nicobarese family have been discussed. In the third chapter the entire process of socialization, life cycle and Nicobarese at the "axis of self" have been discussed.

The third part on "Spirit" deals with the Nicobarese and their spirit world. The Nicobarese believe that their destiny is guided and controlled by the spirits, locally known as the *Iwi*. They also believe that there are both benevolent and malevolent spirits, and they could be pleased and propitiated by the help of the witch-doctors. Thus, the "Sacred Complex" of the Nicobarese is dealt with in this part.

Finally, in our concluding chapter we have discussed the theoretical and methodological importance of the study of the Nature-Man-Spirit Complex of the Nicobarese, and its use in understanding the society and culture as such.

NATURE: COCONUT AND FOREST ECONOMY

The natural setting of the Nicobarese habitat comprises the forests and the sea. The forests that abound in the Nicobar

Islands are mainly tropical. Owing to excessive rain and proximity to the sea, the trees in the Nicobar Islands receive adequate requirement of rain and sunlight. Therefore, the forests are very thick there, and the trees are, sometimes, as tall as, 100′, with a crown foliage on the top.

The land of the Nicobar Islands varies from one island to another. Whereas, Car Nicobar is flat and sandy, the rest of the islands are rugged and hilly. As far as Chowra is concerned, the entire island is as flat as Car Nicobar, except its southern tip where there is a cliff as high as 300′. The cliff is locally known as "Tahop", meaning thereby, the "Devil's Abode". Great Nicobar is the biggest and the most rugged island of the Nicobar group. Teressa, Kamorta, Nancowrie, Trinket and Bompoka are semi-hilly.

The general features of the forests are that they are not very far from the village settlement. A village in Nicobar is always settled in between the forests and the sea. The growth of the forests is more dense and thick towards the centre of the island. Forests are also full of shrubs and bushes.

From the very childhood a Nicobarese comes in contact with the forest. All the gardens (locally known as Heom) are made inside the forest. Generally, a small hut is constructed near the garden. The Nicobarese keep their chickens and pigs inside the jungle.

The Nicobarese also believe that their *Iwis* (spirits) reside in the forests. Therefore, even in the day time a Nicobarese dare not go inside the forests alone. When a Nicobarese dies falling off a tree the people observe complete taboo to go to the forest for three days. Often sacrifices are offered inside the forest and in the gardens, to appease the spirits.

From the very childhood, the impact of the forest penetrates so deeply into the life of the Nicobarese, that it appears as it were in the very 'ethos and world-view' of the people. The familiarity of the Nicobarese children with the ecological setting develops gradually from their early infancy, as they are taken to the forests with their parents for collecting fruits, roots, grasses, herbs etc. They also learn the names of the plants and trees, and recognise the roots and herbs of medicinal value, which help them in times of need.

Thus, the forests are, no doubt, one of the most significant factors of the Nicobarese culture. The Nicobarese love the forest and sing songs in its praise, because it is the source of their livelihood; it provides them with the raw materials for making canoes, mats, baskets, huts etc; and it is the forest where their spirits live. Thus, the forest is one of the main sources of the Nicobarese subsistence.

In accordance with Professor Vidyarthi's study of the Maler forest economy, we have also categorised the important economic functions that the forest plays in the life of the Nicobarese:

(1) Forest as a source of food and drink.
(2) Forest as a source of providing shelter.
(3) Forest as a source of canoe making.
(4) Forest as a source of providing raw materials for cottage industries.
(5) Forest as a source of providing herbs and roots of medicinal value.

FOREST AS A SOURCE OF FOOD AND DRINK

The main food items that the Nicobarese receive from the forests are coconuts, arecanut, pandanus, a variety of fruits and vegetables, animals and birds.

Coconut

A major part of the Nicobarese forest is occupied by coconut trees. Coconut trees are so profuse and abundant that nobody in the Nicobars knows the exact number of the trees he owns. In Car Nicobar, coconut trees of a family are owned by the captain of that respective family.

Pilferage of fruits is seldom practised. In a coconut grove the mark of *Takoya* signifies prohibition to pluck coconuts from the trees. The *Takoya* mark is represented by two sticks erected on the ground under a group of coconut trees, on which are hung a few pieces of cloth, and sometimes the mandible of a pig. When a mark of *Takoya* is seen, it is prohibited to pluck coconuts from the trees around. Such prohibition is observed to commemorate a departed soul. When a person dies, a mark of *Takoya* is erected near the coconut plantation of the respective family. The reasons behind the erection of such a mark are numerous. A number of expensive rituals and ceremonies are observed after the death of a person. To meet the expenses of such functions, coconuts are preserved and saved from wastage.

Takoya is not removed until a lot of money is made out of the coconuts. If the rules of *Takoya* are violated by anybody, the guilty are liable to be severely punished.

Coconut is the mainstay of the Nicobarese life. They eat coconut, they feed it to their pigs, chicken and dogs; coconut is used at the time of their canoe worship; tender coconuts are offered to the canoes and hung around them; coconuts are also offered to appease spirits.

No part of a coconut tree is left un-used. The trunk of the tree is used for making stilts for their houses; the dried leaves of the coconut tree are used for making torches; the torches are used for fishing and catching octopus in the night hours and also for roasting pigs. Small and tender coconuts are used at the time of canoe worship. A small baby is fed with the most tender and delicate cocount kernel. Coconut kernel is a delicious item of Nicobarese diet. They quench their thirst with coconut water. Coconut shells are used as toddy and water containers. Hundreds of coconut shells are hung near every hut which contain water. From the flower of the coconut they extract toddy. Thus, we find that the Nicobarese utilise coconut not only as an item of food and drink, but also for use in all the magico-religious practices. They make oil from the coconut. Copra for oil, made out of coconut, is sold in the Panamhinengo (Co-operative Society) to earn money and purchase different articles of use.

The coconut is associated with every aspect of the Nicobarese life. It would be no exaggeration to say that there is the presence of the coconut-complex in the Nicobars. Whether it be the birth ceremony of a child or the death of a person, a political dispute, or a canoe race, the inauguration of a canoe or a hut, a marriage or merely an exchange of articles or an act of witchcraft, the coconut is indispensable, and quite ubiquitous on all occasions. If a coconut is plucked from a prohibited area where the mark of *Takoya* stands, the guilty are not only punished, but the very sentiment of the Nicobarese is hurt.

There are legends, songs and tales in praise of the coconut. It is held by the Chowrians that their earliest ancestors had brought coconuts with them, and had planted them near Hiva (a sacred place near the cliff at Chowra).

As we have earlier stated that the Nicobarese extract toddy, and oil from coconut, they also make copra for sale. The methods of extracting oil and toddy are very simple. However, their simple method of extracting offers very little yield. The oil that a Nicobarese family prepares is only sufficient for their family use, and not for business.

Copra Making

Nevertheless, copra-making is one of the most essential works done by the Nicobarese. It is so because, only by copra-making, can they make money. There are two processes for making copra. In the first process, they pluck coconuts, and by the help of their iron blades, split it into two halves. They let it dry in the sun for two days. The coconut kernel is then removed from the shell and is kept in the sunshine for eight to ten days. The quality of such copra is very high, but the yield absolutely depends upon the bright sunshine, and as we know that there is tropical climate in this archipelago, and the annual rainfall is approximately 122", the sky is most often covered with clouds. Therefore, Nicobarese seldom practise this method of copra-making.

In the second method, the coconut is first plucked and split into two halves. In the same way, the kernel is removed. Instead of keeping them in the sun, a wooden platform is raised, under which a fire place is made. The ripe coconut kernel is put on the platform, and the fire is lit underneath. Precaution is, however, taken so that the flames should not touch either the platform or the kernel. In this way the kernel is dried by the heat of the fire within a couple of hours. In this method of copra-making one has not to depend upon the sun nor upon the weather. This method is universally applied in the Nicobars. Even during the rainy season a Nicobarese can easily prepare copra for his needs.

From the aforesaid discussion, it becomes evident that the coconut is not only economically useful, but it is also useful in the socio-cultural and magico-religious functions of the

Nicobarese. However, it is desirable here to know that the Nicobarese do not exactly understand the economic importance of coconut. According to a rough estimate, every two out of five coconuts is consumed by the Nicobarese themselves. They feed their pigs and chickens with two coconuts, and they leave one for making copra. In fact, a great amount of coconut is left unutilised by the Nicobarese. If they feed their pigs with some other article of food and instead make copra out of the available coconuts, they would earn more money than at present. It is also to be noted here that the number of pigs owned by a family is more than its members. It can be easily assumed that a greater amount of coconut is consumed by the pigs than by the human beings. On the contrary, the pigs have little economic utility. The pigs are mostly killed during a festive occasion, and ceremoniously consumed. Moreover the pigs are a menace to the well-fenced Nicobarese gardens. Most often they invade the well planted gardens and destroy them by uprooting the plants. Also, the husk of the coconut is left absolutely unused. If the economic importance of coconut is realised by the Nicobarese, and it is appropriately made use of it can, to a great extent, boost the economic condition of the Nicobarese and their fortunes would be enhanced.

Pandanus

Pandanus is one of the delicacies of the Nicobarese. Pandanus trees are wild as well as cultivated in the gardens. Pandanus is not consumed in their daily diet. On festive occasions, they pluck pandanus and, a cheese like preparation, locally known as *Taluva* is prepared out of it. *Taluva* can be kept for a couple of days without its being spoilt. On a ceremonial voyage, the Chowrians and the Car Nicobarese carry *Taluva* with them. It serves as an item of food during their voyage to the other islands, at the same time, they distribute it to their friends of the other islands.

Arecanut

Arecanut is a kind of cash-crop to the Nicobarese. Though, to a little extent, it is also consumed by them. The Nicobarese are habituated is betel-chewing. The arecanut also after drying is sold by the Nicobarese at the *Panamhinengo* at a price fixed by the administration.

Other Fruits and Vegetables

Important among the fruits and vegetables that the Nicobarese produce in their garden are banana, papaya, yams, pine-apple etc. Coconuts, pandanus and arecanut are produced in the forests, and little care is needed for their growth. They are mostly self-sown. But the fruits like yams, banana, papaya etc. are always produced in the gardens. The gardens are well-fenced, though the fencing differs from one island to another.

When discussing the Nicobarese gardens, we should note that while all the families in the Nicobars have a certain number of coconut trees for their livelihood, they do not have necessarily land for making gardens. In fact, only few old and reputed families possess surplus land. In such circumstances, the landless Nicobarese approach the land owners to seek permission to make garden for a particular season. Such gardens are generally shared by many families, and are collectively constructed. The process of garden making is as follows:

Garden Making : Clearing

Owing to excessive rain and its proximity to the Equator, there is a luxuriant growth of forests in the Nicobars. When a garden is to be constructed, all friends and relatives are called upon to contribute in the clearing of the jungle. When a particular site for the garden is selected, on a certain date after consulting the witch-doctor, all the members of a family along with their friends, go to the site with their axes and iron scythes. In the jungle the host prepares food for all. In food preparation mostly the women are engaged. The men clear the jungle with their tools. They first clear the bushes and the shrubs, and then they cut the big trees. If a big garden is to be constructed, it sometimes takes two days to clear the jungle.

Burning

After a few days of clearance, lifeless plants and trees become dry enough. With the consultation of a witch-doctor, a day is fixed for their ceremonious burning. All men and women who have their shares in the garden, make torches of dried leaves of coconut and go there. They start burning the cleared forest from all corners. Within a few hours the shrubs and bushes turn into wild flames and ultimately into ashes. The remaining trunks of the big trees, are later used by the villagers as firewood for copra-making.

Fencing

For a few days after its burning the place is left unused so that the ashes become manure. Then fencing starts. It is done with stakes and shaped in a circular form. After its fencing, division of the area for each shareholder is made. At the centre of the garden, some banana trees are planted. Thus, from the centre each shareholder gets a triangular area. When this demarcation is complete, all the shareholders consult a witch-doctor for the selection of an auspicious day for plantation. Plantation is done generally on the sixth day of the full moon. It is so because the Nicobarese believe that blood is sprinkled from the moon on the earth. They believe that this is harmful for new plantation. Thus, on the plantation day, accompanied by a witch-doctor the Nicobarese go to the garden one morning and firstly kill a pig. Blood is sprinkled at the centre and all around the garden to appease the spirits. It is thought that if the spirits are not appeased, the vegetables and fruits would not grow and death and disease would be caused in the families of the garden makers. For fear of spirits, they roast the chicken or pig, and a few pieces of it are offered to the spirits. After offering sacrifices they start planting.

Demolition of a Garden

The extent of superstition and fear of spirits can be realised from the fact that in the Rhion village of Chowra, the captain of the village named Kamichut fell ill while constructing a garden. There were nineteen shareholders in that garden. When his health deteriorated very much, he consulted a witch-doctor, who after detecting the cause of his illness, advised him to demolish the entire garden, as the spirits near the garden were not appeased at the time of its construction. He also suggested that if the garden were not demolished, the captain would die. Thus, within hours on 27th February 1974, the author witnessed the destruction of entire garden and its saplings which were collectively uprooted.

A garden normally lasts for three years. After the lapse of three years, a new site is selected and, similarly, the entire process of garden making is repeated. Thus, we find that the Nicobarese are *shifting horticulturists*. The Nicobarese do not move from one place to another. They dwell permanently in a village. Their garden, however, is shifted from one place to another. It is also not necessary that a Nicobarese should have a garden only in his own village. He may ask his friend, living in a distant village, for a share in the garden.

We have earlier mentioned that there are only a few land-owners in the Nicobars. Nevertheless, it has been observed that there is hardly any competition found among the Nicobarese. The people are very co-operative. In recent years, however, the pressure on land is increasing and the land-owners are, unlike in earlier times, getting conscious of their property. Now the inheritance of property is strictly being followed on hereditary lines. Half a century ago, the captain of a family was selected purely in a democratic form. It was subject to seniority and leadership quality. But now, due to the introduction of education and their exposure to the modern developments, the eldest son of a captain generally becomes the next captain. It has been observed that unlike before the children of a captain enjoy more privileges in Nicobarese society than their other poor counterparts. It has also been suggested by some writers that there has been the rise of a feudal system in the Nicobarese society.

Thus, besides the use of forests, as adumberated in the foregoing paragraphs, the Nicobarese obtain a number of birds and animals from the forest. For the purpose of shooting birds they use a cross-bow. They use spears while hunting pigs in the jungle.

FOREST AS A SOURCE OF PROVIDING SHELTER

The Nicobarese huts are raised on wooden stilts, thatched

with grass, their floors made of bamboo, and the platform below the hut of wood and bamboo. There is no mud or brick wall nor is there a tiled roof. There is no window, nor is there any artificial ventilator. For the purpose of shelter, all the Nicobarese depend upon the forest.

Their houses are a unique feature of the Nicobarese. They are best suited to their environment. The floor of the houses is raised on stilts about 6′ to 8′ from the ground level and rest on strong posts. The materials used in the construction of the houses, are wooden legs, timber, trunks of coconut or arecanut trees, bamboo, thatching grass and coconut leaves. It has been observed that there are four types of houses in the Nicobars:

(1) Dome-shaped round houses raised on stilts.
(2) Rectangular houses with sloping wagon type raised on stilts.
(3) Improved type of houses, raised on stilts.
(4) Pucca houses which are not on stilts.

As mentioned earlier, the Nicobarese houses are best suited to their climate, availability, adjustment, social norms and social values. Owing to excessive rain and thereby to avoid dampness of the ground, and for fear of snakes and insects, the houses are raised on stilts. The ladder is removed and taken upstairs in the night hours. Thus, all the family members feel secure inside the hut. In all the houses there is a hearth, where cooking is done. Hearths are so safely arranged that there is no danger of fire. Mats are spread on the floor on which people sleep comfortably. Inside the house, the Nicobarese are fully insulated from cold, heat and rain. Articles inside the house are only a few. Life size wooden images of human beings and scary devils, locally known as *kareyava* are kept in a corner. Normally, a Nicobarese hut lasts for thirty years.

While making the houses, the Nicobarese propitiate a number of spirits by offering sacrifices of pigs and chicken. It is also interesting to know that while the male members of a family manage to bring all the necessary articles needed for the construction of a house, and erect the post, it is the females who mainly thatch and build the house.

FOREST AS A SOURCE OF CANOE MAKING

In former days, canoes were the only means of communication between these islands. A Nicobarese canoe is a dug-out hull of the trunk of a big tree. Even today, all sorts of inter-island as well as intra-island communications are carried out by canoes only. And the canoes are made in the forest. Thus, to exploit the sea-economy, the Nicobarese depend upon the forest.

Canoes are perhaps the most loved objects of the Nicobarese. There is no family which does not possess a canoe. Though in Car Nicobar people ride on bicycles, they still prefer the canoe to any other means of communication. Small islands like Chowra, Kondul, Pulomilo etc. depend absolutely upon the canoe for communication. Canoes differ in their shape and size depending upon the locality. They are named as the Chowra type, the Nancowrie type and the Kondul type.

Broadly speaking, the canoes are of three sizes i.e. the mini, the midi and the maxi. A mini canoe can accommodate only two persons only one at the front end and the other at the rear end. It is only used for fishing. Long journeys are not undertaken in it. This size of canoe is found in almost every Nicobarese family.

A midi has two useful purposes. It can accommodate 8 to 12 persons, and is utilised for fishing as well as journey purposes. It has, generally, two sails.

A maxi canoe is mostly used for ceremonial voyages and racing competition. It accommodates 25 to 40 persons and can go a long distance. All the trade voyages are carried on such canoes. Canoe race is prevalent in all the islands of the Nicobar group. It is held in the Nicobars that the bigger the size and the higher the number of such canoes one owns, the higher the social status he commands in the society.

The people of Chowra and Kondul are the main canoe makers. The people of Teressa, Bompoka and Car Nicobar do not make their own canoes. They get them from the Chowrians. Similarly, the people of Great and Little Nicobar get theirs from the people of Kondul Nancowrians are capable of making only small canoes.

Process of Canoe Making

The author has witnessed the Chowrian canoe making process. In fact the canoes are not made in Chowra owing to the deficiency of suitable flora in their land for the purpose. Therefore, Chowrians go to Teressa or any other island of the Nancòwrie group for this purpose. The Chowrians do not ever go to the islands of the southern zone, because of their deep rooted belief that even a particle of sand from there would lead to the destruction of Chowra.

Thus, a Chowrian when he wants to make a new canoe, goes to one of his family friends on any island for some work. It is notable here that the Chowra people whereas, are regarded on the one hand as the spiritual leaders of the Nicobarese, on the other, they are also valued for their manual labour and skill in house construction, horticulture, roof thatching and copra-making. They do such work for their friends and in lieu of wages they demand a big tree for making canoes to their liking. So long as a Chowrian stays in the house of his friend, he is treated as a guest. His friend does not want to offend or displease his Chowra counterpart for fear of misfortune in consequence. Thus after the completion of the allotted work to him, a Chowrian is asked to choose a tree for his canoe. After the selection of a suitable tree, the Chowrian returns home to persuade his friends and relatives to help him in canoe making.

First they clear the jungle and make a path from the seashore to the tree site. It should be noted that the selection of a tree for canoe making is always done near the sea-shore. The tree is cut down and the branches are removed. A place for temporary settlement is made and many persons are employed on the job. The manual co-operation among the Nicobarese can be understood from the fact that on such occasions, no wages are given to the persons employed thus. As long as they stay there they manage their food together. When the canoe is half ready, both its ends are horizontally stretched in mild fire. The finishing work is not done on the spot. An out-rigger is made and the canoe is brought near the sea-shore. All this takes about a month.

Thus, the half made canoe is brought to Chowra. The finishing work, to make the canoe sharp and beautiful, is done at Chowra. Artistic designs are engraved on the front and the rear end of the canoe. The Nicobarese keep their canoes with great care, and from time to time offer sacrifices to appease the spirits to save themselves from disaster at sea.

When the canoe is completely ready, a date is fixed for its inauguration. On the inaugural day, the canoe worship is held with great pomp and show, and is followed by a canoe race in the evening. The main market for Chowra canoes is the island of Car Nicobar.

FOREST AS A SOURCE OF PROVIDING RAW MATERIALS FOR COTTAGE INDUSTRIES

Though there is sufficient potentiality for the development of cottage industries in the Nicobar Islands, and the quality of the articles that the Nicobarese produce is very high, there has been little development of it so far. This is more so because the consumption of such articles is very low. Whatever they produce is for their domestic use only, and not for a market sale.

Mats and baskets are made in Car Nicobar, Teressa, Bompoka and Nancowrie group of islands. Canoes are made particularly in Chowra and Kondul. Pots are made exclusively in Chowra. Inter-island exchange prevails in the Nicobar Islands. Mats are made of pandanus leaves, baskets are made of bamboo and are of various sizes and shapes. Thus, we find that for every article of cottage industry the Nicobarese depend upon the forest. Even for pots the Chowrians depend greatly upon the forest.

A Chowra pot has two significant purposes among the Nicobarese. First it is considered to be the harbinger of fortune and prosperity, therefore, meals are cooked in it on special occasions. Secondly, it is thought that if a child is bathed in the water boiled in Chowra pots, he/she would be immunised against black magic. Therefore, it is held sacred and universally employed for use by all the Nicobarese. People make ceremonial voyage to the island of Chowra to fetch such pots.

The making of a Chowra pot is very interesting. The Chowrians are ignorant of wheel pottery. They prepare it by their hands only. As the pot-clay is not available in Chowra, they ceremonially go to Teressa to fetch it. There are a lot of rituals associated with pot making. (The details have been published in the *Journal of Social Research*, Vol. XIX, No. 2, 1976). When the pot-clay is brought to Chowra, it is handed over to the women-folk. They go to another sacred place in Chowra named Hiva to fetch sand to be mixed with the clay. The preparation of such pots is an exclusively female prerogative. For a Chowrian girl pottery is a necessary skill.

To sum up, we can say that all the necessary articles of cottage industries in the Nicobar Islands are dependent upon the forest.

FOREST AS A SOURCE OF PROVIDING HERBS AND ROOTS OF MEDICINAL VALUE

Hospitals are a new introduction to the Nicobarese life. Owing to complete geographical isolation, the Nicobarese have been using folk medicines from the time immemorial. Except on Car Nicobar, the medicine men still abound in the Nicobar Islands. Besides the witch-doctor, there are numerous experienced old males and females on all the islands, who prove to be helpful in curing a sick person.

While discussing folk medicines it is notable that the people of Teressa are regarded as the experts in folk medicine. It is believed that the Teressans have an extremely good knowledge of 'abortive medicines'; the medicine men of this island could successfully sterilize a woman; people from Nancowrie group of islands, often consult the Teressans for such medicines. It was also astonishing to find that the married couples in Teressa, had either no child or only a few in number. When enquired about the cause of such a state of affairs, it was told that many women practised there, either abortion or sterilization. It was further told by our women informants that they practised abortion or sterilization in order to maintain their beauty. In their opinion, if a woman gives birth to a greater number of children, she would become bulky and ugly. There would be no charm to her face. Consequently, she would no more be able to attract the attention of men during any festive occasion.

All the folk medicines are collected from the forest. The persons who know the names of the plants do not disclose these easily. They also believe that according to the necessities, the spirits, under the man's control, comes in a dream and tell the name of the medicine and its whereabouts. And before plucking any leaf from the plant or the tree he begs for the excused and auto-suggests, "I pluck you, because we want it for cure and for good purpose. O! dear plant, kindly don't be offended and cure the person, to whom the medicine is applied." Thus, the Nicobarese have an idea that there is life even in plants and trees.

NATURE : SEA ECONOMY

We have mentioned earlier that if the forest is on the left hand side of the Nicobarese, then sea must be on the right side. Sea plays an equal and important role in determining the culture of the Nicobarese in general and economic life in particular.

Waters around this archipelago abound in fish. Sea is not only useful in procuring fish but, they get small octopus, varieties of snails, turtles, crocodiles etc. from the sea. Above all, communication is the most important advantage that the Nicobarese gain from the sea. The utility of the sea can be classified into these categories:

1. as a source of food,
2. as a means of communication,
3. as a source of entertainment.

SEA AS A SOURCE OF FOOD

The Nicobarese are very fond of fish. It is also one of their staple diets. From the very childhood a Nicobarese comes in contact with sea. Nicobarese huts are, sometimes, so near the sea that often during the high tide hours, sea waters reach underneath the hut.

Fishing is done by all age groups and sexes. The method of fishing, however, differs from one age-group to another. In the harbours where fishing is devoid of any risk, men and women are found going far into the sea, specially in the night hours.

Fishing Methods

The most common method of fishing is by hook and line. A fishing hook is attached to one end of the line. A bait, generally made of a small fish, is attached to the hook. In open sea, the fishermen on a canoe, throws the line in the sea holding the other end is maintained in his hands. Occasionally, a shark is also caught. In such cases, fishermen are very cautious, and with great precaution they bring the shark onto the canoe, where it is immediately struck with an iron blade and killed.

The Nicobarese also use spears and iron blades for fishing. During low tide, the Nicobarese fish with the help of sticks, rods and their iron blades. They also use a kind of intoxicant locally known as *kinyaya* for the fish. They use it in the still waters along the shore. During the night hours when there is low tide, the Nicobarese go near the shore with torches of dried coconut leaves and practise fishing with their tools. Besides the aforesaid methods of fishing, the Nicobarese now-a-days, also use fishing nets. But as nets are very costly, only the rich Nicobarese can afford them.

Loss of lives and property is very common in the Nicobars during fishing. When there is such an instance, the Nicobarese try to appease the spirits by offering sacrifices. Also, before going to the deep sea for fishing, they worship their canoes to prevent them from any natural calamity or disaster. They believe that through canoe worship the spirits residing in the sea could be appeased. If a man dies by accident while at sea, the witch-doctors forbid people from going into the sea for fishing for a limited period, until the appropriate rituals are over to calm down the wrath of the sea spirit. The taboos connected with fishing are also very elaborate. For example, the Chowrians do not fish around the shore near the *elpenum* (community huts) during their festival of *bunglav*.

Ceremonial Fishing

The Nicobarese fish not only satisfy their hunger and meet the economic demand, but often they organise communal and ceremonial fishing. The most remarkable and elaborate ceremonial fishing expedition takes place in Chowra. Between Chowra and the uninhabited island of Battimalve there is a huge deposit of coral reef. It is spread over an area of a few hundred square yards. The Nicobarese believe that this area is full of different species of fishes. After the festival of *Vee-fop-lach*, the Chowrians organise an expedition to the coral reef. The Chowrians go to the reef in odd numbers and as soon as they reach there, they all maintain silence. They talk by signals only for fear of spirits. They further believe that a spirit in the form of a monster lives near the reef, and any violation of the rules would make him overturn their canoes. Therefore, strict sanctity is maintained in such an expedition. In all the islands of the Nicobar group, similar communal fishing expeditions are organised at the village as well as island level. The day and hour of such expeditions are fixed by the captains and the witch doctors. During calm weather and the mild season, when there is no probability of rain and storm, the Nicobarese, on small and big canoes, set out on a long voyage miles away in the deep sea with their hooks and lines. If they have an enormous catch of fish, they dry it and preserve it for future consumption.

Fish from the sea is the counterpart of coconut from the forest. It is no exaggeration to say that the entire commissariat of the Nicobarese revolve round the coconut and the fish.

Besides fish, the Nicobarese hunt small octopus along the coast, and big turtles and crocodiles in the outer sea. The turtles and the crocodiles are killed with the help of their spears.

SEA AS A MEANS OF COMMUNICATION

The varying sizes of islands in the Nicobar group also vary in their physical features. On big islands, to make a cross-country visit, is a difficult task. For example, in Car Nicobar there is only one circular road, which covers the entire island.

Likewise. the Great Nicobar is so rugged and hilly at the centre that it is really difficult to make a cross-country visit on foot. It is for this reason that no such road has so far been built there. Moreover, in many of the Nicobarese Islands, the hill starts right from the back of the village settlement. Therefore, if a Nicobarese has to go to another village, situated at the other end of the island, he always prefers to go by canoe, rather than on foot or by bicycle.

A long canoe journey is planned with great pomp and show. When a group of Nicobarese decide to go to a distant island they consult the witch-doctor of either the village or the island. A date is fixed for the voyage. The date and time of departure is coterminus with the favourable hour of the tides and the currents. The departure is always preceded by canoe worship. A chicken or a pig is sacrified on such occasions and the canoe is tastefully decorated with the tender leaves of coconuts. Several tender coconuts are hung on the canoe and the inner soft edible part of it is squeezed and mixed with the blood of chicken or pig for pasting on the different parts of the canoe. It is believed that the canoe worship must be performed before a journey, lest any misfortune befall upon the voyagers. From the above discussion, we can easily affirm that communication is mostly by the sea-routes, whether inter-island or intra-island.

SEA AS A SOURCE OF ENTERTAINMENT

Besides the sea being helpful in maintaining the sources of livelihood and means of communication, it also provides recreation to the Nicobarese men and women. It is a common sight to find children and males and females of all age groups, taking a bath at any hour of the day and night. While they take a bath they splash water on one another. Though the Nicobarese often swim in the sea they are not good divers.

The chief entertainment of the Nicobarese is the canoe race. The canoe race has a socio-religious significance for the Nicobarese. Any occasion of happiness or sorrow is followed by a canoe race. It be the inauguration of a canoe, or the birth of a child, or the *kindrak* of a dead soul, or new establishment of friendship between two persons or even dispute between them, it always ends with a canoe race.

The most spectacular race is organised in Chowra. The date of the race is announced a few days earlier. Both the parties keep themselves engaged in collecting toddy, yams, banana, chicken etc. for the occasion. On the racing day all the people of the island, with toddy containers in their hands, assemble in front of the houses of both the parties. The canoes are also tastefully decorated in the morning with banana leaves. A pig is also sacrificed. The pig is killed by inserting a sharp stick in its heart. Consequently the heart gets punctured. The pig is then roasted over a fire made of dried coconut tree leaves and is brought on board the canoe. In the meantime people keep themselves busy with eating and drinking toddy. They also dance and sing. In the evening all come near the shore with their canoes and the canoe race begins. There is no competition in the race. They row their canoes from one end of the island to the other. It does not matter who wins the race, but all the participants are given a piece of cloth.

Thus, canoe race is very often organised between two persons. The interesting feature of the race is that even if two persons quarrel, they decide their dispute by a canoe race. To sum up, we can say that the sea has not only an economic function in the life of the Nicobarese, but its social significance is also immense.

MAN: THE NICOBARESE SOCIAL SYSTEM, THE TRIBE, THE LINEAGE, THE VILLAGE

The Nicobar Archipelago is inhabited by two distinct tribes viz. the Nicobarese and the Shompen. We have mentioned that the Shompen live inside the thick forests of Great Nicobar. They are forest dwellers, food-gatherers and hunters. On the contrary, we have also mentioned that the Nicobarese are coast dwellers and shifting-horticulturists, but settled villagers. Their temporary gardens shift from one place to another, but the Nicobarese live a real settled life. The Nicobarese are neither divisible into tribes, nor is there any evidence of clan or totemic groups. Their conception of community is that all the people of the Nicobars, except the Shompen are Nicobarese. Nevertheless, the people of each island feel their separate identity. Also, they have separate Nicobarese names for their islands.

The Nicobarese prefer to marry within their island only, however, inter-island marriages are widely prevalent today. There are instances of marriages outside the group, but as a rule, it is strictly prohibited. It has been observed that territorial division did not comply with the cultural division. As already mentioned, territorially the Nicobarese are divided into three zones, whereas, culturally they can be grouped into four. It should also be noted that besides the majority of Christian population, there is a small minority of Muslims also in the Nicobar Islands. Thus, we can say that there are three sections of Nicobarese living together there, viz. the Christians, the Muslims and the traditional Animists.

CULTURAL ZONES IN THE NICOBARS

The four cultural zones in the Nicobars are the Car Nicobarese, the Chowrians, the Nancowrians and the Great Nicobarese. This division has been made on the basis of culture traits like inheritance of property, marriage rules and customs. These traits, however, depend upon the size of the island and distribution of population there. In our opinion, these traits play a determining role in the formation and variation of the Nicobarese culture.

Society in Car Nicobar is most systematically organised. It is 49 sq. miles in area consisting of more than 16 thousand souls. The joint family system is found in Car Nicobar. The head of the family is known as *makupati*. The property of the family is owned by him. He is to look after the other members of the family. Pigs are also supposed to be the family property in Car Nicobar. Though the pigs are owned by different individuals, they cannot be killed as fancied by any individual. One has to seek permission from the captain of the family. The head of the family in Car Nicobar inherits the entire property. Thus, owing to the high density of population, there is high pressure on land also, consequently, we find, that in Car Nicobar, women do not possess the right to property. This results in the prevalence of a monogamous form of marriage there.

South of Car Nicobar is the island of Chowra. It is one of the smallest islands with the highest density of population. It constitutes a population of 17 hundred souls in an area of 2.80 sq. miles only. Food is not found in plenty. Male members have to go to other islands in search of jobs and a livelihood. Women are not independent, therefore, monogamy is the rule here.

The case is different in the islands of Teressa, Bompoka, Katchall, Kamorta, Trinket and Nancowrie. These islands are bigger in size than their proportionate distribution of population. Women on these islands do have the right to property. Therefore, they live independently and though, monogamy is practised there the marriage-tie is not very strong and there is a great frequency of divorce on these islands.

Finally, in the southern group we find that property is owned both by males and females. Marriage customs are similar to the Nancowrians.

Nevertheless, because of a clear-cut territorial division in the Nicobar Islands we find two distinct zones of interactions i.e. the inter-island and the intra-island. They are in interaction with each other for economic, social, religious and political functions.

Marriage Ring: A Region of Interaction

Marriage can be easily arranged with any suitable match, from amongst individuals in the same village or another, or on the neighbouring island. The only taboo, as it has been reported is that the match should not be with each other's consanguinal relative, up to three generations, on both father's and mother's side. This is, however, the case only with the Christian Nicobarese. Because surprisingly enough, it is for a Chowrian to tell anything about his great-grand-father. It was astonishing for the present author that while collecting the genealogies, the Chowrians could hardly tell about their five cousins.

Marriages take place in the villages located in all directions. Villages and islands, falling within the marriage zone, are in closer social contacts with each other, and frequent visits on many social, religious and economic occasions take place. Pre-marital relations often result in marriages. In Car

Nicobar, mostly inter-village marriages take place. The Car Nicobarese, however, go to other islands in search of jobs and marry there. Therefore, inter-island marriage is also very common. The Chowrians mostly marry in Chowra. Only a few of them have married in Teressa. This is so because there are strong economic ties between the people of Chowra and Teressa. Almost all the families in Chowra have shares in the gardens of their friends in Teressa. As the Chowrians mostly remain on different islands in search of a livelihood they do not want to marry on other islands. And, they do not also want to stay away from their own island for more than 60 days, for fear of their wives being seduced by others.

In the Nancowrie groups of islands, inter-village and inter-island marriages are equally common. Many people have married in any of the four islands of this group. In fact they believe that they are one people.

Exchange of Mutual Labour

The exchange of mutual help and labour prevails at the inter-island and intra-island level as well. Be it for garden making, or a canoe race, or a birth or death ceremony, or any occasion when the people of the entire village or island assemble together, for a communal feast, the host cannot afford to entertain them alone. In such cases he contacts his friends in the same village or island, and seeks their economic support. Such support is rendered liberally. In return, the host also helps his friend in need. Canoe making or garden making is not done by an individual. It is seen that during the kindrak (re-burial) people from different islands come to help their friends in celebrating the feast.

Festival Ring: A Region of Interaction

The Nicobarese feel pride and satisfaction in celebrating a festive occasion. On different islands different festivals are celebrated. As a matter of fact, we know that the Christians, the Muslims and the traditional Nicobarese are living together in Nicobars. They live in complete harmony, devoid of any animosity. They briskly participate in each other's festivals.

The Traditional Exchange Ring: A Region of Interaction

It is the most significant factor that brings about closer contacts among the people of different villages and islands. There is complete absence of an open market system in the Nicobars. The Nicobarese exchange with each other the articles of indigenous manufacture. The inhabitants of each island are experts in making a certain article of use. The articles of exchange are mats, baskets, pots, canoes, honey, bamboo, pigs, coconuts, fabric and occasionally money. An institutionalised ring of exchange system works in the Nicobars.

This traditional system of exchange in the Nicobar archipelago is the only factor that unites all the islands. There are some islands where direct trade does not prevail, but they get the articles of their use indirectly through other parties as in the case of the Chowrians and the people of the southern zone (*For details see the illustration of the Trade Route*).

Nevertheless, production and consumption are not done on a large scale. As the articles are manufactured mostly by hand, the consumption always exceeds production.

The Chowra pot and the canoe are the most important items of trade. The Car Nicobarese come to Chowra to fetch such pots and buy canoes also. The Chowrians, in return receive pigs, coconuts and cloth. Reciprocal visits are made by the Chowrians to the island of Car Nicobar. As the Chowrians do not go to the islands of the southern zone, people from there come to the Nancowrie group of islands to get such pots. The Chowrian give such pots to the Nancowrians, who ultimately supply it to the Great and the Little Nicobarese.

It is important to note that in the absence of a market system like the mainland, the Nicobarese developed friendship with other islanders. Such friendship is maintained through generations in order to help a needy person in time. The author would like to term it as *family-friendship-bonds*. After the death of a person, such friendship is further maintained and strengthened by his sons. It is very apt to say that *once in bond always in bond*. Such bonds are inter as well as intra-island. Maintenance of such friendship bonds become necessary in case of inter-island trade. Many islands are situated far off and devoid of any lodging facilities for an outsider. In such cases if a person goes to another island, he can be accommodated and entertained by his family friends, and by none else. If he does not have such a friend on any island, it would be futile for him to go there ever. He may have to starve there. Hence the people of these islands are interested in, and wish to strengthen and develop *family-friendship-bonds* with the people of other islands, so as to make this trade flourish and also to maintain the solidarity of the Nicobarese society.

Political Ring: A Region of Interaction

Besides marriage, economic, festival and trade ties, the political set-up of the Nicobarese adds to the unity and the interaction among the inhabitants of several islands. The captains play a key role in the Nicobarese political set-up. This is the indigenous system of leadership there. In fact a man who enjoys more respect and command in the society is selected a captain. Every Nicobarese house has a captain. Similarly every Nicobarese village has three captains. These captains look after every affair of a Nicobarese house or a village.

Thus, we find that a Nicobarese is first surrounded by his family, then by the joint family, to be looked after by a captain who is under the orders of the village captain and finally, he is surrounded by an island which has a Chief captain. The Nicobar Islands are, though, in complete geographical isolation from the rest of the world, but due to marriage, economy, rituals and politics they are in close contact with each other. The Nicobarese today, unlike in former days are in contact with the other islands of the Andaman group. Car Nicobarese frequently go to Little Andaman to see their relatives at Harmandar Bay, a Nicobarese settlement there. Besides this, the employment of the Nicobarese in the various governmental and private companies, has accelerated the extension of the Nicobarese villages today.

UNITY OF THE VILLAGE

Although, Car Nicobar is a small island with 15 villages, specific traits are observable in all the villages. Every Car Nicobarese is conscious that he belongs to a particular village. He remembers the rich heritage of his village. A man of Mus village is proud of the fact that he belongs to the village of the Bishop John Richardson. Likewise the people of Big Lapati are conscious that they belong to the parent village of the Nicobarese. Villagers of Kinmai are proud of their sweet language. A Nicobarese of village Small Lapati is proud of the fact that the only school in Car Nicobar is in his village. The people of Kakana village are proud of their robust qualities. Similarly, people of Kinyuka are proud of their meekness.

Chowra people are proud of their spiritual powers. They are treated as the Brahmins of the Nicobar Islands. People of Rhion village in Chowra are further proud of the fact that they consider themselves to be the earliest settlers in Chowra. Similarly, the people of Nancowrie group of islands believe that they are the most courteous and soft spoken. In Nancowrie, people of village Enunga claim that it is the first village of the island.

A Nicobarese village is a cluster of families. A number of nuclear families from a joint family; and several such joint families constitute a village; and the island comprises a number of such villages. The size of the family, however, differs from one island to another. Thirdly, a church is a special feature of a Nicobarese village. It is also one of the important elements of the unity of the Nicobarese village. Early morning and evening, young and old people go to church and attend the assembly. In Chowra and some other islands, where Christianity has not made major inroads, there are certain sacred centres where people often pay for sacrifices of chicken.

Fourthly, the unity of the Nicobarese village is reflected in its political village organisation i.e. in the institution of 'captainship' of which references have been made earlier. The village council of 'captains' acts as a great unifying force at the village level, and builds up powerful influence for the smooth and integrated functioning of the village organisation.

INFORMAL CONTACTS AND VILLAGE UNITY

In addition to the above mentioned formalised and traditional institutions, there are numerous informal occasions when the villagers come together. These are the sea beach of a village, the proximity of residences and occasions for companionship in the forest and in the garden, visits to the daily and weekly assembly in church etc. add to the natural feeling of cohesion of the co-villagers. In a Nicobarese village the huts are arranged at random, barring any scope for by-lanes. At the centre of the village, there must be a neat and clean sandy small field. Often there is a volleyball ground at the centre. The central place provides them with a venue where they could discuss the affairs of the village, and decide about the plans for observing festivals at family or village level.

Thus, the forest, the sea and the gardens provide ample opportunity for informal contacts to the Nicobarese.

MAN: THE NICOBARESE SOCIAL SYSTEM, THE FAMILY

To our misfortune, all the books and articles about Nicobarese, published before, describe the homogeneous nature of all the islands of the Nicobar group. Whereas, from our intensive study, it is revealed that the family organisation, by and large, differs on every island the size of the family depends upon the density of population and the availability of food on an island. If the sources of their livelihood are obtained with difficulty, then people, though industrious, maintain a small size of family i.e. nuclear family. The husband-wife relationship in such islands is very strong because the economic dependence of women leads to a strict form of monogamy there. It is not possible for a Chowrian to maintain more than one wife at a time. Morever, the continued spread of Christianity in the Nicobar Islands also discourage them now from practising polygamy. It is also to be noted that in some of the islands a small section of Muslim population has lately emerged. However, the Islamic faith has not been able to overcome the economic hardship of the people, and therefore, the Muslim Nicobarese also dare not afford more than one wife at a time.

The practice of widow marriage and marriage after the death of one's wife as well, is however, widely prevalent in the Nicobars. Except in Chowra and Kondul, divorce is very common in other islands. Without any social or legal implication, a widow or a widower, or for that matter divorcee, can easily obtain a partner in Nicobarese society. A marriage-tie immediately ends with the separation of any partner. It is interesting to note that in Teressa, a man and a woman, quite often establish a verbal contact with each other to live jointly for a specific period. When the period is over they live separately. More interestingly, there is no problem as such, for the legitimacy of the children born by them. Thus, we find that especially in bigger islands, like Teressa, a traditional Nicobarese marries several times in his life. However, it is also a fact that at one time a Nicobarese has only one wife.

Initially, a Nicobarese family consists of husband, wife and their unmarried children. However, in Car Nicobar, the joint family system is practised. Several nuclear families make a joint family there. In a joint family, as many as 80 to 100 persons live. They are looked after by a captain. A joint family lives in a cluster of huts. The captain also owns the coconut trees. He is responsible for fair distribution of the fruits and vegetables jointly produced by the family. The cooking is though done separately by each small family, but on festive occasion, there is a common hearth. He settles the family dispute. After the death of a captain, a new head of the family is selected on the sis of seniority and leadership qualities.

In the case of Chowra, we find that though there is a village captain, there is no joint family. Although, the Chowrians make collective garden, they have to maintain their livelihood separately. Males in Chowra go to different islands, work in the garden, thatch the roof of the huts, make canoes and exchange pots for pigs, cloth, tobacco etc. with the other islanders. Females make pots and look after the gardens in Chowra.

In contrast, in Teressa, Bompoka, Nancowrie, Katchall, Kamorta, Trinket and in the islands of the southern zone, the size of the family is even smaller.

The distinct features of the Nicobarese family are its rule of residence and descent. We have mentioned that in order to make economic adjustment between the two families, either the wife or the husband, according to necessity, become *gulam* (servant) at the other's place. This bilocal rule of residence is a unique feature of the Nicobarese life.

Similarly, anybody who does not have any source of livelihood can become the member of a family, provided he does not create any trouble. There are several instances of such unusual membership of a family.

Nevertheless, all the major economic, social and religious activities of the Nicobarese centre around his family. Thus, the most primary kin-group are the parents and their unmarried children. Besides them, any member, be it consanguinal or affinal relative, can easily be accommodated in the family.

A Nicobarese family dwells in a hut. The huts are generally one roomed. All the members of a family consume toddy together in the evening. In the night hours, all the family members sleep in one hut. The huts are generally dark at night. This makes a tremendous impact on the sexual life of the Nicobarese. The unmarried boys and girls are often aware of their elders indulging in a sexual intercourse. It is a good reason why pre- and extra-marital relations are quite common in these islands. In terms of the number of the members of a family, we may categorise them into the following types:

(1) Single member family.
(2) Double member family.
(3) Three-five member family.
(4) Five to twelve member family.
(5) Over twelve member family.

A single-member family is an example of a broken family. Such families are rare in the Nicobars. It is only when a man is excommunicated from the society, that he lives separately. In a double member family, only a wife and husband live together. This is mostly found in Teressa where women do not want a child and practise abortion and sterilization. In the case of the third category the husband, wife and their small children live together. After the spread of Christianity, a good number of such families are found in the Nicobars. Also, those who work in the offices, prefer such families. In the fourth type of family, the members are husband, wife, their married and unmarried children as well. Such a type of family is mostly found in the Nancowrie group of islands. The fifth type of family consisting of more than twelve members is found in Car Nicobar.

Initially, a Nicobarese family is patrilineal. After the death of a man, his property is inherited by his sons. However, in the bigger islands this rule of inheritance does not work. At the time of marriage a girl is also awarded certain number of coconut trees by her father. Thus, the Nicobarese society can be understood as patrilineal and bilocal.

PATTERN OF RELATIONSHIP: WIFE AND HUSBAND

Quite often, though, a husband becomes a *gulam* in his wife's house, but as a rule, the husband has a primary say in a Nicobarese family. He commands a superior position and his wife is always subordinate to him. Nevertheless, the relationship between them is that between partners, co-operating with each other in all social, economic, domestic and emotional activities. A wife is supposed to be the economic asset of the Nicobarese family. The daily routine of a Nicobarese wife consists of working in the gardens, going to the sea-shore for fishing with her husband, collecting fuel from the forest, preparing meals, looking after the children and sleeping with her husband. She always accompanies her husband in social gatherings. A husband tries to give maximum physical and mental satisfaction to his wife. She also co-operates with her husband in copra-making.

The pattern of relationship between husband and wife can be observed in terms of their ritualistic roles. When a wife is pregnant, her husband, also shares the pollution and observes a series of taboos. In spite of such healthy relations of co-operation and co-ordination between the husband and the wife, there are occasions of conflict and tension which often lead to divorce. When a husband becomes suspicious about his wife's extra-marital relations, or if he suspects her as to be long-handed, or if she does not bear a child, then he prefers to divorce her. Moreover, if a Nicobarese woman is known as a witch, she is divorced. Despite such facts, quarrelling among them is perhaps absent. Beating one's wife is regarded as a disqualification. This shows that the status of a Nicobarese woman is high in the society.

PARENTS-CHILDREN RELATIONSHIP

In a Nicobarese family, rearing and nursing of the child is mostly done by a mother. The father is, however, equally careful about the nursing of the infants. Wherever the wife and the husband go, they alternately carry the babies along with them. A female child mostly lives with her mother, and when she grows older helps her in cutting arecanut, making copra and oil, cleaning the house etc. A boy generally knows the expectations of his parents. He helps them in plucking coconuts, and most often he goes alone for fishing. He knows that his parents would be happy if he were to bring fish to his home.

The parents' relationship with their young daughters is equally cordial. The Nicobarese do not make any distinction, nor do they show any preference either to a son or to a daughter. The Nicobarese seldom scold their children. They affectionately tell them the beliefs, customs and practices of the Nicobarese society. The small children are however not allowed to drink toddy or smoke *pops* (local smoke). Strict form of avoidance is not observed between the parents and the children.

PATTERN OF RELATIONSHIPS AMONG THE SIBLINGS

The relationships among the siblings vary in terms of their age-groups. While the young boys and girls below ten years of the same family and village mix freely with each other and jointly play different games, the grown-ups are expected to mix only with the members of their respective sex. The Christian Nicobarese boys and girls however mix with each other quite freely. Young brothers and sisters are not expected to be seen with their suitors by each other. After marriage, however, no sign of avoidance is maintained. In case of affinal relatives, the relationship is one of respect. The closest kinship tie is found among the parents and their unmarried children.

In a Nicobarese family, a number of ritualistic performances are done. In every family, many Kareyavas and scare devils are placed inside the hut. The Kareyavas and the scare devils are the objects of worship in a Nicobarese family. Often sacrifices are offered to these objects at the family level.

MAN: THE LIFE CYCLE OF A NICOBARESE

In the study of the life cycle of the Nicobarese, the interaction with ecology, man and the spirit world is clearly observable. To examine a Nicobarese 'at the axis of his self' it is desirable to know him from even before his appearance on earth. A Nicobarese husband and wife have complete knowledge about the biological consequences of mating. However, the general attitude of the people towards pregnancy is that without the will and the blessings of benevolent spirits, no child can be conceived. The Nicobarese do not have any special liking for a male or a female child.

CONCEPTION

The idea of conception is easily known by the Nicobarese. As soon as the menstruation of a woman is stopped, and she feels a tendency of vomiting, she is understood to have conceived a child. However, conception before marriage is very much looked down by the society. In such a case, the Nicobarese apply all indigenous devices of abortion. Till five months of conception of a wife, the husband continue to maintain the sexual relations with her.

DIET AND TABOOS DURING PREGNANCY

During her pregnancy, a Nicobarese woman is delicately taken care of. She is not allowed to do hard work, and never left alone. She abandons going to the forest or to the sea for fishing. The normal diet of a pregnant woman is pandanus, rice, yams, chickens and birds. Few species of fishes and certain varieties of fruits are prohibited for her. Pork is also not given to her. Experienced ladies of the village often massage her body with coconut oil.

Soon after the confirmation of her pregnancy, a series of taboos are maintained by the woman and her husband as well. Splitting and cutting of woods are prohibited for the husband. No member of the family eats a cannibal fish or pig. The wife and the husband abstain from plucking coconut, pandanus, arecanut, banana or any other fruit or vegetable. A coconut, which is to be given to the would-be mother of a child is plucked from the bunch of an odd number, and is not allowed to fall from the tree, instead it is brought down by the climber with his hands. Binding anything and knotting is also not done by her or her husband. A pregnant woman neither asks anyone for food nor does she accept the food given by people outside her family, for fear of the child becoming greedy and a beggar. She does not look at an eclipse, for fear of the child being handicapped or deformed. Also, for fear of evil spirits, she does not go the jungle or the sea alone, and keeps her belly always covered with a white piece of cloth, hung from her neck. In no case does she or her husband attend a funeral. The wife and the husband always carry an umbrella when they go out. All this is done by the Nicobarese in order to protect the child from evil spirits and to ensure a normal delivery. They believe that if hard work is done by either the husband or the wife, it would affect the good health of the child. Therefore, a husband is also under obligation to maintain the taboos during the pregnancy of his wife.

In fact, the limitless beliefs of the Nicobarese in nature and spirits have compelled them to observe a vast number of taboos. This provides them with a great deal of mental satisfaction and security.

Birth and Infancy

In Car Nicobar, Chowra and many other islands, the birth and death houses are found even today. In the final stage of delivery, a woman is taken to the birth house. This is done so as to maintain the pollution period after the birth of a child. In Chowra, some of the witch-doctors have especially constructed small huts in the jungle, where a pregnant woman is taken for normal delivery. In any case, the hut is made completely vacant. The would-be mother stays there with a number of women. An experienced woman works there as a mid-wife.

As soon as the labour pain starts, the pregnant lady is advised to kneel down, spreading her legs and she is advised to give inward pressure, and after a few minutes the new born child comes out. When enough of the placenta comes out with blood, then, with a sharp bamboo stick, the umbilical cord is cut. The mid-wife is given a piece of new cloth. At the time of the delivery, all the knots in the house are united. This act of the mid-wife is often performed by a witch-doctor in Chowra, who also advises the family members to perform a lot of rituals for a safe and normal delivery. In case of a delayed delivery, in Chowra, the witch-doctor suggests the woman to lie down with her back on the floor and her feet touching the wall of the hut. A rope hangs from the top of the ceiling. The rope is caught by the woman, and she presses her feet against the wall and tries her best to bring the baby out. Some medicines of local make are given to the patient. After the successful delivery, the witch-doctor is rewarded with cloths, yams, chicken and tobacco. After the birth of the child, the placenta and the umbilical cord are collected by a lady in a basket and during the evening hour, are buried inside the forest. However, now a hospital is opened in Car Nicobar, and some educated Nicobarese prefer to go to the hospital than to the traditional birth houses.

Naming

A few days after the birth of a child, in a small ceremony, it is given a name by the parents. The Nicobarese attach little importance to the naming pattern or ceremony. A Nicobarese can change his name anytime he likes. However, the priest christens the Christian Nicobarese.

Suckling

Soon after the birth of the child, if the mother remains very weak, then another woman who has a child of the same sex, offers to suckle the new-born. But ultimately the real mother offers her milk to the child. She keeps the head of the infant in one of her palms and the body in her lap. Then she puts the nipples into the mouth of the child to suckle it. Before offering her nipples, she presses her breasts so that some milk comes out. She does not suckle while in a sleeping position. The mother offers her two breasts alternately. There is no fixed time for offering milk.

Weaning

If the mother conceives once again, or she finds her breasts dry, she avoids offering her milk to the child. When the child reacts for it and weeps, it is given extremely tender kernel of coconut, and a paste-like preparation of pandanus.

The first eating ceremony of the child is an auspicious occasion. A witch-doctor is called, who after sacrificing a chicken, prepares the pandanus paste mixed with boiled banana and coconut milk and kernel. The mother, in the presence of all the family members, feeds the child with the preparation. Then all the members drink toddy and enjoy the food. Gradually, as the child grows, he becomes habituated to different kinds of food.

Speech

A Nicobarese child is not given training for speech at a given time and space. He learns it from his parents and other members of the family. People make repeated efforts by laughing and talking with the boy, and in course of time, the child learns to communicate with words.

Bathing

Soon after the birth of the child, the mid-wife washes the baby with hot water. Until the child learns to walk, the mother bathes him with water boiled in a Chowra pot. They believe that the water boiled in a Chowra pot is capable of immunising the effect of black magic. However, when the child can walk easily, he is taken along to the sea-shore with his parents for a sea bath. After the introduction of modern habits and ways of living, some of the Nicobarese now use soaps and other toilet articles.

Childhood

An infant is made to sleep maximum number of hours. While sleeping, he is not disturbed. His head is rested on a pillow. The Nicobarese are very careful in bringing up their children, but they can be hardly seen beating or scolding their children. If at all they slap their children, it is always mildly. Also, we find that the Nicobarese have hardly ever run into a food crisis. This is one good reason why the Nicobarese are not a warlike people and rather submissive. The Nicobarese children are seldom hungry, and least bothered about the next meal. When they are hungry, either they ask their parents for food or if they are able to, they climb the coconut tree and pluck the fruit.

The Nicobarese parents are however not very careful regarding the clothes of their children. The children are semi-naked. The climatic condition of this region also does not permit them to wear many garments. The traditional dress of loin cloth of the Nicobarese is getting obsolete now. In Chowra alone it is still worn by the people. The rest of the Nicobarese use only shorts.

The dress of a Nicobarese girl is a lungi and a blouse in the Burmese style.

The Nicobarese children though, do not perform any productive work in their early childhood, but they are never left isolated by their parents to roam about meaninglessly in the village or in the forest. While the Nicobarese parents go to the garden they carry their children with them. Thus, a Nicobarese child learns the economic activities from the very childhood by watching his elders and parents working in the garden or fishing along the sea-shore. He learns all the social norms, customs, activities and discipline from his observations and imbibes them through continued association with his parents in every aspect of their life.

Late Childhood

Between eight to twelve years of age, a Nicobarese child undergoes his late childhood. At this very age Nicobarese boys and girls exhibit their worth and their economic utility. The boys and girls of this age-group are assets to their parents and to society. From incessant observations in their early childhood, they learn every piece of work that is expected of him. They also take much care of their personal cleanliness. As we know that education has successfully made its way in the Nicobar Islands, so the Nicobarese children at this age are also sent to schools for study. However the non-going school children are economically more useful than their school-going counterparts. The boys of this age-group often go with fishing hooks and lines along the shore. By this time they have learnt all the methods of fishing, and when they have a big catch, they feel proud and return home triumphantly. Besides fishing, they become expert in climbing coconut trees and in other activities of gardening. With their cross-bows, they also hunt birds in the forest.

The girls on the other hand, are mostly occupied in their household work. A girl helps her mother in cooking. She goes to the gardens and helps her parents in all the work there. She is also helpful in copra-making. Thus, she proves herself to be a dutiful Nicobarese girl at this very tender age.

Thus, we find that this period is very important in the process of socialization of a Nicobarese boy or a girl. In this very period an innocent boy or girl becomes a true Nicobarese by learning and adopting all the norms and activities of the Nicobarese society.

ADOLESCENT AND PUBERTY

The period of puberty and adolescence is hailed with pleasure. When a girl is recognised for the first time to have attained puberty, an initiation ceremony is held. In case of boys no initiation ceremony is done. The first menstruation of a girl is hailed with joy. From thence, a girl is understood to have attained puberty and to be capable of procreating child. The author witnessed an initiation ceremony *Annahanam* on Nancowrie island.

As soon as the first menstruation of a girl is recognised the news of her attaining the puberty is spread in the village. Herefrom a long series of rituals start. In an empty room the girl is kept for fourteen days. She is told to keep together her legs. She is given very restricted food. A pollution period is observed by her. No male member enters the hut. She is brought down from the hut only during the night hours, escorted by elderly women, the women give her profuse lessons in becoming a Nicobarese girl. She is advised not to mix with the boys any more. She is told that she should behave properly as she is now an adult. A number of taboos are also observed by the girl as well as the other members of the family. The last three days of the *Annahanam* are spent in merry making. The guests from different villages and islands come to the girl, offer her presents, gives her some advice to improve her conduct. The elderly women often beat the girl mildly, with a stick suggesting her that if she ever committed any mistake, she would be beaten severely. In this way after fourteen days of undergoing the initiation ceremony, the *annahanam* ends with a lot of food and drink.

PRE-MARITAL RELATIONSHIPS

Despite the fact that a girl is profusely advised by the elderly persons of the village as well as the islands during her initiation ceremony *annahanam* to behave like an ideal Nicobarese woman, pre- and extra-marital relations are often found in the Nicobar Islands. The reason behind it is of course that the girl is influenced so much by her social environment that within a short time she forgets all the teachings rendered to her by the senior ladies of the society. Ideally, a Nicobarese girl is supposed not to fulfil her sexual desire until her marriage, but in reality, this author did not come across any instance of a woman who did not enjoy sexual intercourse much before her marriage.

The ecological condition and the social environment of the Nicobarese are such that pre- and extra-marital relations are inevitable. The forest provides ample opportunity to the young boys and girls to mix freely. The young ones also see their elders having intercourse in the same hut where they sleep. On festive occasions also they find opportunity to mix freely. Moreover, there is hardly any severe punishment for those who ever indulge in pre- or extra-marital terms with the opposite sex. These reasons are sufficient to explain the frequent occurrence of such relationships among the Nicobarese.

Marriage

Selection of a spouse is done by mutual consent. There is hardly any example of an arranged marriage in Nicobar Islands. The role of parents in a marriage starts only after the boy and the girl have agreed to marry.

However, the form of marriage differs from one island to another. Divorce is seldom practised in Chowra and Car Nicobar, whereas, it is frequent in other islands. It has been observed in the Nicobars that the bigger the size of the island, the more frequent is divorce found there; and the smaller its size, the less frequent it is. In fact in bigger islands the density of population is very thin. And because food is found in plenty there, women are economically independent. In such cases she lives with a man for as long as she likes. She need not take any legal or social sanction before getting divorced. Soon after their separation they are divorced. There is no problem for the legitimacy of the child. The child lives with anybody with whom he feels comfortable.

Marriage Rituals

Marriage celebration is most elaborately done in Chowra. A big feast is organised for the occasion. The invitees also bring presents of pigs, coconut, banana, yams and cloth. A witch-doctor supervises the marriage ritual. Bride price is also given of pigs and clothes. After the marriage the couples are advised to hide themselves in the jungle for a fortnight. They are given ample food to eat during this period. After a fortnight they appear publicly before the villagers. This isolation enables them to understand each other.

In other islands, marriage is celebrated by a small feast. We have also mentioned that even after marriage, there are extra-marital relations found among the Nicobarese.

Gulam System

It is found in all the islands of Nicobar group. It signifies the rule of residence and the rule of inheritance of property. In fact a husband or a wife can live at either's place after marriage. It depends upon the economic condition of both the parties. If the parents of the girl have a greater number of coconut plantations, than the parents of the boy, then the husband lives at his wife's residence. He is known as a *gulam*. On the other hand, if the wife is brought to the house of the husband, she is known as *gulam*.

In fact it is an economic adjustment that the Nicobarese make after marriage. Moreover, if the parents of the boy have a larger family than that of the wife, then also the husband lives with the wife. Besides, when a husband lives with his wife, he loses all rights to property of his father. The children born by such married couple would inherit property from their mother's side.

Adulthood

Soon after marriage, the social and economic responsibilities of husband and wife increase. The Nicobarese men and women are expected to behave as adult members of the community. Wherever they are they take up agricultural work, go to the gardens, make copra and procure children. They together participate in all social and religious functions.

The average life span of the Nicobarese is 50.5 years. Taken separately for the male and the female, the average age comes to 51 in the case of male, and 48.5 years in the case of female. When they become old, they spend most of their times in drinking and attending feasts and festivals. It has been observed that at the dusk of their life, the Nicobarese men and women live melancholy. When they become physically invalid, they neither go to the forest or to the garden, nor do they go for fishing. Their children serve food for them. And finally, they come to an end and meet the inevitable event of life i.e. death.

Death

The extent of co-operation and solidarity of the Nicobarese society can be easily understood from the ritual and ceremonial surrounding death. The death of an old man or woman is considered to be natural. When a death occurs accidentally, it is believed that it is because of the wrath of the spirit.

Death is followed by a series of rituals over a very long period. The Nicobarese exhibit very primitive customs after death. If an old man suffers from incessant illness, the Nicobarese know that his end is near. In Car Nicobar the remnants of very old customs still persist, and a dying man is taken to the death house. In other islands where there is no provision of any death house, a certain hut is made vacant there. Inside the house a death bed which consists of a mat and some pillows is prepared. Beside the dying person, some *kareyavas*, which are supposed to be of the benevolent spirits, are placed and a *minluana* along the relative stands by the side of the dying man. In the meantime information is sent to the relatives of the dying man to the different villages and islands. All those who come to pay their last homage to the dying man, stay there till the death of that person. They return home only after his death and burial.

It happens sometimes that the man dies even before the arrival of his relatives. In such a case his body is not immediately buried, but is kept for several days till the persons informed come and see him. Sometimes even the corpse becomes decomposed and a stinking smell emanates from it.

While lying on the death bed, a *minluana* always remains there. It is thought that the *minluana* would protect the man from evil spirits, and the man would die in peace. The *minluana* also offers some sacrifices to drive away the evil spirits.

When the man ultimately dies, all his friends and relatives cry and lament, remembering how the old man loved them and looked after the family.

Death Rites and Burial

Soon after the death of the man, the corpse is washed three times. The relatives are also informed. All those who come, bring chicken, coconut and clothes with them, and the corpse is wrapped with cloth. The death rites vary from one island to another. The Car Nicobarese mostly follow the Christian rite of burial. Though earlier the Car Nicobarese also performed equally elaborate methods of burial. The Chowrians have an absolutely different method of burial. It is known as open burial.

As soon as a man dies in Chowra, some trees are cut down and earthen pots are broken. The corpse is brought to the *elpenum*. The entire island is informed about the death. The children members are not allowed very much to enter the hut where the corpse lies, and some coins and silver ornaments are hung around their neck to protect them from the evil spirit. They all wear black loin cloths and a red scarf around their neck. Such persons are supposed to be unclean.

The Chowrians do not delay the burial of the corpse. They split a canoe into two halves and the body is put on it to be covered by the other half. Some elderly women go to the grave-yard to dig the grave. When the grave is ready the funeral procession silently starts, led by a witch-doctor. People walk with hands folded at their back. Near the grave people have a last look at the corpse and slowly the coffin is lowered into the grave. It is interesting to know that if the corpse is of a female its head is kept towards the sea, and feet towards the forest, and if it is of a male, the feet are put towards the sea, and head towards the forest. It is so because, the males are considered as sea voyagers, whereas, the females mostly go to the forests.

After the burial, they return home and cut down some trees and break some pots again. All the family members shave their heads near the shore. For six days, all the family members attend the grave every morning and evening. After six days they dig the grave again. When the grave is dug, the coffin is lifted and is put on two 'Y' type of sticks erected on the ground. Then the lid of the coffin is removed and the half rotten body is left there. This method of open burial is not practised on any other island. When the entire work is finished, light refreshment is given to the women who dug the grave, and then a pig is killed near the grave itself, and after offering a few pieces to the spirits and the dead man, the rest is consumed. Then everybody goes to the sea and takes a dip there.

After a few weeks all the flesh disappears and the bones only remain there. It is then buried again to be redug during the 'reburial' festivals. Thus, we find that the Chowrians bury their dead twice over.

In Nancowrie, an interesting feature of the burial is that, before the funeral procession, the head of the corpse is shaved. It is also to be noted that in these islands, there is no common burial ground. Therefore, the burying is done not very far from the house of the deceased. In all the islands, however, one thing is common that a series of taboos are observed after the death of a person, and the near relatives, who are supposed to be unclean ritually, undergo a long period of ritual pollution. It is also worth mentioning that in Nancowrie, just before the burial, people organise a stick fight.

Purificatory Rites

In all the islands it has been observed that a number of purificatory rites are observed in three different stages. In fact after the death of a person the near relatives maintain food and drink taboos on different items. In three successive stages they lift all such taboos. In the opinion of this author, they maintain such taboos because it always reminds them that the *kindrak* (reburial) must be performed for the dead man, and performing kindrak, they have to be economically very strong. During these purificatory rites, the Nicobarese make new gardens, domescate a number of pigs, make enough copra to purchase cloth for kindrak and when sufficient amount of cloth, and fruits and vegetables are ensured, they lift all taboos by performing the last of the purificatory rites. Then they consider themselves to be ready to meet the expenses of the kindrak.

Kindrak

The ultimate aim of a Nicobarese is to celebrate the kindrak of his dead relatives. It is a very laborious and costly festival commemorated every third or fifth year with much ceremony, commingled with joy and sorrow. It was earlier known as *kiala* in Car Nicobar. Due to spread of Christianity, it is not celebrated there now. But in the Nancowrie group of islands it is still regarded as the most expensive of all festivals.

During kindrak, the bones from the grave are dug and lifted. The bones are kept in the house for several days. All the villagers and the invitees pay their respect to the bones. After three months the bones are again placed inside the grave, only to be dug and lifted again after three years.

The special features of the kindrak are that people first strengthen their economy. They invite all the friends and relatives, and all the invitees bring presentations of yams, banana, cloth, chicken and pigs. The kindrak is celebrated in ten different stages. The most important feature of the kindrak is that people sing only ancient songs as long as the bones are kept in the house. After the reburial, people start singing the new songs and making merry. And also, soon after kindrak, all the taboos on food are lifted and people live a normal life.

SPIRIT AND THE NICOBARESE SACRED COMPLEX

The indigenous religion of the Nicobarese is an undisguised Animism and all their very frequent and elaborate rites, ceremonies and festivals are aimed at exorcising and scaring away spirits. Fear of *iwi* (spirits) is the guide to all ceremonies and the life of the Nicobarese is very largely taken up with scaring and controlling spirits and feasts of all kinds. Most of the ceremonies take place at night, and whether directly religious or merely convivial, it seems to have an origin in the overmastering fear of spirits that possesses the Nicobarese.

Nevertheless, unlike earlier, the Nicobar Islands are fast progressing; and the days, it appears, are not far off when the inhabitants of all the islands would be engulfed "under the shadow of the Cross." Even then, it is surprising to find that the Christian Nicobarese also pay their respect and fear to the indigenous worship of *iwi*.

CONCEPTION ABOUT IWI (SPIRITS)

The Nicobarese believe that any fortune or misfortune is caused because of benevolent (*ivi-ka*) or malevolent (*iwi-pt*) spirit. It is omnipresent. An unnatural death is caused because of the wrath of *iwi*. So is the cause of the decease of a man. If a man or a *minluana* is good, he is possessed with good *iwi* and if he is bad then a bad *iwi* lives in him. Also, if a man dies of a tree fall, the *iwi* residing in the jungle is propitiated.

In former days, the Nicobarese believed that their captains possessed more *iwi* than the rest. The Europeans had obviously more *iwi*, hence only they could make bigger boats and even in rough weather, they could come to them from unknown destinations. If a canoe capsizes in the sea in a rough weather, a pig is killed and the blood is poured into the sea to appease the *iwi* residing in the sea.

Chowra is the most superstitious and orthodox island of the Nicobars. This island is supposed to be the land of the wizards. They believe that all the Chowrians can control and pacify the wrath of *iwi*. They can change the direction of the wind and the waves. The pots made by the Chowrians can immunise the effect of black magic. The canoes made by them can withstand the turbulent sea in stormy weather. For the people of the other island, except the islands of the southern zone, a journey to Chowra is like a pilgrimage. This is solely because they believe that the *iwi* in a Chowrian, is stronger than in them.

The Nicobarese believe that *iwi* also guides the behaviour of men and women. All the rituals are performed in order to gratify the benevolent spirits and frighten away the malevolent spirits. There are eight kinds of *iwis* classified into two groups.

Besides *iwi*, the Nicobarese try their utmost to appease the Reuse, and the Minluana. Therefore, in order to understand the supernatural powers and those who hold it, we have classified them into three categories, viz. (1) the *iwi*, (2) the Reuse and (3) the Minluana. Minluanas are also known as Kamassun or Tamilnuana.

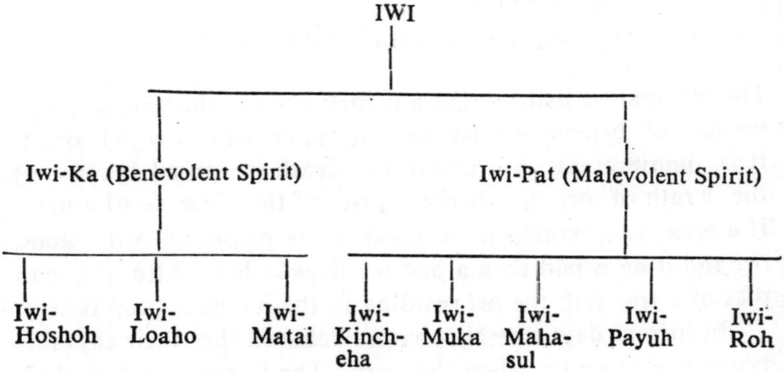

Reuse or Deuse

We have earlier described about the conception of IWI among the Nicobarese. Reuse is the conception of God in the minds of the Nicobarese. It is the degraded form a chief of the spirits, which is frequently represented as a man in quaint European garb, with a wine glass in his hands, surrounded by various weapons, implements and articles of daily use, including a table, chair, watch, telescope and whistle. It is really interesting to know that all this shows that the people regard REUSE as a European spirit, embodied in a ship's captain, because in the former days the captain of a ship was supposed to be the most powerful human being of their acquaintance, who could control the strongest of all IWIS.

As a matter of fact, the idea of Reuse is not indigenous in the Nicobars. We have examined earlier that during the missionary phase of the history of the Nicobarese, the people of these islands came into contact with the Portuguese. In the Portuguese language, it has been examined, that the Reuse means God. Though, the Portuguese, then failed in their effort to evangelise the people, they left behind them valuable religious terms of European origin, such as, *Pater* for sorcerer and *Deos* or *Reuse* for god. Thus, the term *Reuse* ultimately stands for a purely anthropomorphic chief of the spirits to be feared and revered.

Reuse is also omnipresent. It protects the life and fortune of the Nicobarese. It brings rain and because of the mercy of Reuse, yams, banana, coconuts, pandanus and other fruits and vegetables grow in the garden. It does not harm anybody.

In order to appease the Reuse, the Nicobarese in all the villages celebrate an annual festival before the advent of *Samhav* (West Monsoon). In Car Nicobar, where Christianity has made its full impact, the old people still remember Reuse. In Chowra, a festival known as *Vee-Fop-Lach* is celebrated to appease the Reuse. While celebrating the *Vee-Fop-Lach*, the Chowrians march in a procession, led by a witch-doctor, and shout and pray to Reuse, saying, "O Reuse! give us yam, give us banana and give us all the fruits and vegetables. Thou art merciful." In Nancowrie, people celebrate *Wani-La-Ol-Matai* just before the advent of *Samhav* and *fuel* (East Monsoon). Tall posts of bamboo, approximately 60′ in height are erected along the sea-shore to call the Reuse. Thus, we find that the idea of Reuse, is of late origin in the minds of the Nicobarese, but it is very deeply rooted.

Minluana, Tamilnuana or Kamassun

The supernatural belief of the Nicobarese is further exhibited in witchcraft. It is practised by a male or a female, and one practises it is known by the aforesaid terms. However, it is believed that a Kamassun always causes harm to the people. He controls the evil spirits and can employ them for the misfortune of any member of the society. Whereas, if a man is sick, he consults a Minluana or a Tamilnuana, who not only gives him folk medicines, but he also tells about the wrath of any spirit, if it be the cause of his sickness. There is a common thing that both the Kamassun and the Minluana or Tamilnuana have spirits under their control. There is no such recognisable demarcation between them. The Chowrians believe that if a Minluana is possessed with an evil spirit, he becomes a Kamassun. Earlier, on many occasions such a Kamassun has been killed by the unanimous decision of the villagers. This practice of killing a *Kamassun* is known as 'devil murder'. They believe that they do not kill a man but they kill the devil in him.

Thus, we find it clear that there are three types of supernatural powers; the *Iwi*, the *Reuse* and the *Kamassun* or the *Minluana*. They have their respective importance in the Nicobarese society. It is also evident that the *Iwi-Pat* and the *Kamassun* are the malevolent and the negative forces in the spirit world of the Nicobarese, whereas, the *Reuse*, the *Iwi-Ka* and the *Minluana* are the positive forces.

Sacred Geography

In the coming paragraphs, the Sacred Complex, under the three analytical concepts—the sacred geography, the sacred performance and the sacred specialist of the Nicobarese as propounded by Prof. Vidyarthi in his study of the Maler (1963), has been dealt with.

In the Nicobar archipelago, there are certain islands, places and certain parts of the sea universally considered as sacred by the Nicobarese. The island of Chowra is first among them. It is known as the land of the wizards. Likewise, the island of Tallinchong is also held sacred. Ceremonial voyages are made by the people of Nancowrie island to Tallinchong. Between Chowra and Battimalve, there is a coral reef which is held sacred by the Nicobarese. Ceremonial fishing is done there by the Chowrians annually.

Sacred Centres

When one enters any of the Nicobarese villages, he comes across certain common symbols, such as, a mark of Takoya, birth and death houses, the grave-yard, a number of Kareyavas and scare devils, Elpenum, erected poles etc. All these are the Nicobarese sacred centres or shrines. These sacred centres representing different *iwis* of the villagers are located in many places in the village and surrounding hills and forests, and they constitute the sacred geography of the village. Besides these, the churches and the mosques serve as sacred centres for the Christian and the Muslim Nicobarese respectively.

Elpenums are cleanly maintained. In Chowra all the ceremonies take place in the Elpenum. In Car Nicobar all the villages have their own Elpenum. Near the Elpenum in Chowra, there is a grave-yard and a place for open burial. The guests from different islands are always kept in the Elpenum.

The birth and the death houses are the other important sacred centres of the villages. Occasionally, sacrifices are made near these houses, and blood is sprinkled on the pots.

The location of the grave-yard varies from one island to another. In Car Nicobar, all the villages have separate but common cemetery. In Chowra there is a common burial ground for all the villagers.

In Teressa, Bompoka and all the islands of the Nancowrie group, there is no common place for burial. A man when he dies is buried just near his hut. A plant is erected over his grave and all his personal belongings are either buried with him or hung on it.

In Chowra, there are some other places held sacred. The cliff at the southern end of Chowra, known as *Tahop* is considered sacred. It is also known as the 'Devil's Abode'. Ceremonial hunting of crabs is done annually there. If a man climbs atop the cliff, he has to kill a pig and sprinkle blood on himself after his getting down from there. 'Hiva' is another sacred centre for the Chowrians. At the south east point of this island, there is a place known as Lampcho, held sacred, where the Chowrians go in procession, during their festival of *Vee-Fop-Lach*. Besides these, there is always a particular place in all the islands for throwing the umbilical cord of a child, which is also held sacred.

There is no trace of tree worship in Nicobar Islands, but it was found that the Chowrian witch-doctors made their special houses for the treatment of a pregnant lady below the shade of a *Pipal* tree. They believe that the benevolent spirits reside in such trees, which help the Minluana in healing a sick person.

There is also a broken canon in Chowra near the Elpenum, left by some unknown ancient traveller, or perhaps by the pirates. It is known as *Hanvooh*. Periodically, sacrifices of children are offered there.

As a matter of fact, the Nicobarese live in such constant fear of spirits that anything unusual is held sacred by them. It was surprising to find that a doll floating in the sea was also picked up by these people and such objects were also held sacred and safely kept in the houses.

A Nicobarese hut is also considered sacred. Inside the hut a number of kareyavas and scare devils are kept. Pots are also held sacred in Nicobars. A Nicobarese well is also considered sacred.

In all the villages there are certain prohibited areas locally known as *tayuech*. Such areas are temporarily held sacred. In addition to the concept of *Iwi*, the people of Nancowrie and Chowra believe in some form of animal having supernatural powers. In the central group of islands there is a common belief that *tamakung*—a monstrous animal—lives in the dense forest along the sea-shore. Thus, the main sacred centres in Nicobar Islands comprise the huts, the Elpenum, the death houses, the birth houses, the grave-yard, the village well, the garden, the coconut plantation, the takoya, etc. These are the common sacred centres of all the villages in all the islands of the Nicobars.

Sacred Performance

Endless sacred performances are made during the life time of a Nicobarese. It is neither suitable nor is it possible to describe each of them here. But an effort has been made here to describe in a nutshell the methods and processes common in all the acts of sacred performances.

The sole motive of a ritualistic sacred performance among the Nicobarese is either to appease the *Iwi-Ka* (benevolent spirit) or to pacify and drive away the *Iwi-Pat* (malevolent spirit). And in all the acts of sacred performances a chicken or a pig must be sacrificed.

When a chicken or a pig is sacrificed, its mouth is forcibly opened and cut by an iron blade between its lower and upper jaw. When the blood comes out, it is thrown on everybody sitting or standing around there. If the Nicobarese want to collect some blood of a pig to be mixed with the folk medicine, then the legs of the pig are tied with ropes and the pig's tail is cut, and blood is collected in a coconut shell. The main act of a sacred performance can be seen when a Minluana applies his treatment to a sick person. When the preliminary treatment fails to cure the sick person, the Minluana then, takes the help of the scare devils to detect the responsible *Iwi* for the sickness of that person. Though all types of sacred performances are mostly done by the Minluana, ordinary people also sometime do ritualistic works. The owner of the house from time to time washes the Kareyavas and also offers sacrifices and food to them. Women are not allowed to do many ritualistic works, except for digging the graves. They, however, can witness any sacred performance done in the village or in the house.

There are two aspects of sacred performance in the Nicobar Islands, viz. the ritualistic aspect and the secular aspect. The ritualistic aspect of sacred performances mainly include sacrifices and driving away the evil spirits or healing a sick person. The secular aspect of the sacred performance consists of eating, drinking, singing and dancing. All the ceremonies are followed by the aforesaid secular acts.

Next to pig or chicken, coconut is the most important item to be offered to the *Iwis*. We have noted that coconut is offered to the *Iwis*, to the huts, to the Kareyavas, to the canoes, to the Elpenum, to the dead person and to all the persons and the things, whom they hold sacred. We have earlier described that coconut is associated in every walk of the Nicobarese life.

Besides coconut, the offerings are made of yams, banana, pandanus and several other fruits. It is highly surprising that though fish is found in abundance in this archipelago, and it forms one of the mainstays of Nicobarese life, it is never offered either to the Iwis or to the Reuse.

The other types of sacred performances are reflected in the acts of a *Mafai* (a novice witch-doctor). A *Mafai* continues to remain more or less under shamanistic influence for a couple of days and has mainly roles to perform under the influence of spirits.

Sacred Specialists

Altogether there are four categories of the sacred specialists found among the Nicobarese, viz. Minluana or Tamilnuana (one who chases and drives away the evil spirits for healing a sick person), the Kamassun (one who employs evil spirits to cause harm to a person or group), the *Mafai* (an inspired person) and several others, such as the *Yom Aap* (guardian of a canoe), *Yom Elpenum* (guardian of the public houses) etc.

Discussion about the Minluana, Tamilnuana and Kamassun has already been done in the above paragraphs. However, the number of Minluanas is decreasing gradually in all the islands. At present there are 14 in Chowra, one in Nancowrie, 3 in Trinket, two in Kamorta, two in Katchall, two in Bompoka and thirtyone in Teressa.

Mafai

Mafai is another peculiarity of the Nicobarese social organisation. Earlier, the Car Nicobarese also took great interest in the creation of the Mafai, and in conducting Mafai performances. In Chowra and Nancowrie group of islands, people still give hold much of their time and property and labour to a Mafai and take him as somewhat sacred. Mafai is in fact a man who recovering from his serious illness, decides to take rest from work for sometime. In fact he continues to be invalid, and therefore, he does not obtain any food nor does he cook food for himself, but is supported by his community as long as he undergoes the course of a Mafai. The word *Mah* means 'Sir', and is used to indicate one who is superior, and is employed as a term of respect. *Fai* means 'inspired'. *Mafai* therefore means "an inspired man".

A Mafai can also become a Minluana or *Yom Aap* or *Yom Elpenum*. Besides the aforesaid sacred specialists, the women who do the acts of mid-wife and cut the umbilical cord of a child are also considered as sacred specialists.

Thus we find that the concept of Sacred Complex that Prof. Vidyarthi developed in the study of the Maler, absolutely fits in the study of the Nicobarese society. The Nicobarese have well recognizable sacred centres, they maintain elaborate sacred performances and they have a well organised band of sacred specialists. And also, in tune with the concept of Redfield (1955), the sacred complex of the Nicobar archipelago is a little traditional, and structurally, it is exclusively of local importance. The reason behind this has been of course the socio-economic and geographical isolation of these islands.

SUMMARY AND CONCLUSION

This study is an attempt to understand the Nature-Man-Spirit Complex of the Nicobarese. An attempt has also been made to test the terms and concepts used by Vidyarthi (1963) in his study of the Maler tribe. Besides an intensive understanding of different items of culture, this study helps us to understand the very configuration of the Nicobarese culture.

In the course of my long stay in different villages of Nicobar Islands, a Nicobarese village appeared to be like a little community, where several families lived in clusters of huts, sharing a common garden for yams, fruits and other vegetables, and also organising fishing expeditions at the family, village and sometimes at the island level. I also realised that unlike the other tribes of the mainland of India, the Nicobarese have been little exposed to the impact of industrialisation and urbanisation. Above all, the Nicobarese have lived from time immemorial in complete geographical isolation, which eventually forced them to be in socio-cultural isolation too. Though Christianity has made its inroads in the Nicobar Islands, it also spread due to efforts from internal sources only. All the earlier efforts by the foreign missionaries during the sixteenth and the seventeenth centuries met with a futile end because of the very fatal climatic conditions of this archipelago for the Europeans. As a result, the Nicobarese came in little contact with the outside world till a recent period. Also, except with the Shompens in the Great Nicobar, the Nicobarese have never been in through socio-economic interaction with any other tribe of the Bay Islands.

I

While at the initial stage, I started to study the ecological setting of the Nicobarese, I found unlike many other tribes of India, the Nicobarese were not only surrounded by rich forest but by sea too. Thus, the sea and the forest are the two dominant elements of the Nicobarese eco-system. They believe that there *iwis* reside in the forest. The forests help them in fulfilling their most basic needs i.e. sex. Whenever young boys and girls find an opportunity, they slip inside the forest and satiate their desire. They love the forest and sing songs in praise of it, because it is the source of their livelihood, it provides folk-medicines to them, it also provides materials to them for making canoes, mats, pots, baskets and huts. We have also noted earlier that a major part of the Nicobarese forest is occupied by coconut trees. Coconut is the mainstay of their life. It is also associated in all their socio-economic and religious rites and functions.

If forest provides coconut to the Nicobarese, the sea provides them with an abundance of fish. Fishing is done by all the Nicobarese of all age groups, young and old, men and women. Besides food articles of different kinds, it also provides them with the means of communication and entertainment. Canoe races have a very important social and religious significance. On any occasion of happiness or sorrow, a canoe race is organised in the sea.

II

The Nicobarese have a very profound conception about their community. They are not divisible into different tribes, and clans nor is there any evidence of any totemic group. They prefer to marry within their island only, however, inter-island marriages are now widely prevalent. Marrying outside the group, as a rule, is strictly prohibited.

We have also found that territorial division did not comply with the cultural division. However, marked differences are observable among the peoples of different islands. But the differences may safely be referred to their habitat and physical difficulties, of communication between the islands. Nevertheless, it is universally true in the Nicobars that their social structure is mainly on kinship, there is no caste or class among them. Village entity as a territorial group is recognised. The inhabitants of one island are mostly related, to one another, closely or distantly, by blood or by marriage, and they feel themselves to be members of the same family.

There are three sections of the Nicobarese viz, the Christians, the Muslims and the traditional Animists, but for all practical and socio-economic and religious purposes they live in complete harmony. There are various dimensions in the zone of interaction among them, such as, the exchange of mutual help and labour, the festival and political ring, the traditional exchange ring etc. On such occasions people of one village or island come in closer contact with each other.

In the absence of an open market system, people develop friendship bonds with people of the same village or island and with the other islanders too. They maintain such friendship bonds through generations. It is apt to say that 'once in bond always in bond'. Maintenance of such bonds become imperative in case of inter-island trade.

The organisation of a Nicobarese village is very systematic. A Nicobarese village is a cluster of families. We have observed that all the families have a captain known as Makupati; several such families constitute a joint family which is looked after by another captain, and several such joint families constitute a village. A village has three captains, who manage to solve all the family or economic disputes of the Nicobarese. Thus, the political organisation reflects the unity of a Nicobarese village. A Nicobarese village is always situated along the shore, therefore, the sea and the forest are always on either side of their huts. The common features of a village are a church, death and birth houses, Elpenum, grave-yard etc.

Among the Nicobarese, the elementary or nuclear family is recognised as an important social unit. Initially, a Nicobarese family consists of husband, wife and their unmarried children. However, in Car Nicobar joint-family system is practised. A Nicobarese family is neither patrilineal nor matrilineal. In fact, after marriage, the families of the bride and the bridegroom make economic adjustment and then decide the rule of residence. If the husband goes to the family of his wife to live after marriage, he is known as 'Gulam,' and vice versa is also true.

In a Nicobarese family, the husband has always a primary say; even though his wife is understood as a subordinate, she participates in all functions with him in the society. They maintain very cordial relations. And also we find that during the pregnancy of one's wife, a Nicobarese husband observes all the taboos that his wife does.

III

In the study of the entire process of socialisation of a Nicobarese, we have found that their limitless beliefs in nature and spirit have compelled them to observe a vast number of taboos in different walks of life. We have also found that from childhood, a Nicobarese comes in contact with the sea and the forest, and he or she learns also about the Iwi and all the economic activities of the society. For the boys there is no initiation ceremony, but as soon as a girl attains puberty, an initiation ceremony known as the *Annaham* is celebrated.

The ecological condition and the social environment provide them with ample opportunity for pre- and extra-marital relations. The forest plays an important role in this regard. Selection of spouse is done by mutual consent. It is mostly done either in the forest or during a festive occasion. Divorce is more frequent in the bigger islands than the smaller ones. It is so because, in the bigger islands due to sufficient amount of food women are economically independent. No legal or social sanction is needed for divorce.

The extent of co-operation, reciprocity and solidarity in Nicobarese society can be understood from the details of death and death rites. They exhibit very primitive customs after death. The ultimate aim of a Nicobarese is to celebrate the *Kindrak* i.e. reburial of his relatives. All the people of the island as well as people from other islands also take part in it. It is celebrated for three months. In the final stage of the *Kindrak*, the bones of the dead relatives are dug from the grave and after a few days of paying homage to the soul, the bones are buried again.

IV

The study of religion of such a people is more than rewarding. The indigenous religion of the Nicobarese has been Animism. There are elaborate ceremonies and festivals aimed at exercising and scaring away spirits i.e. *Iwi*. Fear of *Iwi* is the guide to all ceremonies. Witches and of course witch finders abound there, and it follows that the mind of the people is so largely occupied with superstition that every man's fortune and sickness are understood to be spirit-caused or witch-caused, and the remedy in each case is believed to be in special exorcism by the help of *Minluana*. The aim of all the rituals is to gratify the good spirits (Iwi-Ka) and frighten away the bad spirits (Iwi-Pat). Besides Iwi they believe in Reuse, the idea of which is not indigenous but of foreign origin.

From the analysis of the sacred complex of the Nicobarese it is clear that as far as the sacred performance and the sacred specialists are concerned, they are fully developed among them. But they do not have any specific sacred geography. Sometimes, the entire island is held sacred, and any object that appears to be unusual to them is considered as sacred.

V

Thus, keeping the focus on Nature we discovered its interaction with the Nicobarese Man. This approach of describing the tribal cultures in the line of Evans Pritchard (1940), Redfield (1953) and Thomas (1956) was of course important in the study of the Nicobarese culture. But as explained by Vidyarthi (1963) in his study of the Maler, when I proceeded from the observational level to the level of abstraction, I found that the socio-physical environment of the Nicobarese was filled with beliefs in supernatural, mainly in Iwi, and a series of rituals modifying and influencing the Nature-Man relationship took place. It was observed that in their entire economic, social and religious activities, their belief in Iwi was a regulating factor of the Nature-Man relationship, and it overall moulded their culture. Thus, in accordance with Vidyarthi's study of the Maler (1963), focusing on Iwi, it was also recorded that with the 'sacred centres', 'sacred performance' and 'sacred specialist', it constituted a 'complex' in itself. With these ideas in mind it was resolved that the wholistic portrayal of a society like the Nicobarese could only be useful when depicted in terms of "Nature-Man-Spirit Complex".

VI

The study of the Nature-Man-Spirit Complex of such a people is interesting in the sense that they have lived isolated throughout the ages, not only geographically but socially too. Our study of the Nicobarese is on the same line as Vidyarthi's study of the Maler, but we find marked differences observable among the Maler and the Nicobarese. Whereas the Maler are the tribes of the mainland, practising shifting cultivation, and their main eco-system consists of forest, the Nicobarese live in different ecological conditions, and sea and forest both are the dominant elements of the Nicobarese eco-system. The Maler are comparatively more in communication with the people around them. They have frequent contacts with many other tribal and non-tribal groups. This is not the case with the Nicobarese.

It is our intensive study of the three villages of the different islands of the Nicobar group, we have discovered that the size of the island and the density of population in it determine the various aspects of Nicobarese life. For example, the smaller the size of the island, the more industrious are its people; and the bigger its size, the lazier its people. Further, the bigger the island, the more frequent the divorce cases; and the smaller the island, the less frequent. Also, it was observed that in smaller islands, people were in greater fear of the Iwi. Thus, we find that despite the spread of Christianity, improved means of communication and government's effort to introduce education and multipurpose development schemes, the Nicobarese still maintain a life style of the Nature-Man-Spirit Complex, and are not easily prepared to undergo drastic changes.

It can also be concluded that as compared to the Maler, the life of a Nicobarese is in greater interaction with nature on the one hand and spirit on the other.

TEN

Ramesh Chandra

ECOLOGY AND RELIGION OF THE KINNER
Mountain Dwellers of North-Western Himalayas

IN HIS study of the Maler, a tribe living in the Rajmahal plateau of Santhal Pargana in Bihar, Vidyarthi observed the significance of 'Nature, man and spirit' complex under the theme of 'cultural ecology' and 'functionalism' (Vidyarthi, 1963). This gave rise to a school under which many of the scholars conducted studies and confirmed the concept propounded by Vidyarthi in different ways. There are several studies made in this direction which deal with the concept of 'Nature, man and spirit' complex directly or even indirectly (Morab, 1980; Prasad, 1978; Sandhwar,1978; Verma, 1977). Some more studies made in the area of cultural ecology and anthropogeography revealed further importance and significance of such studies to understand interplay of ecology with that of social systems and material culture of different people specially those living in somewhat distinct ecological settings. "It cannot be denied that geographical fronts have helped anthropologists in India and abroad to their understanding of social phenomenon. In later years, the correlation between external ecology and social explanation has been increasingly brought forth and stressed upon. The deeper implications and interpretations, where certain areas of two disciplines come closer, can be searched through concepts like cultural ecology, human geography, anthropo-geography etc." (Mann, 1979: 261). It is largely true that the geography of a particular area or ecology in the broader sense, helps to a great extent in shaping the society at its value system level (social aspects) as well as its cultural level (material cultural aspects). But it is also to be considered at the same level how well other institutions help people to respond in a cohesive manner to the needs arising out of ecological settings satisfying demands of institutions simultaneously. A sense of reciprocity between the institutions and ecology fulfilling the requirements of the people deserves attention from anthropologists for its elucidation. It is noted that various social and religious institutions in any society are largely shaped in the manner, or present set of prescriptions, which fit in the framework of need—direct or indirect at different levels—of the people to which terms given for their recognition are 'adjustment' and/or 'adaptation'.

The present paper is an attempt in the direction where religion has been viewed in the context of ecology at the local level in north-western Himalayas. Religion, both as a 'dogma' and as a 'way of life' helps in maintaining a well adjusted plane with the ecology thus satisfying people to fulfil their requirements—in terms of (1) deriving remedial treatment to their problems, and (2) achieving psychological satisfaction. This hypothesis is being examined here in the light of data collected among the Kinner. The paper is a part of research I conducted in Kinnaur (field research was done in 1970-72); however, the concept and framework for analysis are also based on some further research conducted among the people living in almost similar ecological conditions in the north-western Himalayas. Following the 'Nature, man and spirit' complex I propose to deal with the material intended for the present discussion in the manner that I introduce the area of field research first followed by a description of the people and only then I would take up the issue of religion and its reciprocity to the ecological setting keeping the Kinner at the middle who experience and reflect the adjustments in their day-to-day life.

II

ECOLOGICAL CONTEXT

Kinnaur is a considerably secluded and rugged area in the north-western Himalayas. It is situated between 31°-05′-55″ and 32°-05′-20″ north latitude and between 77°-45′-0″ and 79°-00′-50″ east longitude. Kinnaur is one of the twelve districts of Himachal Pradesh. The entire state, excepting some areas can be considered hilly having lofty ranges of north-western Himalayas. Kinnaur consists of rugged terrain of the Himalayan range all over. The district is stretched over an area of 6679 sq. km. It is spread about 80 km in length and 64 km in breadth and constitutes nearly 11.7 per cent of the total state. Kinnaur is surrounded in three directions by Lahul and Spiti in the north, Garhwal, U.P. in the south and by Simla in the west. In the easterly direction Kinnaur has its boundary with Tibet and forms an international border. The district is situated at a height of nearly 2000 metres to 4500 metres. The face of the region presents high mountains and low dales and are marked by precipitous sky high mountains with their peaks covered with perpetual snow (District Hand Book, 1961). The Kinner Kailash mountains of the great Himalayan range lie between the eastern and north-eastern faces of the area and western Tibet. Villages are scattered all over the district at different heights in the plateau, plain land, spur of hills and on slopes as well.

In general mountains are of different geological formations. At some places these are quite stony, hard and stable whereas at other places they are quite loose in nature. Khatra Dhang in Pooh subdivision needs a special mention in this regard. Kinnaur is divided into six valleys each being geographically isolated either by some range of mountain or river etc. Bhabha, Kalpa, Ropa and Hargarang are some important valleys of the district having sizable population in each of them.

The Sutlej is the main river flowing through this area. It originates from Manasarovar in Tibet and passes through a 128 km course throughout the district. There are many small rivers flowing through the district which merge with the Sutlej at different points. The rivers Spiti and Baspa are worth mentioning here. A few small tributaries like Shiaso, Titan, Kiran and Solding also give their water to the Sutlej. Rivers flowing in the hilly tracts through the district can hardly be used for irrigation purposes. Only some *khads* or streams are often used for irrigation purposes by diverting their water through *kuhls*.

Kinnaur presents a varied picture with regard to its climatic conditions. These varied conditions depend upon the nature of rocks and soil, nature of vegetation and intensity of rainfall. Geographically speaking Kinnaur is divisible into three areas or zones which incidentally by and large correspond to administrative sub-divisions as well. These zones are Nichar, Kalpa and Pooh, each having some distinct climate. Rainfall in Kinnaur is from usual (in Nichar) to scanty (in Pooh) with ordinary in the middle zone Kalpa; i.e., it rains considerably well in Nichar, to some extent in Kalpa and almost nil in Pooh. Based on rainfall Nichar and Pooh areas are alluded to as moist zone and dry zone respectively. While Kalpa is considered to be the intermediate zone in this respect. Annual rainfall in Kinnaur varies from 46.51 cm. to 90.72 cm. with an average of 21.51 cm. Kinnaur being situated in the interior of the Himalayan range experiences heavy snowfall. During November to March the area remains covered with thick snow. The average snowfall recorded is 2.16 metres per year. There are several surrounding mountains covered with perpetual snow. In general the climate is cold. The temperature varies from place to place in the district depending upon the extent of forests, altitude, rainfall and snowfall. The mean maximum temperature in the dry zone or Pooh area varies from 58° F in October to 78° F in July and the mean minimum temperature varies from 50° F in April to 67° F in August (District Hand Book, 1961).

So far as the moist zone or western part of the district is concerned, Kinnaur is considerably rich in forests. The dry zone or eastern and north-eastern parts present almost a bare look as no thick forests are seen. It is believed that until a century back there were plenty of large mature trees in the district. Before the forests were demarcated as reserved and unreserved, people took the liberty to cut down forests and start cultivation wherever they liked. This resulted in destruction of forest soil remaining bare, eroding hills, deepening gullies and extending slips. The Kinner in some parts face a problem even to get large size trees for house construction and fire wood is not available to them so easily. This situation has made an impact on the life style of Kinner living in different parts in different ecological settings. As mentioned earlier the climate is cold and is best suited for *Pinus* trees, *chir*, *chilgoza*, walnuts and apple orchards. Therefore *Pinus cederous* and *Abies* are some commonly found genuses in the forests of Kinnaur. "*Pinus gerardiana* forms a thick belt of forests along both sides of Sutlej valley and the side streams between the cliffs of the gorge below and alpine pastures and eternal snows above" (District Hand Book, 1961). Other species of *Pinus* viz. *longifolia* and *wallichiana*, and *Cedrus devdara, Picea smithi*, and *Abies pindro* also contribute to a great extent to these forests.

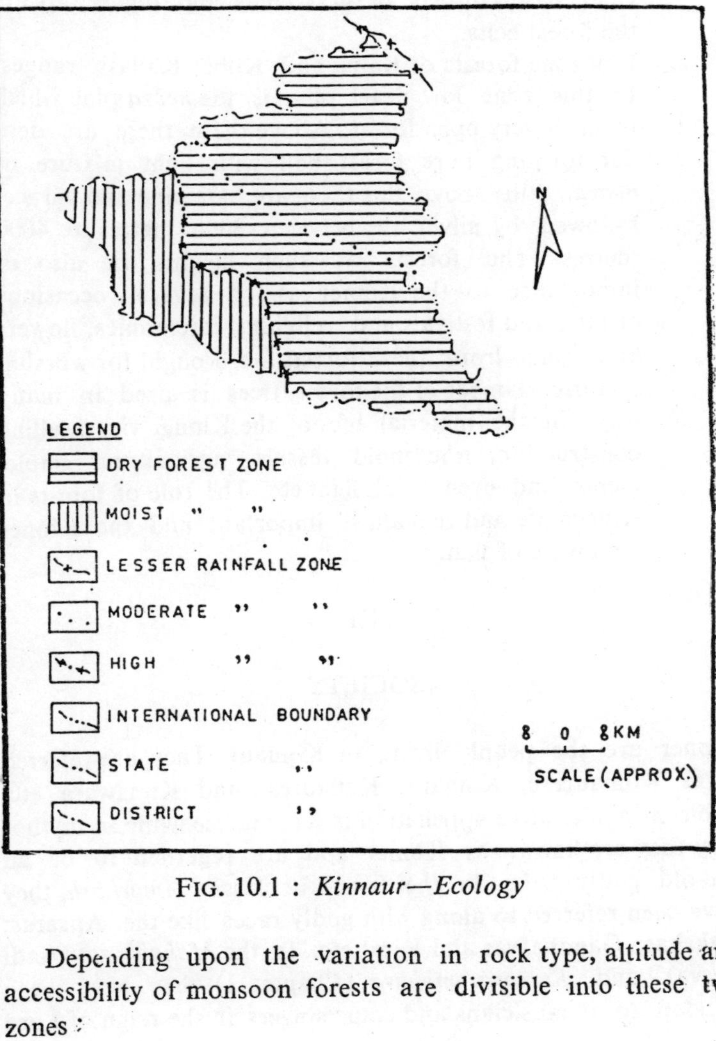

FIG. 10.1 : *Kinnaur—Ecology*

Depending upon the variation in rock type, altitude and accessibility of monsoon forests are divisible into these two zones :

1. The moist zone forests can be seen in western Kinnaur. They comprise the Taranda range forests. On the left side of the valley with northern exposure, forests come much lower down towards the river than they do on the right bank, while isolation of direct sunlight restricts the spread of vegetation. On the left side, the forests are particularly continuous. From the river side at about 1000 metres to alpine pasture at 4000 metres on the right base consists of grasslands and higher up are the forest belts.
2. Dry zone forests of Kalpa and Kilba Kailash ranges. In this zone low level pine is the *neoza* pine which forms a very open forest. Above these there are deodar forming pure forest belt with light mixture of *neoza*. Still above this there are blue pine and spruce, followed by silver fir between 3000 metres to 4000 metres. The forests at such heights are also of importance to the Kinner as on several occasions of fairs and festivals and religious ceremonies, flowers and fruits from these forests are brought for worship and use. Timber of the forest trees is used in many ways in the material life of the Kinner viz. dwelling construction, household vessels, agricultural implements and even torch light etc. The role of forests in Kinner life and religion is important and the Kinner are aware of that.

III

SOCIETY

Kinner are the people living in Kinnaur. They are referred to as Kinnaurese, Kinnara, Kanaurese and Kunawara etc. Their administrative appellation is Kinnaurese while in mythology they are known as Kinner and are regarded to be an age-old godly tribe. In the Sanskrit classic, *Amarkosh*, they have been referred to along with godly races like the Apsaras, Yakshas, Gandharvas and Kirat etc. In the *Mahabharat* (Aadi Parva) and *Kumarasambhava* (Chapter 1) they have been alluded to as musicians and court singers in the reign of Lord

Indra. *Ramayana* (Uttarkhand), *Manusmriti*, *Vachaspatyan* also provide some reference about these people. In the *Raghuvansham*, Kinner have been referred to as a polyandrous tribe in the Himalayan region (Chandra, 1972; Raha, 1978). It is believed that the Kinner were not known until the Rigveda period. Chakravarti traced their origin from Sumarians, a branch of whom became famous by the name Simbeari and the consecutive distribution of Simbeari in the Himalayan area gave rise to the people called Kinner (Kaushal, 1967). Often they have been taken as 'half man and half giant.' As an appellation *Ashvamukha* is also used for the same people (Shashi, 1971). The Kinner themselves are believed to have belonged to Khash or Khasa stock. The Khasa are prominently known people living in Jaunsar-Bawar area of Dehra Dun.

Kinner is the term used for five different ethnic groups inhabiting Kinnaur. They are the Kanet, Badhi, Lohar, Koli and Nagaloo. The Kanet are the dominant group followed by the Koli, then Badhi and Lohar; and Nagaloo is the least populated group. The Kinner are divided into mainly two divisions, one the Kanet who are classified as a scheduled tribe and the other including all remaining four groups is called scheduled caste. Though each ethnic group occupies a definite position in the social hierarchy yet it follows by and large some set of rules, norms and beliefs to give it a shape of an integral constituent of the homogeneous society of Kinner. The cultural differences present among the Kinner are not only at the inter-ethnic level but also at the intra-ethnic level depending upon the geographical isolation and ecological conditions prevailing at the local level in which the particular group of Kinner live. As such cultural variation may exist, at smaller levels, between the ethnic groups of the same identity living in two different geographical and ecological settings. For example the Kanet living in Pooh area show some differences when compared to the Kanet at Nichar or even Kalpa, but have least difference when compared to those living in Hangarang valley. The same is the case with the Koli and other ethnic groups. Nevertheless in the broader sense all groups put together present the picture of a homogeneous society. The presence of any particular ethnic group in the region depends upon the potentiality of pursuing its specialized occupation. To illustrate the point the Nagaloo live only in the western parts, i.e. in Nichar area where they get *nangal* (a climber species) in plenty to pursue their traditional occupation of basketry. So is the case with the Badhi who also dwell in this part only as there is much potential available for their carpentry etc., which is not the case in eastern parts; hence the Badhi do not dwell there.

Kinner are fraternal polyandrous people. All the brothers of a particular generation usually share one common wife. Polyandry forms the societal profile. At least once the Kinner give their sons in a polyandrous marriage. Tying of *pagri* by one and the same piece of cloth on the heads of all brothers partaking of the marriage ceremony, and offering of *neoza* garland by the bride to all her prospective husbands symbolises polyandrous marriage. Sometimes brothers share several wives in common among them. Such form of unions are only next to polyandrous form and are called as 'polyandry and polygyny' form. Often it is observed that in a polyandrous union younger husbands find it too difficult to adjust with the common wife who is considerably older as compared to their (husband's) age. In such cases either new wives are brought in to be shared in common, or younger husbands desert the polyandrous union and go in for monogamy. The former situation gives rise to 'polyandry and polygyny' while the latter one gives rise to 'poly-monogamy'. In poly-monogamy husbands who have enjoyed polyandrous status, for reasons of dissatisfaction go in for monogamous marriage. Thus it can be conceived as switching over or passing from polyandrous stage to monogamy. With the changing scene of improving economy, Kinner are heading towards monogamy through this transitional phase of poly-monogamy (Chandra, 1973). Slightly increasing instances of monogamy are also there in the society. Kinner go in for monogamy for the reasons like when the boy is the only son in the household. The changing trend in the Kinner's marriage choice from polyandry to poly-monogamy is also due to improving economy or capability of each to earn cash to run the household expenditure single handed. This situation necessarily leads to such occupations that yield cash and need single handed efforts viz. labour and business. It is observed that in general Kinner economy is of mixed type which no household can run single handed. More so, no single economic pursuit can provide all that is needed for the household. With a single economic pursuit there is always danger, for a household, even for its survival. To run the household economy smoothly many helping hands are required, and a joint venture is almost a must to run the various economic pursuits viz. agriculture, sheep rearing, domestic animals and other jobs. A detailed discussion would be held a little later about the economy of these people.

Kinner households are of either vertically extended or horizontally extended type. The rule of primogeniture operates. The eldest male member (among fathers or brothers) holds the fort and manages the household. Like property children are owned jointly as long as property is not divided which rarely takes place. In eastern Kinnaur parents after getting their sons married, let them get separated and establish separate households. The norm about such fission is based on the Tibetan family system and is known as *Gangum-Nangma*. *Gangun* is the parents' household and *Nangma* is the son's household which takes responsibility to partake in all social and religious activities while parents lead a sort of free life but have to work to earn their livelihood. In the sphere of religion parents get more time to devote to earn merit by chanting religious hymns *Om ma ni pad me hum* of Buddhistic belief ; however, in Hindu Kinnaur this is not the case as parents form the part of vertical extended households and partake in all social religious activities of the household and of the village.

The Kinner are by and large agriculturists, however no single economy is sufficient enough to fulfil the requirements of the household. Besides agriculture Kinner tend sheep and goat herds, domesticate some milch cattle—*zo*, *zomo* and cow. They may have newly introduced horticulture—apple orchards as well. Until recently they had trade with Tibet which came to an end in 1962. Kinner trade items were food grains, cloth and utensils and dry fruits which they sold in Tibet and in turn brought wool, salt, sheep, zo, and such other items available in plenty in Tibet. Gerard found them as "traders who considered sheep and goat as their wealth. They used to come down to Rampur, Simla, Hardwar and many places during the winter to market their commodities. During summers they used to go to Leh and Tibet for trade" (Gerard, 1841 : 80 ; Raha, 1978 : 86). At present with the cessation of trade the Kinner have now almost forgotten this aspect of economic life ; at least this is the case with the young generation; instead they have diverted their attention towards new opportunities opened up to compensate the loss in terms of orchards and cash crops etc. It has already been emphasized that the Kinner ecological setting is tough and poses problems for adjustments. People have to realize from land their requirements of food etc. Land is not much fertile and landholdings are usually small. Agricultural land is divisible into three types depending upon its situation in the hilly region.

1. Kanda land	Agricultural land in the higher reaches usually at a height ranging from 3000 metres to 4500 metres. Such land yields one crop in a year and remains covered with snow over a considerable period.
2. Gaonang land or Kimsaring	Agricultural land situated at the village level. Two crops may be realized with some pressure.
3. Neole land	Agricultural land at the lower level than the village. Usually it is stretched up to considerably low height. It is fertile and produces two crops in a year. In some moist zone areas people realize even three crops.

Agricultural fields are on the slopes of hills in the form of terraces. "The spaces of available land are few, and the cultivation is commonly done in narrow strips along the brows of the mountains" (Gerard 1841 : 63-64). The situation has not changed much since this observation was made and hence this holds true even today. It is to be pointed out here that the Kinner do practise terrace cultivation but shifting cultivation or slash and burn method is not at all in practice in this part as is usually the case with terrace cultivation in north-east India and other areas as well viz. *Jhum* cultivation by several tribes of north-eastern India, viz. the Naga, Apatani, Garo etc. and Saoras of Srikakulam (A.P.). Kinner are settled agriculturists following crop rotation method in the same land. For irrigation in moist zone as well as dry zone, *kuhls* (channels made of hollow tree trunks) are used to channelise stream water to the fields. One to two crops are produced depending upon the location of the field in Kanda, Kimsaring and Neole. Main crops grown are wheat, buck-wheat, lentils, maize, *china*, *kurgni*, *bathu*, *kala bathu*, *kodo*, *ogla* and *phaphra*. At low lands often paddy is also grown. Potato is grown as a cash crop in these regions quite profitably. This has helped the Kinner economy considerably. Considerable attention is now paid towards fruit production. Apricot, wild apricot (*chulli*), grapes and plums are the items, besides apples, receiving Kinner's attention. *Neoza* or *Chilgoza* and walnuts are grown in plenty. *Chulli* (wild apricot) gets an important place in Kinner's life, for it is used as fruit and the seeds are used for extraction of edible oil. *Chulli* fruit is a major item for distillation of liquor. Apples, grapes and other fruits are also used for distillation. Liquor locally called as *ghanti* has special importance in the socio-religious life of these people. *Chhang* or beer prepared from rice is commonly used on all social and religious occasions. Without *ghanti* no religious ceremony can take place. Distillation and brewing is another work done by many Kinner and adds to their economy substantively directly at consumption level and at production of earning cash level.

Besides agriculture which is the main occupation of almost all Kinner, traditional occupations of different ethnic groups of Kinner society are followed by them. Additional occupations for Kanet, are tending sheep and goats, domesticating some milch cattle, maintaining apple orchards etc. Other ethnic groups may also have these as their economic pursuits; however, they are specialists of some particular occupations. The Badhi do carpentry and masonry work, and Lohar are smiths doing ironsmithy and often working on silver ornaments as well. The Kali have besides agriculture, weaving, tailoring and leather work. Nagaloo are specialized in basketry. In eastern Kinnaur some Kanet are engaged in muleteering also. Occupation specialization varies from place to place depending upon its ecological setting at local level ; and presence or absence of ethnic groups in the area depends much on this aspect. It is evident from the case of Badhi and Nagaloo who dwell in western parts only. As discussed, agriculture forms the basis of the economy at household level and all other occupations are subsidiary ; but nevertheless, on less important. All occupations put together make the Kinner self-sufficient to run their life. This is the case specially with the Kanet and Koli. Kinner land holdings are usually small, that too spread in three different places. Agriculture in these tough geo-economic conditions needs many hands to work jointly to get appropriate rewards from the land. A sense of avoidance of fragmentation of land in the larger interest of the household unit is felt by these people. With the fragmentation of land there is a danger of loss of productivity of land due to shortage of manpower and then the land size becomes non-viable for its owner as with the division of land, other property, animals and equipments etc. are also divided. As a result it becomes almost impossible for the concerned members to run their economy smoothly at the household level for want of manpower, animals, and tools etc. In order to maintain the household unit united, estate undivided and many helping hands available for joint venture, Kinner have sought a solution in polyandry and to give it a shape of a condition which is 'must' they traced its origin in their religion and linked the practice with the legendary heroes of the *Mahabhàratā*—the Pandavas; to legalise the practice within the framework of 'ecological setting' and 'need' they took shelter in religion in the interest of easy survival and perpetuity. There is a temple in village Kothi which is said to have been constructed by the Pandavas and also a tank in front of this temple known as *Bahirav ka talab*. Reminiscences of Morang fort are also said to have belonged to the Pandavas. It is believed by Kinner that Pandavas took shelter in this area during their year in hiding when they were in exile.

IV

RELIGIOUS CONTEXT

It is conspicuous that in Kinnaur two religions flourish simultaneously—Buddhism of the Tibetan type commonly called as Lamaic Buddhism in the eastern part, and the Hinduism of the local level in the rest of the district. The spread of each religion corresponds to the ecological setting to a great deal. In general both the religions work on the broader horizon to give a smooth running to the Kinner in terms of deriving fulfilment of their needs arising out of the ecological setting (Figure 10.2). The dry zone has Buddhism while people of the moist zone profess their faith in Hinduism. Of course, there is a meeting point for these two religions in Kalpa region where people believe in the religions as per their convenience. This area could be alluded to as the intermediate zone. Kinner in general believe in the supernatural. "Whatever happens on this earth is the machination of a supernatural power" is the common notion prevalent in the minds of these people. Anything beyond human control is attributed to the supernatural and the subordinate deities. There are gods and goddesses at different levels and orders in the religious life of Kinner starting from the household level to the regional level; and even some more deities are held in veneration for their specific powers, status and jurisdiction etc. As Atkinson noted about the religion of these people, "religion in these hills is worship of fear" (Atkinson, 1884 : 839), it holds good even today.

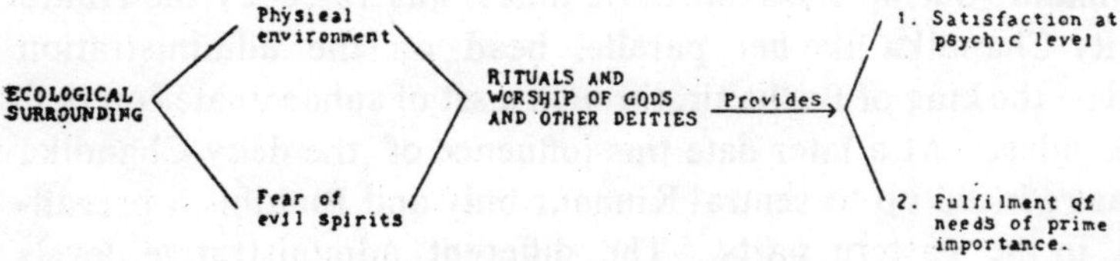

FIG. 10.2 : *Reciprocity of Religion with Ecology in Kinnaur*

Kinner dwelling in these tough ecological settings depend largely on their religious system. As a Kinner starts realizing the tough and hazardous life with the advancing of his age and the fearful surroundings in the form of mountains, jungles and dreadful ecology, his belief in the supernatural and in the gods becomes more entrenched. Routine life and active participation in religious activities of his elders and their sense of complete surrender to presiding and other subordinate deities reinforces a feeling to conceive strong feelings of similar kind in his mind as well. All acts of life, decision-making, dispute solving and even observance of necessary rituals and life cycle ceremonies—all these are observed only after the consent of the deity of appropriate order has been sought. There cannot be any drifting from this set notion else one should be prepared to face the wrath of the deity in the form of some sort of calamity—no rain, or even excessive rain, hailstorm, epidemic at village level, and accidents and personal loss at individual level. "The harder the living conditions the greater will be the faith in religion", gets a strong hold in Kinnaur. Kinner seem to have completely surrendered to their gods. How religion reciprocates in the given ecology will be brought forward in the following discussion by way of describing particular religious traits or elements and thereby providing an interpretation and analysis as well.

A historical view of Kinner religion shows much similarity between traditional administrative patterns and jurisdiction of the deities. In the earlier set-up of administration in Kinnaur there were different officials at some set levels of hierarchy at *Khundt*, *Ghori*, village and household level. Similarly at each such level there is a deity at the corresponding level, of course, this is the case with Hinduism which has its influence in western and central Kinnaur. However, history reveals that once entire Kinnaur (during Bushahir State times) was ruled by the Hindu deity Chandika like her parallel head on the administration side—the king of Bushahir, through a set of subordinates on both the sides. At a later date this influence of the deity Chandika was reduced up to central Kinnaur only and Buddhism prevailed in the eastern parts. The different administrative levels were corresponded by deities on the religious side.

Khundt	—	Khundt level deity Chandika
Ghori	—	Subordinate deity of the region
Pargana	—	Pargana level deity which ruled over the entire pargana villages.

Village — Village god
Household — Kimshoo

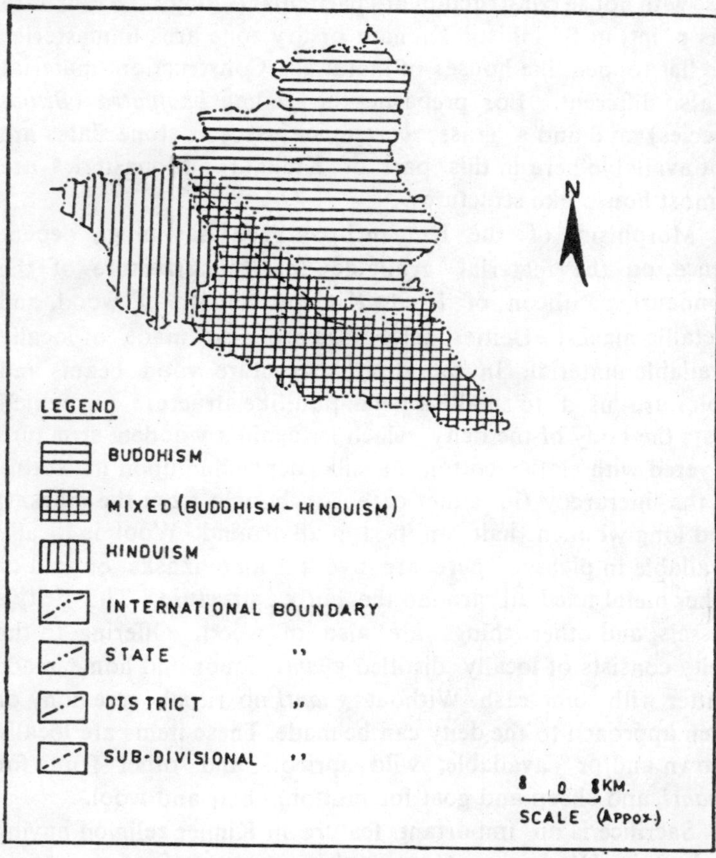

FIG. 10.3 : *Kinner—Religion*

The deities are answerable to the deities of superior level in the same manner as the administrative workers. Visits of the superior deity to its subordinate and vice versa is known as *bonning* and *bioling* respectively.

Reciprocity of religion with ecology can be seen in terms of temple structure, morphism of deity and area of its working. Temples in the moist zone or western Kinnaur are built of the same material as used in house construction—stone and wood. Temples are usually bigger accommodations built by slates and stones and wooden beams and planks etc. Temples are pagoda type having a sloping roof like common houses. The technique involved and material used are the same as is the case with house construction in a particular ecology. To illustrate this point, in Buddhistic Kinnaur or dry zone area monasteries are flat topped like houses of that area. Construction material is also different. For preparing the ceiling *bhojpatra* (*Bitula* species) mud and a grass, *burtse*, are used, as stone slates are not available here in this part of Kinnaur. Monasteries are almost house like structures.

Morphism of the Kinnauri pantheon has much dependence on the material available locally. Structure of the Kinnauri pantheon of Hindu Kinnaur consists of wood, and metallic masks. Deities' belongings are also made of locally available material. In the deity's structure wood beams and poles are used to make a palanquin-like structure on which rests the body of the deity which is again a wooden structure covered with cloth—cotton or silk depending upon its status in the hierarchy (in either case it is bought from the market) and long woollen hair on its top all around. Wool is locally available in plenty. There are five to nine masks of gold or other metal fixed all around the body structure. The deity's vessels, and other things are also of wood. Offering to the deity consists of locally distilled *ghanti*-liquor and home made butter with some cash. Without *ghanti* no ritual, ceremony or even approach to the deity can be made. These items are locally grown and/or available; wild apricots and other fruits for *ghanti*, and sheep and goat for mutton, hair and wool.

Sacrifice is an important feature in Kinner religion having its base in Hinduism. Goat or sheep are sacrificed on important occasions of worshipping gods of different orders from village level to Khundt level, like marriage, fairs and festivals. In this practice an essence of reciprocity of religion with ecology can be seen. An average Kinner does own some sheep and goats in this cold climate for wool, milk and milk products, its skin to be used as sacks, and goat hair for making ropes and *khercha*-mats etc. More so, in cold climates people require rich protein diet full of fat and other rich contents. Since sheep and goat are found in plenty, they have taken place in religion for sacrifice. The reciprocity here lies in venerating the deity by offering animals, with ecology that mutton is distributed as *prasad* which forms a rich protein diet. When deities do not accept sacrifice of animals, it is done to appease malevolent spirits. Kinner fear very much the wrath of deities and evil effects caused by malevolent spirits. Thus in one form or the other an animal is to be sacrificed for the consumption of mutton. There are religious ceremonies requiring ten to fifteen *khadu*, sheep or goat, for sacrifice. The idea implied here is simple: it depends upon the size of the people among whom *prasad* is to be distributed and accordingly the importance of the religious ceremony or ritual is enhanced. Blood and liver of the sacrificed animal are offered to the deity or spirit held in veneration and the rest of the portion is shared by the sacred functionaries (Vidyarthi 1961) and the devotees in the form of *prasad*. By sacrificing animals, Kinner derive a sense of psychic satisfaction that they have appeased the deity or spirit and that they will be saved from the wrath of those deities and spirits. The use of *ghanti* as *prasad* is also based on the fact that in cold climate in order to keep the body warm Kinner require a good amount of in-take of liquor. By accepting *ghanti* as item of offering and *prasad*, the Kinner got sanctified the use of liquor in their life by way of getting it approved by religion. Now a look at the items of *prasad* and offerings, reveal that they contain such items as are needed to keep the body fit in the intense cold climatic condition—warmth, fat, protein and above all a good diet. After the animal is sacrificed its skin and hair are also used in the material culture of the Kinner (Figure 10.4).

Kinner religion claims to protect the source items by guarding them with their powers within the jurisdiction. There are several gods claiming such powers with them in the Kinner religious world. Their status in the hierarchy is fixed starting from *Kimshoo* to the prime presiding deity. *Kimshoo* or *Gharkadevta* is the deity effective at the household level. There is no fixed morphism for *Kimshoo*. All Kinner have their Kimshoo believed to have taken his position in granaries or stores of the houses. For its morphism or conceptualizing Kimshoo some object like box, iron tools and utensils etc. are regarded as being possessed by Kimshoo. Thus the form may vary from house to house. Ecological hazards are so much feared that the Kinner start their day by worshipping Kimshoo. Special offerings are made

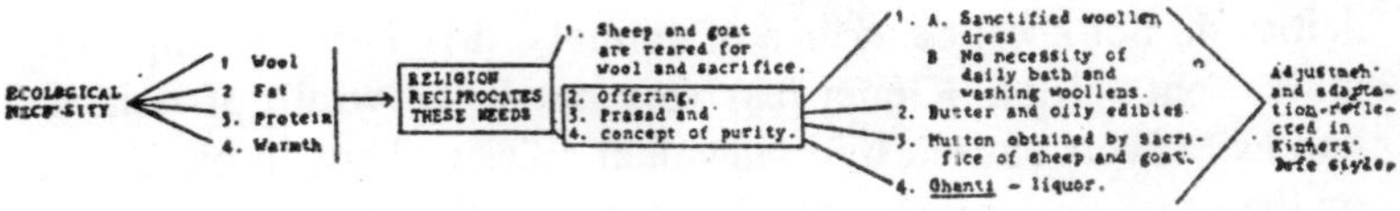

FIG. 10.4 : *Fulfilment of Kinner's Ecological needs through Religion*

on occasions like child birth, marriage, illness, crop failure, harvesting and other socio-economic crises at the household level. The head of the household worships the deity. Kimshoo is the deity at the lowest level of the social unit. Above him is the village god looking after the welfare of the people at the village level and other higher deities working at the still higher level and ruling Kinner life in all respects on the pattern of politico-judicial and administrative system held in tradition.

Besides the Kinner pantheon there are several other deities to help and solve the problems of the people emerging on the ground of tough ecological setting. These deities do not have any kinship affiliation with the Kinnauri pantheon. Kuldev, Bhairon, Bansheer and Shirgul are the deities of this order besides Dahla, Baisaaro and Yulsa who are of Buddhistic influence. Kuldev is a triradiant in morphism and is held in veneration through shamanistic practices. Kuldev keeps malevolent spirits and ghosts away from causing any ill effect on people.

Shirgul seems to have occupied a prominent cognicized position in the life of these people. This has perhaps a bearing on the economic life. Shirgul protects sheep and goats. Kinner economy depends heavily on sheep rearing and tending goat herds. Therefore, they cannot afford to annoy Shirgul in any way. Shepherds moving with flocks of sheep keep a small container having an idol of Shirgul with them. It is widely believed that by doing so flocks are safe from any suffering.

Bansheer is the deity of the forests. It is a common belief that Bansheer protects forests. The wrath of the deity would bring disaster in terms of destruction of the forest hence the deity is worshipped so that people may not be deprived of the benefits from the forests—wood, vegetation, incense, often herbal medicines and pastures etc. Bansheer is worshipped by offering some *puja, ghanti* and often *khadu* is sacrificed. The form of worship varies to some extent but objectives and rewards remain the same as in the case of other deities.

Reciprocity of religion with ecology can also be seen in the pattern of worship and concept of pollution and purity. As the climate is intensely cold, taking a bath daily is just beyond comprehensible thought. The idea of purity and pollution has got much relaxation in this sense. Taking a bath before offering regular *puja* to Kimshoo or even the village god is not a must for the Kinner; even the *pujarar* cleans and washes only his feet and hands and rarely his body before going to perform *puja*. For Kimshoo even this is not done. On special occasions of propitiating deities of a high order it becomes necessary only for *pujaras* and *groksha* (whose body is possessed by the deity during conversation) to take a bath. All other temple functionaries and Kinner laity may attend the *puja* even without taking a bath. Pollution on account of clothing also does not get much importance. It is worthwhile to think in the direction that due to cold climate woollen dresses are worn round the year; and then it is not convenient to wash them so frequently and show concern about such aspects. Above all as a mark of reciprocity, religion does give sanction to woollens as pure, not polluted.

The idea of pollution comes into being on occasions like childbirth and death rituals in the household. Pollution is observed more at the level of ethnic groupings which have a clear cut hierarchy and then within the Kanet group who have several *khandans* associated with the village deities at different levels of hierarchy depending upon the kind of functions they perform in the temple and to serve the deity. For example among Kanet it is clearly defined as to which *khandan* will work as *groksha*, *mathas* who speak on behalf of the people, *chelia* who carry or lift the palanquin etc. At other ethnic levels it is fixed as to which ethnic group will play metallic instruments, trumpets, drums etc. at the time of *puja*. Thus pollution and purity are based more on social organization rather than religion itself which reciprocates with ecology in the interest of its believers.

The Kinner of the eastern region or dry zone profess their faith in Buddhism. There seems some congruence in the spread of Buddhism in this part as in other areas also having similar ecology Buddhism prevails. For example the neighbouring area of Lahul and Spiti, Ladakh and Tibet are dominated by Buddhism. However, how much Buddhism provides in terms of reciprocity to ecology, it is difficult to assess. It is worth noting that Buddhism is in practice in Kinnaur in the eastern part in toto and in central parts also along with Hinduism. Kinnaur Buddhism is of the Lama type which got its origin with fusion of Buddhism with Bon religion of Tibet. It is based on *tantric* practices. This religion has given the institution of *Lama* and *Zomo* which help Kinner in solving some of their problems like 'earning merits' for themselves and adjustment of 'surplus women' due to practice of polyandry (Chandra, 1981). In general Kinner believe in rebirth and for that they have their concern. As tradition holds it, one of the brothers of the household unit goes to join the Lamaic institution to earn merits for himself as well as his household members. In this way Kinner earned merit and in return for his services the Lama (brother) gets his needs of food etc. met by his household people even without working on the "joint estate". The institution of *zomo* helped women having little prospects of marriage and also those who had some inclination towards religious life. In this institution the Kinner saw a remedy to their 'surplus women' created out of the practice of polyandry based on socio, economic and ecological factors, whom they could induct in *Zomoism*.

Devta complex is the universal feature in Kinnaur irrespective of prevalence of either religion. In the Buddhist area Dabla, Yulsa and Chhola are the gods. Like Hindu gods Dabla also claims to have its jurisdiction, protect and look after the welfare of the people. These gods have their jurisdiction in Pooh and Hangarang valleys. Ecological adjustment with regard to their morphism is seen in the form that as the area has no forests or thick forests as are found in the western part or Hindu Kinnaur, Dabla has taken its shape in the likeness of a thin stick; this is perhaps due to shortage of wood. Deities Chhola and Yulsa are said to be represented by cederous tree branches and horns of sheep or goat along with some stone slates with the inscription of *Om mani pad me hum* and figures of *Chhoktans* respectively. An important observation made here is that Buddhism does not prescribe sacrifice in any of the *puja*; but consumption of protein rich diet—mutton and liquor for warmth are equally necessary as in other parts of Kinnaur. As a solution to this problem religion yielded scope for consumption of mutton by giving a morphism of Yulsa in the shape of goat/sheep horns. Then, there are several evil spirits needing goat/sheep sacrifice and liquor to be offered in order to be just appeased. *Zimbo Digyt* and *Lande* are some names assigned to these evil spirits. Kinner fear them very much. In order to keep these malevolent spirits away, the services of a Lama are sought who can free the persons being under the influence of any such spirit by using *tana bana* (tantric practices). Sacrifice is also performed and *ghanti* is offered to these spirits and then to people as *prasad*. In addition, in Buddhist villages *Chhoktans* are erected in all the four directions at the village boundary to keep such evil spirits away. Often people erect *Chhoktans* on the top of their houses. Generally three *Chhoktans* of different colours are erected to ward off the spirits. Functions of the *Chhoktan* are manifold. It is a source of earning merit by circumambulating these starting from left to right side; sometimes it reminds of some Lama of repute whose bones are buried underneath and the *Chhoktan* also works as an indicator of human settlement and its territory. Above all, *Chhoktans* inhibit the entry of evil spirits, demons and ghosts. *Kankani* or gateway to Buddhist villages is also an additional guard against spirits of malevolent nature. Buddhist monasteries are house like structures in congruence with the local surroundings where live the Lama and zomos. A central room meant for worship is the additional feature if monasteries are to be compared with any house structure.

The reciprocity of religion is also evident in life-cycle ceremonies of the Kinner. It is noted that a culture develops rituals around the areas of life that are uncertain, that cause anxiety, or which are beyond human control. Rituals developed around life-cycle are primarily festive in nature excepting those observed during death. There are some variations in observance of rituals in connection with life-cycle in different zones in Kinnaur depending largely upon ecological conditions. There is no particular ceremony observed at the time of first pregnancy in western Kinnaur. However, in central and eastern parts a ceremony called *Dolmasepcha* is observed. On such occasions, a Lama is called to recite the religious hymns and spells of Buddhism. This ritual is observed in the interest of the safe arrival of child on the earth. Here immediately our attention is diverted to the point as to why no such ritual is observed in Hindu Kinnaur ? It is prudent to place an argument that as compared to western parts this region is more hostile and life is tougher. Chances of safe delivery in such hard conditions are perhaps remote as women have to work hard throughout for their survival and face challenging natural conditions. Hence religion takes its role to give strength to the expectant mother and other household people. No particular ceremony is observed after delivery, locally called *Keshong*, until seven days to ward off the pollution. The first ceremony in the Kinner life cycle is *chhangshiming* (*shuddhi* ceremony). On this occasion the house is cleansed by sprinkling *gomutra* (cow's urine) and mother and child are given a purificatory bath. This denotes the end of pollution. In order to protect the child from effects of evil spirits when the child is brought out of the house the first time after five or seven months, the deity Kali in western part and Chhola and Baisaro in eastern parts are worshipped. It is believed that by worshipping these gods the child gets protection and strength to countervail the effect of evil spirits. In the Kinner mind gods are so pervasive that they name their children after gods whether they believe in Hinduism or Buddhism. Some names like Ramchandra, Raghudas, Govinda, Yashoda in Hindu area and Panma Medup, Rinchin Dawa, Medubdorje, Dolma and Yamchin etc. in Buddhistic area are quite common. In marriage consent of the village god is a must. Participation of the village god in marriage is symbolized by some object brought from the temple by the temple *Kardar* who attends the marriage on behalf of the god. Before observing rituals and ceremonies permission is taken from the deity. Sacrifice of goat is a must. It is important to note that at death rituals Buddhist belief prevails. This is perhaps based on a desire for salvation—*Moksha* which Buddhism claims to help achieve. Death rituals observed in different parts also show some dependence on ecological setting. In the eastern part the dead body is cremated in the nearby jungle or near some water resources. Cremation has posed some problem in eastern parts—devoid of forests. In this part the dead body is anointed with oil and then is bathed. For cremation the pyre is made by wood contributed by each of the households in the village. Contribution of wood is an ecological necessity. Pollution period lasts for 39 days and on the day following the ceremony observed for purification is called *Chhanjung*. The role of the Lama remains prominent during purificatory rituals observed on the 7th day (until seven days the household is treated as fully polluted), and 40th day. *Ating* or *Phullaich* is observed after one year and a feast is accorded to the people. In the western part death rituals are observed in the Hindu way. The temple priest is called for the observation of rituals. Cremation poses no problem as wood is available in plenty. Pollution is observed for 14 days. On the fifteenth day purificatory rites are observed by sprinkling Ganges water all over the house. Well-to-do Kinner immerse the ashes of the deceased in the holy Ganges at Hardwar before the commencement of *Phullaich*—a festival when all dead ones are remembered and a feast is hosted in their honour.

V

CONCLUSION

Being mountainous and situated at a high altitude Kinnaur presents a typical ecology for its inhabitants—that too having some variation at the local level. In the given ecological set-up the Kinner have evolved some adjustments with nature through various sets of arrangements at social as well as religious levels to make their survival and perpetuity easy. The hilly economy, social arrangements and the 'world of religion' all put together provide a well adjusted plane to the Kinner. Religion has played an important role in their life by providing a balanced approach to meet the challenge of ecology of the area. The concept that "the adaptation of social arrangements to the requirements of surviving in the harsh environment by means of a certain technological inventory'' (Steward in Vidyarthi, 1963, ii) gets a further dimension to be added in it, as it is evident from the case of the Kinner; and that is the contribution of religion in shaping norms, beliefs and concepts of purity and pollution and functional needs of the society. Kinner religion has reciprocated within the given framework of local ecology for the interest of the people irrespective of the fact whether the Kinner are benefited directly or indirectly from the prescriptions of their religion.

ACKNOWLEDGEMENT

With a deep sense of gratitude I express my indebtedness to the Director, Anthropological Survey of India for awarding me two research fellowships, Junior (1970-72) and Senior (1972-74) which enabled me to carry out my research in Himachal Pradesh.

I am grateful to my colleagues Dr S.G. Morab and Dr A.K. Singh who gave some valuable suggestions on this paper and provided generous help in the preparation of the same. I also like to thank Miss S.V. Rajam, for her neat and efficient typing of the manuscript.

SUGGESTED READINGS

Census of India, *District Handbook of Kinnaur*, Simla 1961.

Chandra, Ramesh, "Socio-economic study of Kinnaurese of Himachal Pradesh" Report. Anthropological Survey of India, Calcutta (Unpublished) 1972.

Chandra, Ramesh, "Types and forms of marriage in a Kinnaur village", *Man in India.* Vol. 53 : 2, 1973.

Chandra, Ramesh, "The Kinners : A study in their society and religion". Ph.D. dessertation. Lucknow University, Lucknow, 1980.

Chandra, Ramesh, "Sex role arrangement to achieve economic security in northwestern Himalayas" in *Asian Highland Societies, An Anthropological Perspective* ed. C. Von furer Haimendorf. Delhi. 1981.

Kaushal, R. K., *Himachal Pradesh : A Survey of the History of the Land and its People.* Delhi. 1967.

Mann, R.S. "Anthropo-Geography : an important methodological issue", *Man in India.* Vol. 59 : 3.

Morab, S. G., "The Soliga : A study in ecology, economy, society and Religion of a hill tribe" Ph. D. thesis. Ranchi University, Ranchi, 1980.

Prasad, Rama Kant, *The Paruhiyas : A Study in Cultural Ecology and Tribal Dynamics.* Series Indica 8 Wien, 1978.

Raha, M. K. "Stratification and religion in a Himalayan Society" in *Himalayan Anthropology.* Mouton Publishers. The Hague. 1978.

Sandhwar, A.N. *The Korwa of Palamu : A Study in their Society and Economy*. Series Indica 9. Wien, 1978.

Shashi, S.S , *Himachal, Nature's Peaceful Paradise*, New Delhi 1971.

Singh, A.K. "Shifting cultivation : A case study of Vamberalli village, Srikakulam district," Report. Anthropological Survey of India (Unpublished) 1979.

Verma, K.K. *Cultural Ecology and Population*, National Publishing House, New Delhi. 1977.

Vidyarthi, L.P. *The Sacred Complex in Hindu Gaya*. Asia Publishing House, New York. 1961.

Vidyarthi, L.P., *The Maler : A Study in Nature-Man-Spirit Complex*. Bookland Pvt. Ltd. Calcutta. 1963.

ELEVEN

Pradip Singh

NATURE-MAN-SPIRIT : A CONSTANT? A Note

THE NATURE-MAN-SPIRIT Complex was originally conceived by L.P. Vidyarthi (1963) as a theoretical and methodological model to describe the 'soul' of the culture of a hill tribe of Bihar—the Maler. This was later on re-examined by other researchers in the context of different tribes living in different ecological settings. They found the tool useful and true.

The whole culture has been divided into three parts—Nature, Man, Spirit—which in turn are closely inter-related, inter-dependent, inter-woven and interacting, so much so that the existence of one simply cannot be thought of in the absence of another. Each division, among themselves, comprises every aspect, every component of culture and, viewed as a whole—as a complex—gives the total and comprehensive picture of the culture in its proper perspective. Or, mathematically speaking, the sum product of all the three components gives the value of the total culture, which always remains constant.

Thus :

Nature × Man × Spirit = Culture

Let us see how.

It is established that with every change in any one component, any aspect, any trait in a complex, there will be a corresponding change in other components, other aspects, other traits too.

In the part 'Nature', the interaction between man and his environment is dealt with. That is, how man exploits the environment with the help of whatever productive technology he has at his command. The lower the efficiency of this technology, the lesser will be the quantum of energy produced, and thus, the more dependent upon nature man will be. So the dependence of man upon nature is directly related to the technology he employs. *With every change in the productive technology there will be a corresponding change in man's dependence upon environment* and this will be inversely proportional.

If technology is t

and dependence upon environment is e

then $t \propto 1/e$ . . . . . . (1)

Now, *with every change in the relationship between man and his environment there is a change in the man to man relationship.* When the technology increases, his energy-exploiting capabilities increase, his food-supply becomes more secure, sure and sustained. Specialization of labour appears. Man, who was self-dependent for all his needs, has now to depend upon others. His needs increase too. Thus, though man becomes less dependent upon environment, his dependence upon other men increases. This is also inversely proportional.

If man's dependence upon man is r

$e \propto 1/r$ . . . . (2)

Again, *with every change in man's relationship with his environment and also in the man to mon relationship, there is a corresponding change in man's relationship with his supernatural world or his gods and spirits.* His beliefs change, many of his religious practices die out. He is less afraid of God, he is less dependent upon God.

if dependence upon God is g

$t \propto 1/g$ . . . . (3)

and

$r \propto 1/g$ . . (4)

Now, by (1), (2), (3), (4)

$t \propto 1/e - t \times e = k1$

$e \propto 1/r - e \times r = k2$

$r \propto 1/g - r \times g = k3$

$g \propto 1/t - g \times t = k4$

or $t \times e \times r \times g = K$ (a constant)

Thus, the sum product of all the components of culture always remains constant, be it a hunting and gathering society or a highly industrialised one. The Nature-Man-Spirit Complex always remains constant.

So, if it is possible to gauge or measure the values of t, e, r, and g, it will be possible to find out the value of K. And once the value of K is determined it will be possible to assess the level of a given culture, as also to predict at what level it is likely to be at a given time in future.

Index